T0110534

Social Work Practice During Times of Disaster

Disasters affect people individually and collectively in their communities, national societies, and the international sphere and in any setting from the home to the planetary level. Furthermore, these disasters can be complex, multi-layered and what happens in one location can affect sentient beings elsewhere directly and/or indirectly. These create interdependencies between people, the flora, fauna, and physical environment that require the holistic, transdisciplinary approaches to disasters that are advocated by green social work perspectives.

Using case studies drawn from practice and research to explore the skills and knowledge needed by social workers to practice within disaster situations, this book illustrates what good social work practice during times of disaster looks like. It highlights the theories, skills and expertise needed to intervene effectively in specific disaster situations and provides case studies as a major vehicle for considering ethical dilemmas and skills sets that facilitate interventions in specific disasters. Part I focuses on disasters that afflict the UK, where social workers may be part of the emergency response including floods, droughts, cold-snaps, windstorms, storm surges, fires, chemical discharges, terrorism and COVID-19. Given the interdependent nature of disasters, this section also draws upon knowledge from the international sphere to show how the local and global are interlinked. Part II considers disasters that dominate in other parts of the world, but which have impacts upon the UK, either because its personnel go overseas to provide humanitarian aid, or because the victim-survivors of such disasters seek sanctuary in/migrate to the UK. These disasters include refugees from earthquakes, volcanic eruptions, hurricanes, armed conflict and climate change. The ethical dilemmas that social workers face during all disasters are particularly poignant in the case of asylum seekers and refugees.

This book will be of interest to all social work professionals, practitioners in emergency and health settings working with social workers, academics and students both in the UK and around the world.

Lena Dominelli (Professor) is Chair of Social Work and Director of the MSc in Disaster Interventions and Humanitarian Aid at the University of Stirling. She has undertaken research in projects including climate change and extreme weather events, health pandemics such as COVID-19; earthquakes; volcanic eruptions; disaster interventions; vulnerability and resilience; community engagement; coproduction and participatory action research; and climate risk for young people. Lena has published widely in social work, social policy and sociology, including several ground-breaking classics, the latest on *Green Social Work* which provides a theory and practice of disasters from a social justice perspective that includes environmental justice and sustainability. A key message of her research is using a holistic approach that includes the duty of people to take care of Planet Earth by seeking alternatives to fossil fuel-based patterns of production and consumption to ensure sustainable approaches to meeting human needs and ending wars through the peaceful resolution of conflicts. She founded Social Work for Peace to this end. She currently chairs the IASSW Committee on Disaster Interventions, Climate Change and Sustainability and attended United Nations discussions on climate change (UNFCCC COP), since Cancun, Mexico in 2010. She also chairs the Special Interest Group on Disasters, SPEDI, for the British Association of Social Workers (BASW) and is a founder member of the England Round Table on Disasters and Social Work. She has received various honours and prizes for her work.

Social Work Practice During Times of Disaster

A Transformative Green Social Work Model for Theory, Education and Practice in Disaster Interventions

Lena Dominelli

Routledge
Taylor & Francis Group

LONDON AND NEW YORK

Cover image: © Getty Images

First published 2024
by Routledge
4 Park Square, Milton Park, Abingdon, Oxon OX14 4RN

and by Routledge
605 Third Avenue, New York, NY 10158

Routledge is an imprint of the Taylor & Francis Group, an informa business

© 2024 Lena Dominelli

British Library Cataloguing-in-Publication Data
A catalogue record for this book is available from the British Library

Library of Congress Cataloging-in-Publication Data
Names: Dominelli, Lena, author.
Title: Social work practice during times of disaster : a transformative green social work model for theory, education and practice in disaster interventions / Lena Dominelli.
Description: Abingdon, Oxon ; New York, NY : Routledge, 2023. | Includes bibliographical references and index.
Identifiers: LCCN 2023001857 (print) | LCCN 2023001858 (ebook) | Subjects: LCSH: Social service—Practice. | Disaster victims—Services for. | Disaster relief. Classification: LCC HV10.5 .D663 2023 (print) | LCC HV10.5 (ebook) | DDC 363.34/8—dc23/eng/20230504
LC record available at https://lccn.loc.gov/2023001857
LC ebook record available at https://lccn.loc.gov/2023001858

ISBN: 978-0-367-61645-8 (hbk)
ISBN: 978-0-367-61644-1 (pbk)
ISBN: 978-1-003-10582-4 (ebk)

DOI: 10.4324/9781003105824

Typeset in Sabon
by codeMantra

This book is dedicated to Mother Earth, the planet that nurtures us all and provides us with all we need. It is also a 'thank you' note to all those wonderful, courageous environmentalists whose voices will never be silenced regardless of dictators, murderers and predators waiting to pounce on every ounce of generosity bequeathed to us by Mother Earth. The Earth has its own song of strength and solidarity to sing. We can but join the choir.

Contents

Figures

Acknowledgments

A book is rarely the work of one person sitting in a garret in front of a dimly lit computer screen for days on end. Rather, it typically involves many people, engaged in dialogue and conversations that end up sharing experiences of the profundities and nonsenses of life, which leave profound insights in one's brain and heart. This book is no different. Countless conversations, some deliberately sought out, others occurring through happenstance, have left their marks on my mind. They have made me rethink the question of how I express the gratitude and thanks that I want to give to those whose words have pushed the 'pause' button and required me to think through my views more clearly, although I did not realise this until much later. I thank them from the bottom of my heart for enabling me to think more deeply to understand the greater complexities of living in a world full of vested, competing and controversial interests.

I also want to thank those students who shared their stories with me and enabled a deep, insightful sharing of experiences that transcended cultural and geographical boundaries in celebration of each other's uniqueness. Similarly, I want to thank those colleagues who encouraged me and supported me through tough times and enabled me to hang on to hope for a better tomorrow. Here, I want to thank Irena Connon whose optimism and enthusiasm made her a joy to work with. To Marius Stratulis and Ruth Allen, I want to convey my humble thanks for their unending and unstinting support of so many initiatives, I have lost count. I also want to thank Jenny Boddy for her wonderful sign of Hope Station in Derbyshire. I shall never be able to go to the Ladybower Reservoir without thinking of the 2022 Lissmore Floods in Australia, the 'tinnies', and the hope for survival through the assistance given by outsiders. Hope will live forever as long as people strive to create and innovate.

Finally, I must thank the many members of my family who were always there for me, cheering me on, even during dark moments when I would realise I could no longer pick up the phone to talk things through with Mom and Dad. Nonetheless, their spirit lives on in all of us and I feel their voices on the whispers of wind that breeze through my communion with nature.

Thank you all!

Preface

Disasters are increasing in frequency and intensity across the globe as human activities keep shifting the balance of harmony between nature and humanity, and as people seek to exploit nature's bounty whether it is animal, plant, other living beings, land, waters, air, minerals or other resources created through millennia of ceaseless action and laid at our feet. It is a tragedy that humanity, with notable exceptions such as indigenous populations who continue to respect nature and its generosity in providing resources that sustain life, has repaid its generosity with greed, indifference and a ruthlessness that has brought the planet, the biosphere and all things within it to the brink of a mass extinction and to the detriment of humanity as a whole.

The bell is sounding its knell of warning. It is still not too late to pull back from the abyss and work with nature to care for our daily needs and the planet that nurtures us in a sustainable relationship whereby people care for this beautiful planet and all it contains to infinity. This means rethinking our lives, especially how we produce and consume the goods and services necessary for living a fulfilled life at peace with the elements and with each other. This vision of moving forward in humanity's attempts to live differently and in harmony with our surroundings is also an important part of social work. However, many practitioners argue that disasters, including climate change and poverty, the symptoms of which they encounter every day, have little to do with social work. They maintain that while practitioners may assist in responding to the needs of victim-survivors of a disaster, once they have done that rebuilding communities, their infrastructures and the wider society within which they are located is the prerogative of some other profession, not theirs. This book takes issue with such pronouncements to argue that social workers are at the heart of every disaster response throughout the disaster cycle – prevention, preparation, relief, recovery and reconstruction. Moreover, it draws upon the green social work model to develop a theory, practice and a curriculum for the brave new social work portfolio of disaster interventions and humanitarian aid. This material is core social work, building on its values, concern for social justice which now includes environmental justice (Dominelli, 2012a), commitment to empowering individuals, groups and communities, lobbying politicians and policymakers to ensure that as the United Nations (UN) put it in its Agenda 2030, 'no one is left behind', and mobilising people for transformative social change. A social change built on peace, reciprocity, solidarity, sharing resources equitably and sustainably, and valuing diversity and inclusivity.

A journey into the unknown by working through what is known is what this book lays out before you. And it asks you to respond to its clarion call with energy, enthusiasm and a willingness to give and keep on giving as we all commit to building this transformative future together.

Lena Dominelli
26 November 2022

1   Introduction

Introduction

Disasters are increasing in frequency and intensity at local and global levels and pose new challenges for social work practitioners, academics and students to consider. Given the absence of coverage of disaster interventions in qualifying social work programmes in the UK and elsewhere except for the TATA Institute of Social Sciences in Mumbai, India, which has trained practitioners in this area since 1947, this unacceptable state of affairs must be corrected quickly. This book will provide crucial material to support the development of social work practice during disasters and a curriculum that equips social workers to assume disaster intervention roles with integrity and effectiveness. It progresses this task by exploring green social work (GSW) theory and practice as a transformative paradigm that redefines social work interventions during disasters within holistic, transdisciplinary, socially constructed directions embedded in social and environmental justice and human rights-based directions. This introductory chapter contextualises green social work, a newly emerging paradigm for practice that goes beyond the theory and practice of the 'deep ecology' approach described by Besthorn (2012). Consequently, GSW is a socially constructed integrative, transdisciplinary model that explicitly critiques neoliberal models of production and consumption and argues for the replacement of fossil fuel usage with renewable energy sources and implementing the duty to care for and protect planet Earth in perpetuity. GSW is rarely covered by other social work books considering ecological or environmental approaches. Until very recently, the absence of this paradigm in pockets of the discipline discussing environmental issues was ironically demonstrated by the lack of the inclusion of Dominelli (2012a) as a chapter author in various edited collections except for Gray et al. (2013). However, Dominelli's contribution to that text focused on the general curriculum rather than green social work theory and practice.

DOI: 10.4324/9781003105824-1

Chapter 1 defines green social work, its contributions to the profession, and key institutions and concepts integral to disaster interventions. It will also introduce the rest of the book, explaining its rationale, and distinctiveness from other environmental publications. It argues that green social work interventions during disasters provide an excellent opportunity for widening the practice portfolio for practitioners and students and equip them to provide better services for victim-survivors of disasters and 21st century challenges. Acknowledging social work's contributions to disasters will enable the profession to move out of its comfort zone to meet the challenges posed by contemporary realities.

Disasters: Twenty-first century challenges to social workers

Hazards of varying types have led to disasters when human behaviour impinges on their presence in often unplanned ways. This is instanced by building housing on a flood plain without thinking about taking precautions to deal with potential floods. Flood plains have been nature's way of dealing with a flood hazard, providing space for a river to expand into the surrounding area without causing irrevocable damage, until developers utilised this land to build high density housing. Giving little thought to the risks posed to people living in these properties meant that householders were poorly prepared when disaster struck, as indicated in Chapter 5 on floods.

A health pandemic is another kind of disaster. COVID-19, a respiratory disease which burst on the world scene in December 2019 in Wuhan, China and later became a world pandemic which has impacted everyone globally in a differentiated manner. COVID-19 has had two important effects that have altered the landscape for social workers and governments. One is the horrendous experience of being a victim-survivor in an illness for which humanity has no natural immunity. Another effect was the alterations in daily practice routines. These factors exposed existing structural inequalities in accessing health care and other services. They also altered professional practice responses to needs during this catastrophe and pulled everyone into the remit of the digital technologies to work from home.

Problematic challenges included home visits being disallowed in a relationship-based profession; inadequate personal safety equipment, and fear of spreading COVID-19 among service users and professionals' own families. These significant changes in everyday routines shifted public attention onto the imperative of preparing for the next disaster. Providing professional support for those suffering adversity in disasters indicated key roles for social workers to perform in responding appropriately and adequately to needs during calamities. Professionals, including social workers need appropriate PPE (personal protective equipment) and to be well-trained in disaster preparedness, mitigation, adaptation, and prevention. However, despite the opportunity to embed social work during disaster responses brought about by COVID-19, the public in the UK rarely thinks about its contributions in such tragic situations. Thus, the inputs of social workers and social care workers including loss of life in various disasters, including COVID-19 remain invisible. Social work's invisibility during disasters remains an issue to be challenged (Dominelli, 2014).

Disasters are increasing in intensity and frequency locally and across the globe. Among these are climate change with its associated extreme weather events covering droughts, floods, cyclones, storm surges and wildfires; earthquakes; volcanic eruptions; and more recently, health pandemics and cataclysmic wars. These precipitate environmental and social disasters that challenge people's capacities to live in the world and thrive in it. The lack of capacity in coping with unexpected events is becoming particularly evident and requires political leaders to promote solidarity to enhance resilience and response capacities globally. The current health pandemic, COVID-19, has exposed the general failure of health and social care systems to react to shocks with resilience that encompasses everyone, especially those without state support globally. Disasters have compounded existing social inequalities within and between societies. They have also highlighted the failure of politicians' fine rhetoric to meet basic human needs and welfare rights enshrined in the Universal Declaration of Human Rights (UDHR) that all member states of the United Nations (UN) have signed.

Moreover, the destruction of the biosphere, especially that involving tropical and temperate forests wreaks substantial calamities when people disrespect the people-environmental hazard interface. COVID-19 emanated from people transgressing into the animal kingdom. Others include SARS, MERS, swine flu, H1N1, Ebola and Zika. However, unlike nationally driven responses to COVID-19, global cooperation at governmental levels in these other specific instances of viral spread, prevented their becoming pandemics despite their inherent potential to do so. Such governmental cooperation and solidarity were missing in the COVID-19 pandemic because nation-states have prioritised solving the problems it generated within their own borders. This reaction also ignored interdependencies among nation-states, peoples, flora, fauna, and physical environments, and exacerbated the fears created by environmental degradation and exploitation, particularly among indigenous and disadvantaged populations.

The World Disaster Report (IFRC, 2018: 16) revealed that 84 per cent of natural hazards affecting 2 billion people are weather-related. Many people displaced by weather-induced disasters, might migrate to more clement surroundings, challenging the notion of state boundaries. Moreover, the poorest people in the Global South bear the brunt of the damage disasters cause. One of the drivers behind such destruction is the neoliberal system of industrial production and consumption. It exploits human labour, particularly that of women and children living in the Global South and uses the environment as a sink to extract profits for shareholders in global multinational companies which increasingly include billionaires from China, India and Russia, not just the West. *Forbes Magazine* claims Moscow was the city with the most billionaire's per capita in 2016. However, this position is being challenged by billionaires inhabiting other megacities. Rich people contribute more to global warming than do poor people.

Social workers are involved in all these disasters in the immediate relief and recovery stages, usually in evacuation centres where they provide practical assistance such as water, food, clothing, medicines and shelter, coordinate resources, emotional support, reunify 'missing' individuals with family members, reunite people with pets and/or livestock, and arrange psychosocial support. Social workers acting as community development workers, remain after the cameras have gone, and engage in the reconstruction stage to rebuild societies and communities following a disaster. The social work voice is muted, and the media are full of accounts from other professionals, including health professionals who are prioritised above social workers and social care workers.

Disasters are experienced differentially, and social workers are attuned to this through their micro-level work and commitment to social justice and human rights. Green social work conceptualises environmental rights as an integral part of social justice (Dominelli, 2012a). Practitioners can advocate for marginalised groups whose voices are ignored, mobilise communities and lobby for policy changes and resource re-distributions that cater for their specific needs. The United Nations and its various agencies are charged with delivering humanitarian aid during disasters. Social workers are involved in these structures delivering aid and attempting to influence strategy through their international organisations, the International Association of Schools of Social Work (IASSW), the International Council of Social Welfare (ICSW), and the International Federation of Social Workers (IFSW). Known as 'sister organisations', they were formed in 1928, and have worked together on various initiatives since. The most recent of these is the Global Agenda, running from 2010 to 2030. I consider these institutions below.

International institutions

International institutions form the bedrock of humanitarian aid throughout the disaster cycle including reconstruction. The institutions associated with the United Nations system symbolise the international world order. The United Nations Security Council, General Assembly, and associated agencies are key to delivering humanitarian aid. Crucial among these for social workers are:

- UNHCR (refugees; now UN Refugee Agency)
- OCHA (humanitarian aid)
- OHCHR (human rights)
- UNICEF (children)
- UNWomen
- WHO (health)
- UNCHR (refugees)
- ILO (workers' rights)
- FAO (food programme)
- International Court of Justice (the Hague)
- WTO (trade)
- UNDP (social development)
- Social Work Day at the UN (March)
- Global Social Work Day (March) (initiated by IFSW and now includes IASSW).

Deliberations in the United Nations, especially the Security Council, are governed by two key principles: national sovereignty (sovereignty); and the duty of care (protection). These principles contradict each other. Article 2(1) of the UN Charter restricts international action in the internal affairs of member states. Overcoming this limitation requires unanimous Security Council approval. The Security Council consists of five permanent members: China, Russia (initially Formosa/Taiwan and Soviet Union respectively), France, United Kingdom, and United States of America. A veto exercised by one of them can stymie any action. This occurred recently regarding Putin's War in Ukraine when Russia resisted any attempts to hold it accountable. Among its aggressive actions, it did not declare a conflict of interests and stay away from the proceedings. Article 2(1), initially based on the Montevideo Convention on the Rights and Duties of States, was agreed by the League of Nations in 1933. The 'sovereignty' principle can be used by rulers to disallow delivery of international aid as did Myanmar/Burma when Cyclone Nargis devastated the country in 2008. The UN Security Council eventually approved aid delivery for Nargis victim-survivors when the duty of care trumped national sovereignty. The 'Responsibility to Protect' was agreed by the International Commission on Intervention and State Sovereignty in 2000.

Various UN conventions are relevant for social/humanitarian workers. These include the:

- Universal Declaration of Human Rights, especially Articles 22–27, which address rights to food, clothing, shelter, health, and education can be very useful in providing individuals and groups with these resources (George, 2003).
- International Covenant on Civil and Political Rights.
- Convention on the Rights of the Child (CRC).
- Convention for the Elimination of all Forms of Discrimination Against Women (CEDAW), and Beijing Platform for Action, 1995.
- Convention on the Elimination of all Forms of Racial Discrimination.
- Indigenous and Tribal People's Convention.
- UN Convention on the Rights of Persons with Disabilities.

These agencies deliver aid through the cluster system which is discussed in Chapter 2.

The United Nations Framework Convention on Climate Change

The United Nations Framework Convention on Climate Change (UN-FCCC), considered in Chapter 4, is not an agency, but a treaty which UN member states have endorsed to combat climate change. It meets yearly in the Conference of the Parities (COP) meetings. The COP has delegates (government representatives) and observers consisting of various stakeholders including NGOs such as Oxfam, IASSW, the Sierra Club, universities with expertise on climate change and businesses that are accredited to attend COP meetings. Twenty-seven COP meetings had taken place by 2022. COVID-19 led to the postponement of COP26 in 2020.

Climate change is a key disaster that requires social workers to take more active roles in such eventualities than they have hitherto. Despite decades of messages from politicians and activists in the Global South for the international community to act quickly, fund adaptations, and uphold the 2015 Paris Agreement on climate change, little has changed. COP25 in 2019 which relocated to Madrid, Spain from Santiago, Chile due to social unrest was hugely disappointing. COP26, which took place in Glasgow after being postponed from 2020 to 2021 due to the COVID-19 pandemic following restrictions imposed on social distancing, and travel, was another disappointment. And so was COP27 which took place in 2022 in Sharm-el-Sheik, Egypt. No global action to mitigate climate change and keep global warming to a rise of 1.5°C has been implemented. National self-interest and geopolitical dynamics help perpetuate the deadlock that has hindered international activities on climate change since Copenhagen in 2009.

Boris Johnson sacked Claire Perry O'Neill, the then President of COP26 in January 2020 and replaced her with Alok Sharma who presided over its activities in Glasgow, Scotland during November 2021. The extended wait for COP26 could have been used to secure such agreements in readiness for November 2021, but this time was lost as the work done by O'Neill was ignored. Yet, engaging in pre-meeting deliberations is essential to convincing the many countries involved to put aside national self-interest and reach a global agreement about moving forward well before they reach the convention locale. The limited outcomes of COP26, and absence of the leaders of the key greenhouse gas emitting nations China and Russia, the first and fourth largest emitters respectively from COP26 were other disappointments. Thus, expectations for COP27 in Sharm-El-Sheik, Egypt were subdued. And when that ended in November 2022, little progress had been made in getting firm agreements with deadlines on implementation globally.

Social workers can engage in such arenas. Although, a few do on behalf of the profession, many more should do so. The International Association of Schools of Social Work (IASSW) has engaged in COP deliberations since 2010. Here, it aims to make visible the invisibility of existing social work activities in the climate crisis and ask questions to highlight the dangers of neoliberal forms of production and consumption for the poorest members of the global community and those living in small island developing states (SIDS) that are sinking under the sea, despite having contributed least to the climate crisis (Thomas et al., 2020).

Climate change is a key socially or human-induced hazard, not a natural one, and affects all the Earth's inhabitants. Climate change produces extreme weather events such as wildfires, cyclones, droughts, and floods that lead to both social and environmental disasters, often with catastrophic results. Climate change features in this book as a key disaster which is relevant to social work practice. Another one is the COVID-19 pandemic (Chapter 3). This disease has taken hold because a coronavirus crossed the animal-human barrier and spread through human-to-human transmission. These interactions have been attributed primarily to industrialisation systems that have exploited the Earth's resources while destroying many vegetative and animal habitats, thereby placing humans and animals in closer proximity and danger. There is considerable debate about how far any disaster, including earthquakes and volcanic eruptions, are 'natural' rather than being socially constructed, even if the hazard begins as a natural one (Alexander, 1993; Pelling, 2003). Some researchers consider all disasters as human induced. Consequently, this book explores the controversies around 'natural' and (hu)man-made disasters to see what insights come out of such disagreements for current and future social work practice and its ability to engage with other professionals and researchers to protect human and planetary wellbeing. Social workers are responsible for engaging in such topics alongside other disciplines and professions Matlakala et al., 2022).

Social workers have to claim their place at the decision-making table, engage in transdisciplinary teams, and ask awkward questions about power relations, structural inequalities and inequitable resource allocations that hinder the development of innovations that will unite people in coproducing a more inclusive, equitable and solidaristic world that is better able to stave off disasters.

Structure of the book

The book is structured to explore how disasters affect people individually, collectively in their communities, national societies, and internationally, and in any setting ranging from the home to the planetary level. Disasters can be multi-layered, interdependent, and complex because events in one location can affect sentient beings elsewhere directly and/or indirectly (Van Eck et al., 2021). These interactions can deepen interdependencies among people, the flora, fauna, and physical environment and require holistic, transdisciplinary approaches to disasters as advocated by the green social work model. This model integrates theory and practice devised through coproduction processes in which scientific experts, residents from local affected communities, policymakers, businesses and other stakeholders work together to solve common problems, build resilient, sustainable communities, societies and physical environments by pooling and valuing their separate knowledges. Moreover, those engaged in community engagement and coproduction processes are more likely to uphold proposed solutions because these are embedded in reciprocated caring relationships that bind people, plants, animals, and the physical environment (air, soil, water) in meeting the needs of all those living in a specific biosphere.

To cater for this global diversity and scale, the book contains two, interlinked parts. Part One, focuses on disasters that afflict the UK (as one country composed of four distinct nations – England, Scotland, Northern Ireland and Wales), while simultaneously making links between it and the global arena, through the interdependencies among people and socio-economic and biospheric systems that interact with each other. The chapters in Part I focus primarily on disasters encountered within the UK: fires, floods, droughts, cold-snaps, windstorms, storm surges, chemical discharges, terrorism, and COVID-19. These calamities befall other places, so the articulation between the local and the global is also examined. The chapters in Part II, consider disasters that dominate other places in the world, but which also impact the UK, either because its personnel go overseas to provide humanitarian aid, or because the victim-survivors of such disasters seek sanctuary in or migrate to the UK. These disasters include those migrating away from earthquakes, volcanic eruptions, hurricanes, armed conflict, and climate change. If global warming is not kept within 1.5°C above pre-industrial levels, the numbers of those seeking refuge from climate induced disasters will increase dramatically.

Case studies drawn from practice and research will explore the skill sets, understandings and knowledges needed by social workers to practice within disaster situations. These explore what good social work practice during times of disaster looks like. These disaster case studies will highlight the theories, skills and expertise needed to intervene effectively in specific situations. Through disaster discourses I consider how action research projects can coproduce resilient solutions to disaster vulnerabilities. I conclude by retheorising social work to expand paradigms that link caring for the Earth with meeting people's needs. Thus, I argue that the 'social' should not be trumped by 'economic' exigencies. Other crucial issues include the deconstruction of existing practices through transdisciplinary work, rethinking risk assessment, mitigation, adaptation, and preventative measures alongside a reconsideration of concepts like resilience, sustainability, and producing goods and services that do not cost the Earth. Case studies and exercises will be utilised to consider ethical dilemmas and skills sets that facilitate interventions in specific disasters. This book highlights alternative paradigms for practice rooted in environmental justice and transformative economic approaches to meeting human needs. GSW is key to reconceptualising social work interventions in disasters. Below, I describe the book's contents.

Part I – Disaster interventions in local and national contexts in the UK

Chapter 2 – Contextualising social work interventions in disaster situations in the UK: a multi-nation approach

This chapter sets the scene in the UK, covering UK-wide legislation, that of its constituent nations (England, Northern Ireland, Scotland, and Wales) and socio-political economic contexts that have shaped social work roles and responsibilities in disasters, highlighting similarities and differences between them. Devolution will drive further differentiation between each nation-state. The Aberfan disaster in Wales lacked social work intervention except for those volunteering or working with the Red Cross, but the trauma arising from it persists and requires attention. The chapter also examines the roles of international organisations on social work during disasters.

*Chapter 3 – COVID-19: a health pandemic that challenges
the social work profession*

COVID-19's arrival in Wuhan, China in December 2019 and its global
spread to reach the UK is covered in chapter three. It considers the poor
preparation for this pandemic among practitioners, the networks of
support they devised to adapt to their changing roles within this new
situation, including delivering services through digital technologies and
various practice transformations. It also covers transferable knowledge
and practice skills, lessons from other countries, and making practice
culturally relevant and locality specific.

*Chapter 4 – Climate change: social work responds to political
failures nationally and internationally*

Government tardiness in responding to the dangers of human-induced
climate change, globally is examined in chapter four. The British National
Action Plan (NAP) formulated following the Paris Agreement of 2015,
covers geopolitics and power relations underpinning national responses.
It examines social work's contributions to discussions within UNFCCC
COP (United Nations Framework Convention on Climate Change, Conference of the Parties) through representation and organised side-events,
e.g. COP 26 in 2021. Climate change interventions, critical to twenty-
first-century practice, range from adaptation to reconstruction.

*Chapter 5 – Extreme weather events: flooding and wildfires,
disasters frequently calling upon social workers' contributions*

Floods, a major disaster intervention for UK social workers, are becoming more frequent and more intense, making previous flood plans
and preparations inadequate. This chapter uses case studies to highlight the extensive range of activities that social workers perform in
flooding disasters to mitigate impact on victim-survivors in the different UK nations.

Chapter 6 – The Grenfell fire disaster

The Grenfell fire disaster of 2016 was a wake-up call for the failure
of successive governments sufficiently to address fire protection in high
rise buildings, and indifference to adequately training social workers to
intervene in such calamities. This chapter focuses on the experiences of
social workers who volunteered to support residents. They uncovered
the lack of human rights and social justice in the treatment of residents
who were largely from black and minority ethnic groups, receiving low

pay and facing structural inequalities. It will draw on the findings of the public inquiry into Grenfell, and fears of slow action on fire-proofing similar buildings.

Chapter 7 – Terrorist attacks: immediate and long-term consequences for social work interventions

Chapter seven considers terrorist attacks occurring within the nations of the UK. These include 'The Troubles' in Northern Ireland, Lockerbie and Dunblane in Scotland, the 7/7 tube attacks in London and the Manchester Arena attack of 2017. Lessons learnt from the 9/11 World Trade Center attack in the USA filtered into emergency planning forums in the UK. The chapter demands appropriate training at qualifying level, in-service top-up training, continuing professional development (CDP) and specialist (Masters) levels for social workers to cover the ongoing needs for training, debriefing, self-care, supervision, and support for practitioners.

Part II: Learning lessons from disasters occurring in other countries

Chapter 8 – Storm surges and hurricanes

Storm surges and hurricanes feature regularly in industrialised countries like the USA, and industrialising ones like the Philippines. Social workers working with local populations to survive disasters and rebuild their communities provide lessons accessible to others doing this difficult and complex work. These situations require social work support for extremely disadvantaged communities within a context of differentiated experiences of disasters to provide greater inclusivity in emergency responses and policies.

Chapter 9 – Earthquakes: socio-economic and political structures turn a natural hazard into a social disaster

Earthquakes are a major 'natural' disaster. However, those occurring in the UK go unnoticed due to their insignificant magnitude. Others, like those in Sichuan, China; Concepción, Chile; Christchurch, Aotearoa/New Zealand; and Haiti have presented substantial, serious, and complex catastrophes. These and others like that in Fukushima, Japan and 2004 Indian Ocean Tsunami become case studies covering humanitarian aid, the invisibility of social work interventions in disasters, lack of capacity in social work education and training, and creation of the

Rebuilding People's Lives Post-Disasters Network (RIPL) by IASSW in 2005. This chapter also examines the importance of working with seismologists, other physical scientists, and engaging other stakeholders, especially residents.

Chapter 10 – Volcanic eruptions: a local natural hazard with sometimes unanticipated global impact

Volcanic eruptions were rarely considered in UK-wide social work circles until the Eyjafjallajökull eruption in Iceland in 2010 when flights were grounded for a week and highlighted the need for additional research by NERC (Natural Environment Research Council) and the ESRC (Economic and Social Research Council). This chapter considers the lessons to be learnt from social workers researching this area, including the wearing of masks for protection from ashfall. This became relevant for COVID-19 as preparations include stockpiling masks and distributing them, tasks undertaken by social workers, community development workers, and NGOs in the Global South. This chapter also explores ethical dilemmas and concerns arising from a world order that places greater priority on safeguarding economic interests than people's health or children's education.

Chapter 11 – Financial disasters

The 2008 global financial disaster triggered by the fall of Lehman Brothers – the American bank deemed too big to fail, highlighted the fragility of a neoliberal economic system based on wealth accumulation and insufficient liquidity and assets. This tragedy caused enormous hardship to low-income people in countries across the world and subjected them to years of austerity to revive the financial institutions that drove the economy. This chapter studies the impact of reduced public expenditures on service users who become dependent on state welfare and/or charitable support while case managers developed packages of care that proved inadequate, e.g. philanthropy-driven responses like food banks over rights-based entitlements then and in the 2022 cost-of-living crisis. This chapter argues for rights-based entitlements, and the valuing of public service and civic ethics.

Chapter 12 – Conclusions

Disasters of diverse kinds have challenged social workers to think about structural issues and their impact on human rights, social justice and environmental rights in a way that has not occurred before. This chapter concludes by considering what social workers can and cannot do, depending on specific socio-economic, cultural, political and geographic contexts and differentiated disaster outcomes, dependent upon gender, age, ethnicity, disability, mental ill health, and income. It argues that social workers can play crucial roles in advocating for rights-based approaches to disaster preparedness, mitigation, and adaptive interventions to widen the practice portfolio, become trained to respond to the new challenges disasters create, and acquire the new skills sets necessary for participation in disaster interventions and humanitarian aid. It calls for a rethink of social work curricula to include training for disasters at all educational levels and advocates for changes in policy and practice to endorse support, solidarity and reciprocity locally, nationally and internationally. This envisages a new world order that social workers can promote.

Green social work: A model for disasters and humanitarian interventions

Green social work (GSW) affirms environmental justice within social justice as it promotes social development and sustainability. GSW is a transdisciplinary model for practice. It 'focuses on how the social organisation of relationships between peoples and their interactions with the flora and fauna in their physical habitats create the socio-economic and physical environmental crises that undermine the wellbeing of human beings and planet earth' (Dominelli, 2012a: 25).

Green social workers assess the risks posed by environmental and human-induced hazards and argue for:

- Recognition of interdependence among all living things and planet Earth.
- Profound holistic conceptual and social transformations.
- Sustainable relationships among peoples, other living things, the inanimate world, and planet Earth in a reciprocated duty to care for and about everyone and everything.
- Transdisciplinarity involving all sciences and professions to engage local communities/residents to share expert, local, and indigenous knowledges and co-plan and implement action throughout the disaster cycle.

A transdisciplinary framework enables GSW practitioners to address risk by:

- Working in empowering community-based partnerships to resolve environmental issues through coproduced solutions owned, controlled, and managed by local residents.

• Understanding disasters, their nature, causes and associated secondary hazards. This knowledge, especially the physical science behind disasters, must become easily accessible to non-specialists.
• Knowing the spatial contours or geographic particularities of each disaster because communities are situated in specific physical settings.
• Understanding communities' specific vulnerabilities and strengths to care for the physical environment and not increasing environmental stress with inappropriate demands (e.g. building housing on floodplains).
• Understanding the social, cultural, economic, political, and historical contexts of the locality in which a disaster occurs as central to individuals' sense of identity and belonging.
• Respecting people's attachment to space and place, an under-rated feature of traditional models of community-based disaster risk reduction strategies, to facilitate community engagement.
• Understanding that attachment issues are deep, profound, and critical in explaining people's sense of security and safety in a specific place and space.
• Appreciating the physical environment as an end-in-itself, and not only as the context in which people live and acquire resources they need to survive and thrive.
• Mainstreaming the green social work curriculum for all social work students and practitioners.

There is no agreed definition of the terms multidisciplinary, interdisciplinary, or transdisciplinary; some authors use the terms interchangeably (Dominelli, 2016). Dominelli (2016), Bracken (2017), Sim et al. (n.d.) and Sammonds (2018) have attempted to unravel their definition and usage. These authors argue that transdisciplinarity differs from multidisciplinarity and interdisciplinarity, through its key focus on multistakeholder engagement and emphasis on the processes of coproduction. Dominelli (2012a) proposed:

• Multidisciplinarity: separate disciplines working together on a common problem without developing a common approach, but each contributing from a specific disciplinary perspective.
• Interdisciplinarity: separate disciplines working together on agreed common objectives without sharing an agreed theoretical or common framework.
• Transdisciplinarity: various disciplines working together on a common problem with agreed objectives and sharing a common framework or theoretical approach that brings together diverse stakeholders having an interest in coproducing solutions to a particular problem and valuing diverse forms of knowledge, e.g. expert, indigenous or local.

Transdisciplinarity lays the groundwork for 'doing science differently' (Lane et al., 2011) by working across disciplinary and professional boundaries to solve problems by utilising connectivities in scientific, lay and indigenous or local knowledges. Hirsch Hadorn et al. (2008) claim that transdisciplinarity has four characteristics:

• A focus on real world problems.
• Transcending and integrating different disciplinary paradigms.
• Participatory research (coproduction).
• Seeking unity among knowledges to transcend disciplinarity.

Social work can contribute substantially to and learn from this approach, including valuing locality-specific, culturally relevant, participatory anti-oppressive practice, research, and grassroots-based professional paradigms.

Lane et al. (2011) argue that 'doing science differently' involves transdisciplinarity whereby each group learns from the others to innovate and solve agreed problems for effective disaster management. Doing science differently means that expert and lay knowledges are both valued and used to coproduce solutions. This insight arose from the 26 June 2007 flood in Pickering, North Yorkshire which had flooded in 1999, 2000 and 2002. Working together effectively requires trust and good communication to enable the contributions of different voices to be heard and valued. Stakeholder engagement traditionally focuses on consultation and information-sharing that treat people as passive recipients of scientific expertise rather than promoting and valuing co-participatory stakeholder engagement.

Transdisciplinarity in research and practice is increasing in relevance to disaster interventions (Dominelli, 2018b; Post, 2019). This is because it is expected to: provide time for reflexivity; share materials with others; develop common objectives and goals; undertake joint training; work through problems together (team building); seek innovative solutions to social problems (for disasters it includes saving lives); collaborate with diverse stakeholders, experts, and community residents; and build capacity within scientific and lay communities.

Tensions exist within transdisciplinary approaches. These need to be acknowledged and addressed. They include:

• Professional rivalries.
• Gender disparities.
• Ethnic insensitivities.
• Individualised versus collaborative working.
• Inadequate resourcing and funding.
• Privileging expert knowledge over indigenous and local knowledges.

- Scepticism about the values of equality and coproduction.
- Fear that coproduction shifts power away from experts.
- Other people's assumptions and reactions.

Key concepts for understanding disasters

Disasters are contextualised in the interstices between a hazard which may have a physical component and the social structures within which they occur, especially socio-economic, political, cultural, and religious ones. Moreover, there are key concepts which are critical to understanding what is happening to the people, animals, plants, and physical environments within specific situations. Considered below, these concepts encompass power relations, hazards, risk, exposure, vulnerability, mitigation strategies, capacity building and resilience:

Power relations

Power is conceptualised as the control that people can exercise in social relationships with others. Some adhere to a fixed view of power which is considered a zero-sum game as depicted initially by Parsons (1957). This means that power is a fixed entity that occurs within a binary of one party to a relationship holding power, and the other having none. Thus, a person, community or state either has or does not have it. Those that do not have power are subordinated to the more powerful party and considered inferior and weak. In disasters, those who consider power as fixed and pre-determined, expect people to respond according to pre-planned top-down directions. If this does not happen, they are surprised, perceive people as 'ungrateful' for the help proffered, and blame victim-survivors rather than their top-down approach. Anderson and Brion (2014: 69) utilise this conceptualisation when describing power as a social relationship that assumes 'asymmetric control over valued resources'.

Power can also be considered as a dynamic multi-layered relationship which is continually negotiated and recreated to reflect changing expectations and interactions between people, communities, or states (Foucault, 1980; French, 1985; Dominelli, 2009; Pyles, 2016). This conceptualisation of power means that people are engaged in responses that are not pre-determined. In the context of a disaster, this usually means that people engage in what is happening, although the extent of their involvement may vary according to the stage in the disaster cycle occupying their energies. This extends to the possibility that they may refuse to engage with those offering help. This is accepted as their choice, based on their specific understandings of what is occurring, and what they need. Thus, finding out the basis of their responses, not prejudging them, and anticipating that they may change their minds at another point is important.

Hazard

A hazard is a potential source of danger or risk that can impair (physical and/or mental) health. Hazards are categorised as geophysical, meteorological, hydrological or climatological. They may inadequately portray (hu)man-caused disasters, e.g. technological failures in nuclear plants, chemical spills as befell Bhopal, India, terrorist attacks, and wars. Chartes et al. (2019: 232) define a hazard as 'any natural or man-made substance, chemical, physical or biological agent, that is capable of causing an adverse health outcome'. They argue that such dangers are assessed through a multi-step risk assessment process consisting of hazard identification to determine the circumstances than can produce adverse health outcomes; hazard characterisation which establishes the exposure levels that produce ill-health; and exposure assessment regarding a population's exposure to particular hazards. This assessment helps determine the level of risk posed to susceptible people. Mitigating these risks assists in developing resilience.

Risk

Mitchell and Harris (2012) define risk as the likelihood of 'suffering harm or loss'. In a disaster, judging whether a risk will materialise or the extent of damage a hazard may cause is uncertain. Risk is mitigated by adaptation measures that develop resilience (Lubell et al., 2021).

Risk assessment

A risk assessment, defined as *a function of the likelihood and impact to assess and mitigate risk* in the event of a disaster, aims to reduce the negative impact of vulnerability on an individual's or community's well-being. Ultimately, a risk assessment aims to reduce risk and uncertainty, enhance resilience, or achieve sustainability by encouraging individuals to prepare themselves to cope with unexpected hazards and/or risks (Jongman, 2017).

A disaster occurs when hazards, risks, exposure, and vulnerabilities combine to produce human suffering beyond the victim-survivors' capacity to cope individually and collectively (Cutter, 1996). The formula utilised in planning responses is: *risk = hazard × exposure × vulnerability*. Disaster planning groups examine risk, identify, and prioritise individual and group vulnerabilities to articulate actions that will reduce their vulnerability (Cannon, 1994). As resource availability drives planning processes there can be a gap between the resources needed and those delivered (Alexander, 2002).

Mitigation strategy

Mitigation refers to attempts to reduce potential harm that may be engendered by a specific hazard. A mitigation strategy is a strategic approach to eliminating hazard risk and preventing a disaster or reducing the harm caused upon impact with individuals and society. Effective mitigation and adaptation often involve a holistic approach that acknowledges interdependencies (Dominelli, 2012a; Narayanan et al., 2020).

Exposure

Exposure is defined as the extent to which a hazard encounters people, plants, animals, built infrastructures and physical environments in its proximity in specific locations over a period. It is a key element in the equation, Risk (R) equals Exposure (E) × Vulnerability (V), usually shortened to R = H × E × V. This formula is used regularly when considering the impact of natural hazards on vulnerable social groups.

Vulnerability

Vulnerability is a contested concept referring primarily to the lack of capacity to resist damage or harm when exposed to the danger(s) a hazard poses (Ten Have, 2018). The damage may be physical and/or emotional, and not necessarily functional. Responses vary. Individuals may accept the prevailing social order, roles, and prescriptions to 'fit in', accommodate, or resist being labelled as 'vulnerable', e.g. women (Hollender, 2002). They are deemed vulnerable by 'emphasizing the maintenance and reproduction of normative conceptions ... neglecting countervailing processes of resistance, challenge, conflict, and change' (Collins et al., 1995: 498). This highlights the passive conceptualisation of women's agency. Controlling or reducing vulnerability depends on maintaining functionality, structure and control; having the capacity to organise one's life, socio-economic and physical environments; and strengthening the capacity to learn from past experiences to adapt better to future risks. Füssel (2007: 159) offers a definition of vulnerability that covers 6 dimensions: a temporal reference (current, future and dynamic); a field (internal or external and cross-scale); a knowledge domain (socioeconomic, biophysical, or integrated); vulnerable system; attributes of concern; and a hazard.

Social vulnerability

Vulnerability is socially constructed as *social vulnerability*. This concept shifted the disaster reduction paradigm away from understanding hazards as determinants of a disaster and onto the socio-political and economic realms to focus on risk assessments, adaptive capacity, and resilience building. Wisner et al. (2004: 4) argue that '"Natural" disasters flow from the social frameworks that influence how hazards affect people … [by] putting too much emphasis on the natural hazards…and not nearly enough on the surrounding social environment'.

Bankoff (2001) critiques Western discourses that portray the Global South as 'other' – disease-ridden, poverty-stricken, and disaster-prone, to cast the West as culturally superior. The Global South is formulated as a defenceless geographical space full of vulnerabilities including misrule which leaves populations without entitlements, disenfranchised and disempowered (Said, 1978; Watts, 1993; Hewitt, 1997). Poverty is relevant because it is embedded in 'historical processes that deprive people of access to resources, while vulnerability is signified by historical processes that deprive people of the means of coping with hazards … incurring damaging losses that leave them physically weak, economically impoverished, socially dependent, humiliated and psychologically harmed' (Chambers, 1989: 1). Consequently, vulnerability becomes configured through invisible colonial, predatory relations in disaster discourses (Pyles, 2006, 2016) that establish the scene for technocratic interventions that ignore the structural realities of inequality imposed internationally, and intensified under globalisation, especially neoliberalism with structural adjustment programmes (SAPs) that devastated emerging welfare states in the Global South (Thomson et al., 2017).

Vulnerability, experienced differentially, is usually defined by the socially dominant group to depict women and children across all ethnic groups as weak, vulnerable and requiring protection. While they are more likely to experience violence in camps when due to lack of space, they cannot perform bodily functions safely, women and children are also remarkably resilient despite the shortcomings they face (Drolet et al., 2015). Women's and children's vulnerabilities are structural and rooted in having access to fewer social resources and less opportunities in the public arena than men (Cannon, 1994; Rosenfeld et al., 2005).

In the intersection between gender and ethnicity (Mattson, 2014), white women are deemed more vulnerable than black women, and black men as more dangerous than white men (Dominelli, 1988). However, women's behaviours belie these depictions because they take care of families when men are absent and display strengths in looking after family income and caring needs. Gender stereotypes are resisted or subverted intentionally, by women assuming tasks traditionally associated with men and otherwise participating in gender resistance to challenge power relations controlling their behaviour by exercising power and agency. This enables women to assert their entitlement to be in both private and public spaces independent of men. Yet, women's resistance can be ignored, trivialised, challenged, deemed exceptional, reframed as victimisation, or co-opted into dominant discourses.

Contemporary society is challenged in reducing structural vulnerabilities that impede enhancing women's resilience. These challenges include:

• Lack of equitable access to energy.
• Living in degraded environments.
• Inequitable distribution of income and wealth.
• Compromised health status, particularly for women of child-bearing age requiring maternal health care.
• Violence, including armed conflict to assert control over scarce resources, e.g. water in Central Asia.

These challenges raise questions about building resilience regarding:

• Ownership and use of resources which have inequitable distribution and access.
• Structural denial of access to resources including knowledge and wealth, e.g. prioritising boy children's education over girl children if funds are inadequate.

Overcoming vulnerabilities in the long-term requires:

• Resilience that is sustainable, asserts intergenerational solidarity and conserves planet Earth and all it contains.
• Sustainable use of resources in meeting human and planetary needs for long-term resilience.
• Support buttressed by individual and collective actions to change social relations and cultural traditions among people and within communities.
• Celebrating indigenous knowledges as sources of wisdom and wealth.

Capacity building

Capacity building is the process of equipping people with the knowledge and skills required to make decisions about their lives, how to access the resources they need to survive and thrive, and what action to take to improve their current position (i.e. engaging in personal and structural change). Capacity building is linked to resilience as the ability of people to shape their environment and social standing when adapting to changing situations or acting to improve their condition or status in life to cope with adversity more effectively. Capacity and resilience building strategies can be individual and/or collective. Capacity building may transcend poverty, one of the world's most widespread disasters.

Resilience

Resilience is defined as a concept that describes how a system, community or individual can deal with disturbance, change and unexpected events (Dominelli, 2012b). Resilience in the social sciences refers to people's capacity to overcome adversity and get on with their lives. The IPCC (2012: 34) considers resilience as the 'ability of a system and its component parts to anticipate, absorb, accommodate, or recover from the effects of a hazardous event in a timely and efficient manner'. Resilience means calculating the risk of a natural hazard occurring and then planning, regulating, and training people to ensure that a community is prepared to face that risk. This involves a process of governance that enables risk managers to engage with resilience and protect people and communities from an anticipated risk. Resilience can also be the outcome of mitigation strategies aimed at reducing risk.

Resilience can be basic, support maintaining the status quo, or promote recovery. Basic resilience occurs in the relationship between the risk of a natural hazard occurring and the community's capacity to plan, regulate, and train in preparing to address that risk (Dominelli, 2012b). Recovery relies on a community's understanding of a natural hazard as an entity that can be made worse or its threat lessened by local factors concerning the social structure of a community, its natural environment, and built environment (Pelling and Manuel-Navarette, 2011) and governance structures. Resilience can be robust if it can 'resist or tolerate change without adapting its initial stable configuration' (Meadows, 2008: 77).

Resilience has moved from the physical sciences' concern about the capacity of materials to withstand stress and onto an ecological system's ability to maintain itself before entering the social sciences (via systems management) to contain and control crises. Control and containment are rooted in linear understandings of resilience that can be operationalised, assuming it moves progressively in an upward direction. Critiques of this static, linear view have reconceptualised resilience as the emergent property of a system that has non-linear and fractured characteristics with resilience at one point and its lack at another on a continuum of various states of resilience. The constantly changing nature of resilience makes it an emergent property that can rebalance and refocus a system, before during and after a disaster. It also features in preventative measures, crisis responses and long-term reconstruction. According to Dominelli (2012b), resilience can be on a continuum of failing, surviving, and thriving. Moreover, resilience considered as a property of an individual can be used to blame people for its absence without addressing structural inequalities. Today, resilience has become a buzzword with ubiquitous meanings.

Resilience can be reactive or proactive. In a reactive resilience system, people focus on survival, strengthening the system's capacity to resist change and maintain the status quo. In a reactive system, people focus on adaptation, prioritise the stability of the system, are more sensitive to political imperatives, and become less flexible. This can make them less likely to be resilient if an unexpected shock occurs. In proactive systems, people are flexible, expect change and can deal with it by rapidly changing operational assumptions and institutional arrangements to reduce vulnerability and enhance future viability. Reducing vulnerabilities is critical to developing resilience. Gubbins (2010: 8) favours collective responses to adaptation and argues that community resilience is, where 'communities have the confidence, capabilities, resources, knowledge and skills to address adverse factors affecting their cohesion and development'.

The Natural Hazards Resilience Screening Index (NaHRSI) framework is used to indicate how natural hazard events impact resilience for specific localities. The NaHRSI evaluates those features that shape vulnerability, a community's capacity to recover from an event and to quantify how changing these will (re)shape resilience to specific hazards (Summers et al., 2018). The NaHSRI evaluates five elements to assess recoverability from events. These are: risk associated with specific events; governance structures; social context; built infrastructures; and natural environments.

In the USA, national security considers natural disasters a national security concern because these are economically costly. Resilience initially focused on the persistence of 'natural' ecological systems to one of constant change resulting from human interventions during the human-driven 'Age of the Anthropocene'. Resilience is achieved through planning and taking action to enhance it. How to reach this objective may be contentious.

National and local governments have responsibility for ensuring resilience within communities within their jurisdictions. Their actions include:

- Developing and implementing effective land management systems, planning arrangements and strategic policies on mitigating risk.
- Creating systems that inform people on how to assess risks effectively and reduce vulnerability to hazards.
- Running education campaigns that enable people to understand and enact effective responses to hazards in their community.
- Supporting individuals and communities to prepare for extreme events.
- Ensuring that emergency services and volunteers deliver effective, well-coordinated responses.
- Working swiftly, compassionately, and pragmatically to enhance community recovery.
- Learning from disastrous events to enhance performance in innovating and adapting systems to deal better with future disasters.

Building resilience capacity relies on:

- Mobilising communities and engaging everyone.
- Understanding community dynamics and players and the relationships between them.
- Forming egalitarian partnerships.
- Building alliances to promote egalitarian social justice.

Social workers are involved in resilience practice through Emergency Response Teams, playing significant roles in building resilience capacity and ensuring that it affirms social justice. However, social workers' voice and their specific concerns are usually overlooked.

Professionals using expert driven (top-down) approaches to vulnerability and resilience:

- Want to control people in ways compatible with power-over relations.
- Assume people are passive and will do as they are told (lack agency).
- Tell people what to do (prescriptive).
- Legitimate 'off the shelf' or 'one-size fits all' responses to emergencies (inflexibility).
- Neglect the significance of diversity in communities (unity)
- Are surprised if people respond in unanticipated ways (resist).

Communities adapt to changing circumstances through various means including adaptation and resilience enhancement. Adaption varies according to:

- Who defines adaptation?
- Which issue is being addressed, and by whom?
- What resources are available?

Enhancing resilience requires taking action to enhance individual and structural strengths and overcome barriers.

Adaptive capacity

The American Federal Emergency Management Agency (FEMA) considers adaptive capacity as contributing to collective efficacy and social connections to bring together and integrate the diverse elements of a complex system. For FEMA, adaptive capacity is defined as the knowledge and skills necessary to promote recovery and tackle disaster risk. Collective efficacy occurs when communities work together to enhance their social connections or use social capital and networks to energise people and resources and promote community resilience.

Social workers develop and use adaptive capacities to overcome social vulnerabilities. They achieve this through social connections that can increase capacity and resources, empower local action, and develop community resilience and sustainability. Social workers employ adaptive capacity to support vulnerable groups to survive, rebuild their communities and thrive (Dominelli, 2012c) including in post-COVID societies. Their endeavours are underpinned by social work values including valuing people, social justice, human rights, equality, and inclusivity. These practitioners also ensure that practice: is holistic, locality specific and culturally relevant; builds on people's social connections; listens to the voices of vulnerable people; engages them in coproducing solutions that promote mutual self-help; and enhance resilience, and bring in much needed external resources (Dominelli, 2012a). Adaptive capacity involves both an individual's ability to identify and access resources, whether psychological, social, cultural, and/or physical; and a community's collective capacities to ensure equitable and culturally relevant provision of and access to life's much needed resources. This relational and connected understanding of resilience is embedded in a green social-ecological framework (Dominelli, 2012a, 2012b).

Social capital

Social capital refers to the connective resources that 'individuals bring to a community, and which can be extended by collaborative relationships and interactions with others when lubricated by trust and reciprocity' (Dominelli, 2019b: 40). Social capital is not shared equally across members of a community, but is differentiated according to gender, ethnicity, and other social characteristics (Goldbourne, 1999; Edwards et al., 2006). Social capital occurs as three types: bonding, bridging (Putnam, 2000), and linking (Woolcock, 1998). It is useful in building and maintaining communities before a disaster, and in rebuilding resilient communities afterwards (Mathbor, 2007).

Sustainability

The Brundtland Commission defined sustainability as meeting today's needs without impacting on the capacity of future generations to meet their needs (Brundtland, 1987). In this definition, Brundtland prioritised the social, economic, and environmental spheres, without ranking them. Culture was excluded but added later after being critiqued for its being left out (WCCD, 1995). Sustainability as a concept in disaster studies gained prominence in the 1990s, and was applied to mitigation, recovery, and preparedness responses. It also included indigenous knowledge and insights (Throsby and Petetskaya, 2016). In contrast, the previous recovery model consisted of the:

- Emergency period.
- Restoration period.
- Replacement and reconstruction period.
- Developmental reconstruction period including commemoration and betterment (i.e. 'building back better').
- Opportunity to improve pre-disaster conditions.

This was a sequentially ordered, top-down defined path to recovery. Recovery, as a messy process and experienced differentially by different groups, raises issues of intergenerational equity or the care of resources for use by future generations. Moreover, sustainability introduced the notion of reducing future vulnerability as an outcome of post-disaster mitigation, establishing equity, and creating amenities (Virtanen et al., 2020).

Sustainability is a life-centring matter whose lack currently threatens indigenous people and their cultures with extinction globally (Throsby and Petetskayay, 2016). There are 370 million indigenous people in 90 countries, leading placed-based lives, struggling against dispossession and colonisation, and seeking to reclaim their heritages and lands. Indigenous people focus on sustainability as:

- Context-based relationality, i.e. a concern with collective, not individual wellbeing.
- Community-based governance.
- Education about all living things and their environment.
- Language that depicts the interdependencies between living things and the Earth's environment, i.e. mutual, and place-based relationships.
- Quality of life and health needs using resources judiciously.
- Communal recognition of certain non-humans as life-givers.

Indigenous worldviews acknowledge the interconnectedness of all living things and their physical environments. This endorses spirituality and holism as important components of their worldviews. These characteristics are integrated into the green social work model and thereby reject the primacy given to anthropogenic values (Dominelli, 2012a).

Smith and Wenger (2007: 238) argue that sustainable disaster recovery be defined as the 'differential process of restoring, rebuilding, and reshaping the physical, social, economic, and natural environment through pre-event planning and post-event actions'. It is affected by 'social parameters', [that] different groups can recover at different rates (including not at all for some)'. Restoration covers psychosocial responses alongside material ones linked to the reconstruction of society's social and physical fabric and its ecosystem.

A sustainable recovery framework encompasses public involvement, equitable resources, pre-disaster planning, addressing issues that might hinder recovery, e.g. social vulnerability and existing power relations. Systems theory used in recovery processes can: facilitate the determination of mitigation strategies, link the physical environment, the built environment, and human systems to build local networks, increase capabilities and consensus, generate a holistic governance network; and ensure a comprehensive education and training system.

Disaster recovery is understood through various perspectives: the sociology of disasters; power relations in decision-making; sustainable development; policy implementation; urban planning. Each discipline considers its own focus, particularities, and needs. Furthermore, disaster recovery becomes a messy, variable process involving many actors, differentiated access to resources and knowledge, and unequal power relations.

Not everyone wants to change their community after a disaster. Not changing social structures has been challenged sometimes and exposes tensions between residents who want 'normalcy' quickly, and professionals who demand that change be placed on the agenda.

Friuli case example: recovery processes

Recovery processes are case-specific. On 6 May 1976, a 6.4Mw earthquake struck Friuli, Italy, killing nearly 1000 people and destroying many built infrastructures. Recovery processes in Friuli exemplified the importance of assessing seismic risk, and pre-disaster cultural, social, and economic conditions in determining the path for recovery after the earthquake (Carulli and Slejko, 2005). Local residents helped each other to look for missing people and rebuild their lives. This case, amplifying existing class inequalities and post-disaster initiatives, enabled those who were better off to benefit financially from the disaster, e.g. merchants. While these groups gained, poorer segments of the population, e.g. older people, struggled to restore their pre-disaster circumstances. Areas that were previously declining economically deteriorated further, but areas displaying dynamism earlier engaged more actively in reconstruction and became further advantaged. The Friulian experience indicates that entrenched structural inequalities must be addressed specifically in any disaster situation to promote sustainable equality and resilience.

The conclusions arising from Friuli's case suggest that recovery plans include:

- Community participation and coproduction.
- Information about what has happened, is happening, where people can obtain assistance, and from whom.
- Organising to respond before the disaster (prevention), and during it and afterwards in post-disaster emergency planning, post-disaster evaluation and reconstruction.
- Determining procedures for coordinating different responses and players and supporting those seeking aid.
- Evaluating interventions and damages, including identifying available resources and funding.

The capacity of local government to develop action plans may be uncertain and its activities may be underfunded. Also, involving inexperienced people in devising local recovery plans may be problematic. This occurred during Hurricane Katrina in the USA. Smith and Wenger (2007: 121) argue that state and federal plans should incorporate the following principles:

- A concerted effort to obtain materials and services from state and federal emergency management officials, including those who may not recognise the merits of recovery planning.

- Emphasising the importance of pre- and post-disaster recovery planning, long-term recovery and reconstruction.
- Identifying stakeholder roles in a sustainable recovery.
- Strategising to identify and address local needs in pre- and post-disaster environments.
- Emphasising disasters as opportunities to incorporate sustainable development strategies into post-disaster recovery and reconstruction.
- Establishing education and training agendas focused on building and sustaining local capacity, self-reliance, and commitment to an ethical sustainable recovery.
- Having a sustainable recovery ethic and incorporating a moral code of conduct into daily routines.
- Having sustainable recovery ethics that reinforce self-reliance, hazard resilience, and multi-objective planning.
- Convincing victim-survivors of their entitlement to disaster recovery assistance.

Exercise: the Anthropocene

Working in small groups, consider how you would promote non-anthropogenic strategies in protecting an area of scientific interest that flooded when the flood meadow was replaced by housing. Consider:

- How you engage communities in discussing alternative forms of development.
- What evidence you would collect to demonstrate how house building damages the river's capacity to overflow with minimal risk to life.
- How you would engage different stakeholders – experts, residents, businesses, in sharing their respective knowledges to develop sustainable solutions to provide housing without risking flooding and damage to the environment.

Social workers' engagement in disasters

Fenton and Kelly (2017: 472) argue that 'Social workers who focus on relationship building, understanding service users from a lens of social injustice, and practicing within a social welfare context can find working in a highly risk-averse and defensive system antithetical to their moral compass', which contrasts to 'risk-averse, managerial, and procedural practice', to produce 'ethical stress' and 'moral injury'.

Social work sought to raise the international visibility of the profession through the Global Agenda which aims to:

- Increase social work's visibility and voice.
- Increase social work's influence.
- Strengthen and promote professional social work and social development.
- Increase professional self-confidence.
- Encourage creative and innovative thinking.
- Involve as many countries as possible.
- Share examples of local good practice internationally.
- Support national and regional bodies.
- Focus on four pillars from 2010 to 2020. After evaluation, this was extended to 2030 and included inclusion, diversity and connectedness as depicted by 'Ubuntu' (I am because you are) and 'co-building an inclusive social transformation'.

Social workers engage with businesses in developing resilience because they provide services, built infrastructures and are responsible for maintaining supply chains, before, during and after disasters. Businesses need support to maintain their roles and functions during disasters. The insurance industry is an important business sector in mitigating risk and initiating change that encourages mitigating action. Governments are pushing insurance companies to play even greater roles in risk mitigation. However, their actuarial base limits their exposure to risk. Discovering this, the UK government responded with FloodRe to pool risks collectively. COVID-19 has highlighted the strengths and weaknesses in the capacity of businesses to cope with, survive a disaster, and then thrive. Engagement depends on a business' capacity to take risks or make use of opportunities that arise, e.g. businesses that have sought to profit from the need to provide vaccines for the world's entire population.

NGOs and volunteers are crucial in developing resilience during risk mitigation activities. These are many and varied in any disaster, and often there is a lack of coordination between volunteers and state agencies, and NGOs and state agencies.

Social workers talk about 'risk work' when assessing risk as the probability of harm occurring in deciding whether a situation is 'risky', its seriousness (negative value) and possible realisation. This involves considering potential gains and harms, and whether preventive or mitigating actions can diminish its seriousness or reduce its potential to occur. Emotions including wariness of lurking conflict materialising can induce anxiety, fear, or courage (Whittaker and Taylor, 2017). Social workers work in 'risk averse' environments wherein taking risks is frowned upon because it may endanger someone's life, and not taking a risk (or a chance) can mean that an opportunity to innovate is missed. Keddell (2017) claims that a different conceptualisation or weighting of risk factors arises between practitioners who focus on 'developmental-lifespan' approaches over 'presenting-welfare-needs' ones.

Exercise: Risk-averse social work?

Working in small groups, choose a notetaker to report back to the plenary and a chair to facilitate discussion. Then discuss the extent to which social work is a risk-averse profession. Consider:

- The meaning of risk-aversion.
- How practitioners assess risk.
- How practitioners can mitigate climate-induced risks.
- Whether risk-taking presents opportunities.

Conclusions

Disasters provide a fairly new arena for social workers to take seriously, ensure that the skills necessary to practice before, during and after disasters are included in social work education and training. Social workers also need to develop new paradigms for practice to acquire the necessary expertise. Green social work provides one such model, and should underpin social work education and training from the qualifying to doctoral stages.

Part I

Disaster interventions in local and national contexts in the UK

2 Contextualising social work disaster interventions in the UK
A multi-nation approach

Introduction

The United Nations (UN), through the United Nations Office for Disaster Risk Reduction (UNDRR), defines a disaster as 'a serious disruption of the functioning of a community or society involving widespread human, material, economic or environmental losses and impacts, which exceeds the ability of the affected community or society to cope using its own resources' (UNISDR, 2009). The scale of an event (usually greater than what local communities or organisations can deal with) and disruption to the basic necessities of life such as food, water, clothing, shelter and medicines are key criteria in determining whether a state of emergency should be declared. The International Strategy for Disaster Reduction (IDRR) was promulgated to assist nation-states in preparing for disasters and mitigate the damage done.

An emergency in the UK is generally aimed at dealing with events that have caused substantial risk to human welfare, damaged the environment, and/or threatened local and national security. The 2004 Civil Contingencies Act, amended in 2014, governs current emergency responses in the UK. It replaced the 1920 Emergency Powers Act which had allowed the state to proclaim emergency powers to protect communities across the entire country by Order in Council as required. The 1920 Emergency Power Act (EPA) had been amended in 1964. Interestingly, the 1920 EPA was used primarily to curtail strike action up to the Heath government of the early 1970s. Prior to the 1920 Act, emergency powers were invoked during the First World War, through the 1914 Defence of the Realm Act (DORA). In this chapter, I will describe the socio-economic and political contexts that underpin legislative changes concerning disasters, the legislation and guidance associated with specific laws – nationally and internationally and conclude with a discussion of the legitimation that legislation provides for social work interventions in disasters. Such guidance can inform practice that is enacted by emergency personnel, social workers, humanitarian workers and volunteers.

DOI: 10.4324/9781003105824-3

Socio-economic and political contexts set the scene for legislative initiatives

Legislation is formulated according to government priorities and the social and geographical contexts within which to take care of people's welfare, national security, economic exigencies, and physical environment. These concerns set the approach to what laws are proclaimed to enact responsibilities in each of these areas. Austerity and the Treasury's desire to contain public expenditure often condition governmental responses to social issues. The First World War was lengthy, caused millions of casualties – including those instigated by the significant spread of a health pandemic known as 'the Spanish flu', and massive destruction of built infrastructures and physical environments caused by war, especially on the European continent and in Asia. This created a situation commonly defined as a disaster, that is, an event that results in so much damage that coping with it exceeds the local and/or national capacity to do so. For Europe, American loans and the Marshall Plan of economic support were critical in facilitating the rebuilding of a war-torn continent. The loans took decades to repay, in the case of the UK, 70 years. The COVID-19 pandemic initially belied the austerity imperatives in that the British government authorised expenditures for the National Health Service (NHS) to deal with it. However, austerity pursued over several decades (Maynard, 2017) meant that the NHS was badly placed to respond, and health professionals had to struggle with inadequate personal protective equipment (PPE), bed shortages, poor staffing levels and other infrastructural lack of capacity. The context of austerity raised its head again in 2022, as the government once more sought to shift the cost burden of service provision onto individuals. In the summer of 2022, this situation was exacerbated by another cost-of-living crisis (CLC), triggered primarily by international forces including Russia's War Against Ukraine, shortages in supply chains including of basic commodities and energy.

Responding to such situations through the enactment of emergency powers enables government to: release resources to local areas badly affected by a disaster; ask for external assistance to enhance access to funding and build capacity; and control the population to ensure that law and order are maintained in what may be extremely chaotic conditions. From a government perspective, the Defence of the Realm Act (DORA) was enacted in 1914 and amended 6 times during the First World War to achieve these aims mainly by regulating communications including censorship of the press and troops' personal letters, controlling the country's ports, requisitioning supplies including land from businesses and the population, and bringing civilians charged with criminal behaviour under the jurisdiction of military courts. Violations of security provisions could result in the death sentence and 10 people were executed under its remit. Many of its controls impacted on everyday life, e.g. restrictions on purchases including buying binoculars, starting bonfires, and drinking throughout the day by reducing pub opening times. In 1918, rationing was introduced, and feeding wild animals was prohibited as a waste of food (Hynes, 1914). DORA 1914, amended several times, remained in force until it was replaced by the 1920 Emergency Powers Act.

The 1920 Emergency Powers Act retained many of the provisions of DORA 1914 and subsequent amendments. Strikes were also prohibited. The 1920 EPA was used to prevent the strike of 1921 under the leadership of the Triple Alliance (equivalent to today's Trade Union Congress, TUC), and subsequently the General Strike of 1926 to maintain coal supplies. It was used 12 times until 1974, mainly to curtail strikes (Newsinger, 1999) and remained in force until 2004 when it was repealed by enactment of the 2004 Civil Contingencies Act (CCA). The 1920 Act was amended considerably in 1964, although its provisions did not apply to Northern Ireland. Section 2 of this Act made provisions allowing soldiers to undertake agricultural and other work deemed necessary for the defence of the country, thus bringing permanency to provisions covered by the 1939 Defence (Armed Forces) Regulations. The 2004 CCA, a UK-wide, generic piece of legislation, is intended for use as a last resort at the highest level of an emergency, i.e. category 3, or a catastrophic level emergency. The other two emergency levels are Category 2, or a serious emergency; and category 1, a significant emergency. COBRA, the Civil Contingency Committee meets in a Cabinet Office Briefing Room and is usually chaired by the Prime Minister in the event of a calamity striking the nation. Interestingly, the CCA was not invoked during the COVID-19 crises, when the government relied on the Public Health (Control of Disease) Act 1984 and Coronavirus Act 2020. These two pieces of legislation will be discussed in the chapter on COVID-19.

Other contexts that impact upon resources made available during declared states of emergency or disaster situations are those linked to previous social policies aimed at sustaining economic performance. For example, in the UK, Clement Attlee's government had to restrain the development of universal services as identified by the Beveridge Report 1948, due to the huge government deficit incurred to pay for the Second World War, and American loans. These meant that the Treasury refused to create social services as a universal service available to all at the point of need (Meacher, 1975). Harold Wilson's government had to devalue the pound sterling in 1967 to boost exports over domestic consumption. Free school milk ended in 1971 under Margaret Thatcher when she was Secretary of State for Education: 'Thatcher the Milk Snatcher' was a slogan used to decry this action. James Callaghan had to borrow money from the International Monetary Fund (IMF) in the mid-1970s and the IMF demanded that prescription charges be introduced to previously free drugs. Margaret Thatcher raised public expenditure cuts to a new level during the 1980s and 1990s through the sale of British state-owned public assets to the private sector under a huge privatisation programme (Maynard, 2017). This included utilities and energy companies, council housing and the privatisation of many facilities including water, health and social services in the field of residential care which included the sale of public care homes (Carey, 2006) and the loss of the state provider role through the introduction of care management and the development of packages of care for older people through the Community Care Act 1990.

Thatcherite policies entrenched neoliberalism. These were mitigated for a period under the 'Third Way' introduced by Tony Blair. Ultimately, the advent of the Coalition Government of David Cameron (Conservative) and Nick Clegg (Liberal Democrat) initiated an Age of Austerity which squeezed public service provision, including benefit levels provided to individual claimants. This policy was maintained under the government of Theresa May and continued anew by Boris Johnson, despite his rhetoric of 'levelling up'. Even under COVID-19, Johnson provided greater funds to maintain the economy than enlarge the public sector, even though COVID-19 demanded heroic acts, endless hard work and enormous risks to health and wellbeing among public sector health professionals, social workers and social care workers who lacked adequate personal protective equipment (PPE), and enough beds or places in homes to provide needed services to everyone requiring them. Thus, hard choices about prioritising those most in need, had to be made by professionals who had dedicated their lives to meeting all needs as they arose. Consequently, many people – residents and professionals, especially Black and minority ethnic personnel in their ranks, died disproportionately under these atrocious conditions.

Legislation governing emergency responses in the UK

The Civil Contingencies Act (CCA) 2004 empowers senior government ministers (usually the Home Secretary) to pass regulations without going through Parliament and includes the authority to amend legislation except the Human Rights Act 1998 and the 2004 CCA itself. When bypassing this specific piece of legislation, the regulatory changes made by government are not time-limited by this new legislation. With the new Coronavirus Act 2020, the government could circumvent the CCA requirement of obtaining Parliamentary approval for renewal after 30 days. Johnson's alternative legislation for an emergency (like COVID-19) raises questions about a continued lack of democratic accountability and scrutiny which the CCA had sought to avoid by embedding a time limit within which government had to seek Parliamentary approval to extend emergency coverage. The CCA's provisions also allowed for judicial review. All emergency powers must be proportionate to the perceived threat and of limited duration, even if government is seeking a greater degree of flexibility than that permitted under the CCA. Although the CCA requires that the devolved administrations (Northern Ireland, Scotland and Wales) are consulted on such changes, these can by ignored if time is of the essence. Nonetheless, the CCA emergency powers have not been used during COVID-19.

The 2004 CCA specifies the civil protection duties entrusted to the emergency services, local authorities within which social workers and health professionals are ensconced. It is divided into two main parts: local arrangements for civil protection; and emergency powers. In Part One, rules and regulations specify the guidance linked to emergency preparedness, and the impact of the roles and responsibilities to be fulfilled by category 1 responders. These responders are mainly the emergency services (fire, police, military), local authorities which include social workers, NHS organisations and health services providers. In undertaking their civil protection duties, category 1 responders are required to:

- Assess emergency risk and utilise this for contingency planning purposes.
- Formulate emergency plans.
- Create arrangements and management structures that maintain business continuity.
- Provide the public with information about civil protection issues including early warning, informing and advising the population regarding the action(s) to take in the event of an emergency being declared.
- Support coordination among local responders including those under category 2 by providing information that facilitates such action.
- Cooperate with other local responders to improve coordination among them and efficient service delivery.
- Support business continuity management by providing advice and assistance to companies and voluntary organisations.
- Support local authorities in meeting their responsibilities and ensuring business continuity.

Category 1 responders work with category 2 responders through an area local resilience forum (LRF). There are 42 LRFs in England and Wales (four LRFs for Wales, namely Dyfed-Powys, Gwent, North Wales and South Wales). Each one is contained within the borders of the relevant Police Area. This delineation excludes London which has a Borough Resilience Forum in place for each local borough (Cabinet Office, 2013).

Scotland's equivalent to the LRF covers a Strategic Coordinating Group (SCG) which is based upon a constabulary area and consists of three regions (North, East and West). Each region has an assistant chief constable in charge. Scotland has 13 divisions, each one covering one or more local authority area and headed by a chief superintendent. The LRFs in Scotland are called Regional Resilience Partnerships (RRPs). In Northern Ireland, there are three Emergency Preparedness Groups (EPGs) which sit under the Executive Office in the Northern Ireland Civil Contingencies Policy Branch.

By defining the roles and responsibilities of all categories of local responders, the CCA aims to achieve consistent, efficient, and coordinated responses among all participating responders. The CCA also requires the entire health system consisting of the emergency services, local authorities, and NHS entities to be ready to deal with any calamity or serious event that might arise. In the COVID-19 pandemic, this obligation was discharged by controlling demand for assistance on health service providers, both by those suspecting they had contracted the coronavirus, and by those requiring elective surgery and non-essential medical procedures. Thus, only the most serious cases accessed the services provided in hospital settings, including ventilators which were in short supply.

Disaster interventions: emergency planning and response

Declaring a state of emergency

A government declares a 'state of emergency' to be able to take action to manage a catastrophic situation quickly. Such a declaration enables the ruling elite to:

- Pass regulations without parliamentary scrutiny.
- Ignore statutory duties that government is normally obliged to uphold.
- Take actions that government would not normally be entitled to undertake.

In the COVID-19 pandemic, this included closing retail outlets, requiring people to remain locked down in their homes, and preventing gatherings in groups (freedom of association) and social and physical distancing.

Emergency planning prior to a disaster seeks to prevent disastrous events or mitigate (reduce) the damage they can do to life, socio-economic livelihoods and built and environmental infrastructures. Mitigation activities often involve alert systems warning about a hazard or pending emergency and remedial action(s) to reduce the impact of an emergency on a person, community, or organisation. In compiling an emergency plan, a risk assessment is conducted to ascertain key priorities for action. Emergency plans are either generic or specific. A generic plan focuses on core issues to facilitate organisational responses to an emergency and recover from it. This plan should ensure the welfare of staff and access to appropriate resources in sufficient quantities for the responses required.

A specific plan is concerned with responding to an emergency in a particular site or location and is based on a specific emergency defined at a certain level. In the UK, these are: level 1 (significant emergency) wherein action is led by a designated department in the local authority; level 2 (serious emergency) which requires sustained nation-based government involvement; and level 3 (catastrophic emergency) which is widespread enough to necessitate central government engagement. Specific plans are a set of emergency arrangements based on a generic plan but containing more detail. These will be relevant to an organisation's activities and operational tasks including preparing for situations that might go awry. For example, a fire in a building will have evacuation plans for it, based on a risk assessment of what actions are essential and those that are desirable. Their effective and efficient implementation may depend on effective communication of these plans to those who might be affected, interagency coordination, and easily accessible resources necessary for adequate responses. If, for example, a building that has burnt down is large and considerable numbers of people are affected, a previously articulated specific plan may not have allocated enough dwellings to rehouse those affected, even on a temporary basis. Thus, the plan must be (re)evaluated and rethought. Meanwhile, additional housing units might be brought in from elsewhere and may take the form of tents or trailers (caravans). The 2016 Grenfell Tower Fire in London exemplifies a UK-wide failure of government policies alongside erroneous local authority enforcement of compliance with fire safety regulations (Moore-Bick, 2021).

A local resilience forum (LRF) is a multiagency body authorised under the 2004 Civil Contingencies Act to coordinate the activities of category 1 responders including local authorities, emergency services, the NHS, and Environment Agency. Schools need to be considered specifically. When will they close? When will they reopen? Will school buildings be used as evacuation centres? What will happen to the students normally studying within them? These are among the many issues to be considered and planned for. The LRF collaborates with category 2 responders such as the public utilities companies and Highways Agency, and with the military and voluntary organisations like the Red Cross. Local elected representatives also have a role in supporting emergency responses and linking officials with residents locally. The Meteorological Office provides weather forecasts that are useful in providing early warnings about adverse weather phenomena. The insurance industry also assists in assessing damage and working with the other agencies to determine mitigation strategies that will reduce damage during future adverse events. The geographical borders of the police area determine the boundaries within which each LRF operates. Each LRF identifies and defines local risks, develops emergency plans and seeks to prevent and mitigate the impact of any event on local populations and communities. Thus, each LRF needs to be well-informed, particularly about policies and the scientific information that is available about any specific hazard and the damage that can be inflicted when it encounters centres of habitation.

An emergency action plan is formulated around three key groups: those who are highly likely to be impacted (usually called 'vulnerable' groups); the victim-survivors; and the workers who respond to the emergency. Those implementing an emergency plan should be aware of and be prepared to handle possible secondary impacts such as those arising from media interest in the topic including those supporting long-term recovery and worker protection. Procedures should also articulate how decisions will be made, and who will be involved in making them. These discussions should cover the point at which an emergency can be declared and by whom; and identify who becomes the lead coordinator during an emergency. The coordinating organisation is usually the police who take charge of the control and command centre. Once an action plan is devised, it is monitored, reviewed, and revised in a circular movement that leads to a cycle of action, evaluation, and reformulation to take account of new realities. In the absence of an actual disaster, this cycle of implementation and review draws on regular exercises and training of the personnel involved. The LRF ensures that the emergency plan is updated regularly, using lessons learnt from its activities, other calamities, and research findings. The processes for community engagement and coproduction are outlined in Figure 2.1. The coproduction dimension is critical in ensuring that residents and other stakeholders locally feel that they own whatever the action plan contains. Full engagement helps to assure ownership. Additionally, involving local communities in continuously evaluating the outcomes of their endeavours and in subsequent attempts to amend the plan is likely to cater better for new eventualities that the community might confront.

The processes identified in Figure 2.1 are similar whether the emergency is a health pandemic, an earthquake, a flood or other disaster, 'natural' or human-made. While the entry point in the disaster cycle might vary, the processes of engagement can begin wherever is most appropriate, depending on context, information available, and resources required and accessed. Dialogue and coproduction involving community residents and experts from the sciences is crucial to obtaining meaningful outcomes.

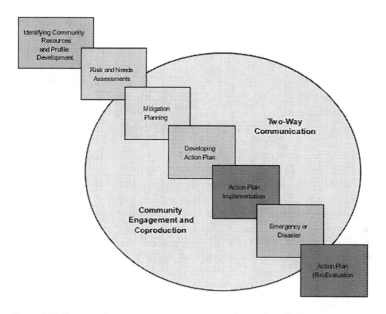

Figure 2.1 Community engagement processes and practices during emergencies.
Source: adapted from Dominelli (2018b)

Disaster interventions: recovery responses

Recovery responses seek to establish a return to more familiar situations, and usually follow the immediate relief or emergency phase. However, thinking about what to do during it has to begin immediately after the disaster occurs, or even in pre-disaster planning, prevention, and preparation. Recovery considerations draw upon extensive risk assessments. These form important elements in deliberations during the immediate relief phase to ensure that the transition between these two phases is smooth and continuous. Recovery tends to last for some time and may require additional resources to enable victim-survivors to rebuild their communities. Later, reconstruction is usually considered in terms of 'returning to normal', which is what many victim-survivors want. Disaster management experts talk about it in terms of 'building back better' (Manyena, 2006). I prefer to recast this dimension as *transformative renewal* or *transformative action* to allow for the possibility of social changes that can reduce existing inequalities. These different definitions indicate a tension between a type of rebuilding that maintains the status quo which may be full of inequalities that are maintained and often reinforced, even when people want to change them because they prioritise getting back to a situation that is familiar to them, and where they believe they can more easily calculate risks. When victim-survivors of the 2004 Indian Ocean Tsunami in southern Sri Lanka were asked what they would like to do once they reached emergency accommodation, they often wished to return to their former homes – including those based on the beach which had been washed away. They wished to re-establish their homes where they had lived for many years, and resume their livelihoods, usually linked to fishing (especially the men) or the tourist industry (Dominelli, 2020). Following the 2007 floods in England, many victim-survivors in Tollbar, Doncaster, wanted to return to their homes or have the temporary caravans (trailers) in which they were housed together as a community or placed in their gardens near their flooded homes to prevent looting (Easthope, 2018).

Those that want to 'build back better' (Manyena, 2006), include the United Nations (UN) and its agencies, and many NGOs (non-governmental organisations) offering humanitarian aid. These have covered what communities had to do to mitigate risk prior to the calamitous event, and the actions to take to redress those elements, e.g. retrofitting houses or earthquake-proofing them in earthquake zones; building flood defences in flood-prone areas. While useful and necessary, approaches that focus only on built infrastructures fail to address social inequalities and marginalisation. Thus, existing difficulties and inequalities that impinge heavily upon the quality of life of many people, especially women and children before the disaster may be retained unless these are resisted explicitly (Hollender, 2002). Women's concerns include intimate partner violence and child abuse, both of which increase significantly during disasters (Parkinson and Zara, 2013).

The lack of integration between 'social' considerations, economic exigencies, the physical environment and built infrastructures, lies at the heart of the critique of current approaches to disasters articulated by green social work (GSW) developed by Dominelli (2012a). The GSW model is holistic, transdisciplinary, and integrative of all those systems that impact upon people's lives and the physical environment beyond people to cover flora, fauna, and the duty to care for the physical environment and biosphere. GSW, therefore, focuses on transformative renewal, which requires victim-survivors to discuss openly their social standing in their communities and become involved in transforming current social relations to address existing structural inequalities, develop alternative models of economic development that do not continue to reproduce structural inequalities or degrade the physical environment and contribute to greenhouse gas emissions. This provides a strategic view of humanity's place in the world and includes a reduction of consumption for the sake of consumption and taking steps to meet human needs sustainably by caring for planet Earth now and into the future. Transformative renewal offers an optimistic way of engaging all stakeholders in coproducing innovative, imaginative, and acceptable sustainable solutions in a post-disaster environment. Dialogues across controversies seek to ensure that a consensual solution that meets the needs of everyone is reached during community deliberations. Reaching a consensus might take time, but it is more likely to lead to equitable outcomes that will be sustained in the long-term.

Social workers and community development workers have key roles in mobilising communities, engaging all stakeholders in dialogues that do not exclude marginalised and unheard voices and thereby promote inclusivity in public discourses and decision-making. This is particularly important for women, children and young people, groups often ignored in such deliberations. Practitioners can form support groups among and mobilise those experiencing communal and individual violence and denied expression of their interests (Pittaway et al., 2007; Neumayer, and Plümper, 2007; Parkinson and Zara, 2013; Svistova and Pyles, 2018; Dominelli, 2020). GSW also espouses the importance of addressing the specific and differentiated needs of men alongside those of women, children, young people, and older people. Such responses attempt to address men's needs during disasters and facilitate the articulation of their emotionality, loss of status and livelihoods as well as address their inappropriate behaviours towards women, children, young people and other men (Dominelli, 2020).

The recovery phase seeks to provide stability by addressing key elements of daily life and communication about what must be done, how it should be done, and who should progress the action (Davis and Alexander, 2015). Alongside a resumption of economic and business activities to keep the economy functioning is giving priority to health and welfare concerns. The recovery phase ensures that financial institutions, economic enterprises, and supply chains are functional and can support economic development by providing loans; facilitating the provision of goods and services; cleaning up debris; protecting built infrastructures and the environment; sharing scientific and lay knowledge and disseminating it; and endorsing community health, cohesion and recovery.

In the UK, local authorities initiate the recovery process by creating a recovery coordinating group (RCG) to facilitate interagency activities. Its work commences during the response phase and runs in parallel with the strategic coordinating group which hands developments over to the RCG when appropriate. The strategic coordinating group is headed by the police, whereas the recovery coordinating group is chaired by the local authority, and when ready, it assumes the control and command role. Once the recovery coordinating group is active and functioning adequately, criteria used to determine the handover point from the police include: the emergency has ended and is not expected to reoccur; public safety is assured; sufficient resources are available to undertake the necessary work; and communication structures are functioning. In the emergency control centre, individual organisations including district councils and other governance structures are operating effectively and ready to engage with the recovery coordinating group and its deliberations. The fire and rescue service and ambulance service should support the recovery coordinating group and should have resolved their own resourcing issues and have the capacity to act independently of the emergency control centre. A handover certificate is signed at the point of transferring duties. The recovery coordinating group should have public confidence in its ability to devise and implement action plans and ensure that it can engage other agencies as required.

The action plans are important in determining priorities as well as activities including roles and who is going to undertake them and when. These action plans cover a range of different topics and identify agency responsibilities (Ferguson, 2018). These include identifying mass fatalities and supporting enquiries into them; prosecutions for criminal behaviour including negligence; military assistance; caring for displaced communities, nationals from other countries, UK nationals returning from overseas; providing humanitarian aid, mutual aid, financial disbursements, economic and business recovery. They also focus on repairing built infrastructures including schools, hospitals, doctors' surgeries, clinics, housing, transportation, utilities, communications, sanitation systems, removing debris including waste, contaminated and polluted materials, meeting health and social care needs, community engagement and cohesion, and the impact of external events on the UK.

The recovery coordinating group also works with volunteers and the voluntary sector. Which voluntary agencies are involved depends on the type and nature of the emergency. The St John's Ambulance and Red Cross are usually involved in most emergencies and identified as category 2 responders. The voluntary sector has expertise and resources that can be made available. These are:

- Welfare provisions, especially those linked to providing water, food, clothing.
- Longer-term-support including the provision of mental health facilities.
- Medical support, especially to ensure that those with medication for pre-existing conditions continue to take their medicines.
- Search and rescue, including bringing together family members.
- Transport, especially important in accessing service providers, including health services.
- Communications that clarify official statements, and facilitate communication with family, friends, and service providers.

- Documentation, especially those involving compiling evidence for insurance claims and accessing various types of resources.
- Training and exercises that help volunteers and other agencies to acquire the skills necessary to support category 1 responders.

Reconstruction usually follows the recovery phase, as people seek to achieve stability and greater degrees of certainty in their lives. Reconstruction activities can reinforce existing social relations, including the structural inequalities embedded within them, or they can become transformative. Much depends on the value system being adhered to, the availability of resources, the views of the different stakeholder groups, social policies, and insurance practices. For example, people caught in several instances of local flooding following unexpected rainfall may find insurance companies refuse to insure them if the actuarial risk entailed in coverage is too great. The reluctance of insurance companies to provide affordable cover for houses built on flood meadows in the UK exemplifies this. The Cameron government created the FloodRe scheme to mitigate this response. Under this scheme, all policyholders paid an additional nominal sum (£1) in their insurance premium, thereby pooling risks to reduce premium rates that would have been beyond individuals with a house on a flood plain to pay.

Links to global international organisations aimed specifically at disaster interventions

Rebuilding Europe after the Second World War

Modern day initiatives in disaster interventions and humanitarian aid are based on the rebuilding of war-torn Europe following the end of the Second World War. The European Recovery Programme, also known as the 1948 Marshall Plan (1948–1951), was a central plank in this rebuilding process. It initially allocated $15 billion in American grants and aid for reconstruction endeavours, with $1.2 billion for humanitarian aid. The Plan was extended in 1949 through the Four Point Program and covered both loans and grants. The key European signatories to the Marshall Plan were the UK, France, Austria, Belgium, Denmark, West Germany, Greece, Iceland, Italy, Luxembourg, the Netherlands, Norway, Sweden, Switzerland and, across the Adriatic Sea, Turkey. Ultimately, 18 countries were recipients of this aid, the bulk of which went to the UK, France and West Germany. A condition of this aid, often called 'tied aid' because it has restrictive clauses attached, was that goods had to be purchased in the USA and taken across the Atlantic in American merchant ships. Although this endeavour claimed to rebuild Europe, it also benefitted the American economy. Moreover, the Marshall Plan assumed that if European economies could be rebuilt quickly, it would halt the spread of communism on that continent. This aim meant that the then Soviet Union led by Stalin and represented by Vyacheslav Molotov in detailed negotiations, the Eastern European states under Soviet auspices, e.g. Poland and Hungary, did not participate in this Plan. They warned that this marked a major negative step in the Cold War that was developing between the East and the West. This concern led to the creation of Comecon as a counter entity to assist economic development in communist Eastern Europe. Economic recovery, particularly in Western Europe, had been achieved by 1953, with rising levels of growth, especially in the engineering, steel, and chemical sectors. Ultimately, this led to the formation of the 6 nation (France, Western Germany, Italy, the Netherlands, Belgium, and Luxemburg) European Coal and Steel Community in 1950. The Marshall Plan also encouraged trade liberalisation and integration among the participating economies and laid a foundation for globalisation and even greater trade liberalisation and integration. Overall, $44 billion were distributed as loans under the Marshall Plan. Of these sums, the UK had $13 billion. Over time, the European states repaid all these monies, although West Germany was asked to repay only one-third of its 'loan'. The USA had made separate funds available to assist reconstruction in parts of Asia, especially those with current or previous links to the British Empire (Tarnoff, 2018).

Besides providing resources and personnel, the Marshall Plan included the Marshall Scholarship Scheme which promoted the training of many humanitarian aid workers, including social workers, who were usually sent to the USA for training. This encouraged the Americanisation of a profession that began in Europe (Kendall, 2010) and to the dominance of one-to-one casework alongside clinical and psychosocial interventions including in areas where these were rarely practiced earlier. This led to a downplaying of community development initiatives which had been key elements of the European tradition built upon insights drawn from the Settlement Movement (Gal et al., 2020). It also undermined many forms of 'indigenous' or locality specific, culturally relevant forms of social work, e.g. in Greece (Ioakimidis et al., 2014). Americanised forms of practice dominated the social work scene in Europe until radical social work began to challenge its hegemony. In the UK, this began in practice through *Case Con*, and then moved into the academy, particularly in the 1970s and 1980s (Corrigan and Leonard, 1978; Hanner and Statham, 1988; Dominelli, 1988; Dominelli and McLeod, 1989). These works were concerned primarily with structural inequalities including exclusion according to class, poverty, ethnicity and gender, and highlighted poverty as among the world's largest longstanding disasters (Dominelli, 2012a).

The United Nations and its agencies in disaster situations

The United Nations (UN), through its various agencies, plays a key role in ensuring that external humanitarian aid reaches a society experiencing a disaster. Its activities involve coordination with the government of the country concerned and operational matters about the delivery of aid and a 'return to normal' as quickly as possible. The Office for Humanitarian Affairs (OCHA), headed by an Under-Secretary General of Humanitarian Affairs, is the main UN body liaising with the relevant government(s) and dealing with developments on the ground. Humanitarian work is extensive and complex and requires considerable coordination of different actors and the resources they bring to a situation. It can be difficult for OCHA to know which agencies are involved in a particular community, who their personnel are, what each specific humanitarian organisation is providing by way of resources. OCHA's lack of capacity, knowledge and reach on the ground can result in coordination becoming fragmented and inadequate. This situation is compounded by the many individuals who unilaterally go to such areas and volunteer their help (Zhang et al., 2012). Their numbers can be substantial and overwhelm local service providers. Concern about the 'hordes' of volunteers arriving to 'help' during the 2008 Wenchuan Earthquake in China gave rise to a saying 'Stay away from fires, dogs, and psychotherapists' among victim-survivors throughout Sichuan's affected areas (Sim, 2015). Fires are a frequent hazard after an earthquake, numerous dogs running amok can endanger already vulnerable people and environments, and unwanted psychosocial volunteers feed victim-survivors' anxieties about losing control over what they want to happen in their communities and to them.

Exercise – Psychosocial social work: a help or a hindrance?

You are a psychosocial social worker, and you are in a flood-stricken country that is suspicious of psychosocial interventions on the grounds that what they need is 'practical help', especially money to rebuild their lives. They reject your offers of assistance, services and keep their distance from you.

Discuss in pairs, how you would respond to this situation as there are many traumatised people who feel accessing mental health services is stigmatising.

Make notes to discuss your views in a plenary with the entire group.

The Office of the Commissioner for Humanitarian Affairs

The local response is spearheaded by the national government and its leaders, while the Office of the Commissioner for Humanitarian Affairs (OCHA) provides support at country level through the Resident Humanitarian Coordinator (RHC). This partnership is responsible for maintaining the coherent effectiveness of international assistance and overseen by OCHA's Under-Secretary General. The Under-Secretary General, nominated by the Secretary General, is appointed by the General Assembly for four years which can be renewed for a further term.

The right of the UN to provide humanitarian aid and coordinate its delivery to victim-survivors of various emergencies and disasters was mandated by a resolution of the General Assembly (46/182) on 19 December 1991. In its role as coordinator, OCHA undertakes a range of crucial activities: prevention, preparedness, capacity building, and appeals for assistance from member states. OCHA facilitates cooperation between different organisations and the national government of the country affected and provides operational leadership throughout the disaster cycle including relief and rehabilitation and post-disaster development. The Emergency Relief Coordinator (ERC) facilitates the creation of the Inter-Agency Standing Committee (IASC) under General Assembly Resolution 46/182. IASC has several sub-committees that assist in devising guidelines for practitioners in emergency situations. These cover many dimensions, e.g. psychosocial social work and gender (IASC, 2007). Humanitarian assistance is expected to adhere to the principles of humanity, neutrality and impartiality. At the same time, the work of the Emergency Relief Coordinator must not undermine the role of the national government in the disaster area under its jurisdiction. The national government always retains the key responsibility in beginning, organising, coordinating, and implementing the distribution of humanitarian aid there. However, there can be tensions between the different players and their interpretation of their roles which can be experienced as disempowering. For example, the United Nations usually waits to be invited to intervene, and rarely over-rides the sovereignty of the nation-state concerned, even when the state neglects its duty to care for residents. In recent history, there has been only one occasion when the Security Council of the UN overrode national reluctance to receive aid. This occurred in 2009 when the military junta ruling Myanmar (Burma) rejected humanitarian assistance desperately needed by its population following the devastation caused by Cyclone Nargis. Only a unanimous decision enables the Security Council to act or challenge the sovereignty principle.

Humanitarian aid workers follow existing norms and standards articulated by General Assembly Resolution 46/182; the Oslo Guidelines on the Use of Military and Civil Defence Assets in Disaster Relief; 2005 Hyogo Framework for Action; *Sphere Handbook*; Humanitarian Charter and Minimum Standards in Disaster Response; and Code of Conduct for the Red Cross and Red Crescent Societies and other NGOs providing disaster relief. The Good Humanitarian Donorship Principles (GHD, 2003) and the Sendai Framework are also relevant to these bodies. Key ethical principles observed are to:

• Adhere to principled humanitarian action.
• Prioritise saving lives.
• Show respect for and promote international humanitarian law.
• Assess needs and provide needs-based assistance.
• Be accountable to the victim-survivors.
• Seek access to assured humanitarian funding.
• Avoid duplication of donor responses.
• Use a strengths-based perspective (without ignoring weaknesses that need attention).
• Engage in coproduced disaster responses that empower and engage affected populations.

Other crucial guidance for international responses to disasters covers both international and domestic aid. It includes the IASC Operational Guidelines for the Protection of Persons in Situations of Natural Disasters, Guidelines for the Domestic Facilitation and Regulation of International Disaster Relief, and the Initial Recovery Assistance Guidelines (IDRL Guidelines). The IDRL Guidelines also address legal preparedness and strengthen a country's institutional, policy and legal frameworks. A key aim is to ensure the coordinated and efficient distribution of aid where needed. Guidance tends to be rooted in the array of norms and standards mentioned above.

The 'cluster' system

The international humanitarian community organises itself in sectoral working groups called 'clusters' to support those government leaders that are responding to an emergency. Known as the 'cluster approach', it encompasses two levels – the global and the country or national levels. In the global sphere, the cluster approach seeks to improve preparedness and technical capacity. Those individuals leading global clusters aim to be accountable about the activities that are undertaken under their remit and provide good leadership among responders. IASC (Interagency

Standing Committee) agrees who will become designated as Global Cluster Leads. Cluster Leads are appointed to cover 11 areas under the aegis of a UN agency and are as follows: agriculture led by the Food and Agriculture Organization (FAO); camp coordination and management organised by the United Nations High Commissioner for Refugees (UNHCR) and International Organisation for Migration (IOM); early recovery headed by the United Nations Development Programme (UNDP); education led by the United Nations International Children's Education Fund (UNICEF) and Save the Children; emergency shelter supported by UNHCR, but convened by the International Federation of Red Cross and Red Crescent Societies (IFRC); emergency telecommunications under the auspices of OCHA, UNICEF and World Food Programme (WFP); health led by the World Health Organization (WHO); logistics which includes transportation and warehousing led by the WFP; nutrition led by UNICEF; protection headed by UNHCR; water, sanitation and hygiene (WASH) under the aegis of UNICEF. Each cluster is required to mainstream cross-cutting elements that include human rights, gender, age, HIV/AIDS, protection, the environment, and efficient and prompt recovery. Those involved in country level responses usually mobilise diverse agencies and NGOs in strategic and coordinated responses across all areas of activity. Overall, the cluster approach aims to strengthen coordination among all humanitarian actors and the government of the country (or countries) concerned at all relevant echelons, and to identify and address gaps in their emergency responses. The Cluster Lead specifies roles, the division of labour between different agencies, and responsibilities of the various sectors responding to the emergency, e.g. health care, housing.

The cluster approach operates at two levels. At the global level, the aim is to strengthen system-wide preparedness and technical capacity to respond to humanitarian emergencies by designating global cluster leads and ensuring that there is predictable leadership and accountability in all the main sectors or areas of activity. At the country level, the aim is to ensure a more coherent and effective response, with each sector having a clearly designated lead, as agreed by the RHC after consultation with the Humanitarian Country Team (HCT) and all other relevant actors. Cluster Leads endeavour to secure:

• communication services
• data connectivity services
• technological support
• service coordination
• information management services
• services for communities.

Country level responses ought to be locality specific and culturally relevant in addressing the emergency needs of those affected. They should utilise local capacities, build these where needed, and ensure that officials know which humanitarian actors are operating in their area, their skills, resources, and activities. Responders should also make certain that they maintain links with the national government, local authorities, state institutions, local organisations, and businesses.

Cluster arrangements for delivering aid

The UN delivers aid through 'clusters'. There are 11 clusters (leads in brackets) and four areas of responsibility. The 'clusters' are logistics (WFP), nutrition (UNKCEF), protection (UNHCR), shelter (IFRC, UN-HCR), water, sanitation and hygiene (WASH) (UNICEF), camp coordination and camp management (IOM, UNHCR), early recovery (UNDP), education (UNICEF, Save the Children), emergency telecommunications (WFP), food security (WFP, FAO), and health (WHO). The areas of responsibility (AoR) are: child protection; gender-based violence; housing, land and property; and mine action.

National clusters or sectoral groups are formed when a major emergency has substantial and complex humanitarian needs that require a wide range of international humanitarian actors involved in multi-sectorial responses. Cluster leads may be IASC members, a UN agency or someone else. Country clusters, established to meet the needs of specific situations, may not align with the 11 global clusters. These take account of local organisational capacities and strengths and may have different leads. An existing coordination group blessed with clear leadership can continue operating. The country cluster structure and corresponding cluster leads are proposed by the UN Humanitarian Coordinator (HC), or the UN Resident Coordinator (RC) if an HC has not been appointed. Government authorities and relevant country level IASC partners agree the cluster lead and consult with the ERC and IASC at global level.

WHO leads the health cluster globally and reports to the UN Emergency Relief Coordinator (REC) in a health emergency, e.g. COVID-19. The global health cluster has 30 partners. It develops normative guidance and tools for assessment, coordination, information management and training. WHO establishes surge capacity by bringing in skilled experts and supporting them with appropriate supplies, logistics and security to enhance national capacity. WHO also contributes to the nutrition, WASH, emergency shelter and protection clusters. With the leaders of these clusters, WHO promotes harmonisation across clusters.

IASC principles focus on improving prioritisation, defining the roles and responsibilities of humanitarian organisations. These are to:

1 Support service delivery with a platform to agree approaches and eliminate duplication.
2 Inform strategic decision-making to enable the HC and Humanitarian Country Team (HCT) to coordinate needs assessments, gap analyses and prioritisation.
3 Plan strategic development in sectoral plans, adherence to standards and funding needs.
4 Advocate on behalf of cluster participants and affected victim-survivors.
5 Monitor the cluster strategy, reporting on results, and recommend corrective action as required.
6 Undertake contingency planning/preparedness/national capacity building as needed and if the cluster has capacity.
7 Uphold each cluster's responsibility to integrate early recovery with humanitarian response plans from the outset.
8 Enable the Resident Coordinator/Humanitarian Coordinator (RC/HC) to establish an Early Recovery Cluster (ERC).

Child protection

The Child Protection (CP) Area of Responsibility (CP AoR) aims to enhance child protection coordination and responses in humanitarian contexts by effectively coordinating national and international efforts to protect children, secure maximum quality and ensure impact. The CP AoR supports 40 countries with inter-agency field-based coordination groups through its international, national, and local members. Its Rapid Response Team (RRT) and Geneva-based coordination staff provide in-country support to field-level child protection coordination groups. The Enquiry Service of the CP AoR answers questions about CP and its coordination, and analyses requests to identify gaps and priorities for global policy and tool development. CP coordinators and IMs form communities of practice to offer peer-to-peer support. CP regional focal points provide in-depth technical support to CP coordinators and IMS (Information Management Systems). RRTs rapidly deploy high quality child protection coordination and technical capacity in humanitarian situations and offer surge support.

The gender-based violence (GBV) AoR, formed in 2008 is a global-level forum to coordinate and collaborate on GBV prevention and response. It is a component of the Global Protection Cluster (GPC) led by the United Nations Population Fund (UNFPA). The GBV AoR brings together NGOs, UN agencies, donors, academics, and independent experts to ensure more predictable, accountable, and effective GBV prevention and response in emergencies.

The UN shifted from disaster responses to disaster risk reduction to reduce the rising costs of threats to human life, damages to built infrastructures, physical environments, and biosphere. It declared 1990–1999 the International Decade for Natural Disaster Reduction. The first international conference, the World Conference on Natural Disaster Reduction ran from 23–27 May 1994 in Yokohama, Japan. The Yokohama Strategy for a Safer World and Action Plan sought to assist individual countries in developing infrastructures to mitigate the impact of disasters. In 2000, the UN International Strategy for Disaster Reduction (ISDR) was formulated. It engaged NGOs, civil society organisations, UN agencies, and regional organisations in developing and sustaining international action to reduce disaster risk. In 2005, the Second World Conference on Disaster Reduction took place in Kobe, Japan. This added preventative action to mitigating action and led to the Hyogo Framework for Action 2005–2015: Building the Resilience of Nations and Communities to Disasters (HFA) and encouraged people in local communities to take seriously disaster risk reduction. At the international level, the HFA required individual countries to address:

- Governance within organisational, legal and policy frameworks.
- Risk identification, assessment, monitoring, and early warning.
- Knowledge management and education.
- Reducing underlying risk factors.
- Preparing for effective response and recovery.
- Introducing risk management in all social development, environmental protection, disaster management, and planning measures.
- Funding the Global Platform for Disaster Risk Reduction to implement the ISDR.
- The International Association for Impact Assessment (IAIA) which defined the impact of social change as 'all impacts on humans and the ways … people and communities interact with their socio-cultural, economic, and biophysical surroundings', and accounted for differentiated experiences.
- Rising social vulnerabilities. People are demanding more health and social services including mental health services and services for people with disabilities.
- Risk mitigation for older people encountering greater risk by living in coastal areas.
- Climate change for increased psychological stress, and greater risks people face during extreme weather events.

Collective approaches to reduce risk can respond more capably to increased risk, e.g. Isle of Eigg Heritage Trust which purchased private land and companies to promote renewable energy collectively on that island.

The Third World Conference in Sendai, Japan replaced the HFA with the Sendai Framework for Disaster Risk Reduction, 2015–2030. It has seven targets and four priorities for action to meet the 2030 obligations. These targets are to:

- Reduce global disaster mortality.
- Reduce global numbers of people affected.
- Reduce direct disaster economic losses in global gross domestic product (GDP).
- Reduce disaster damage to critical infrastructures, disruption of basic services in health and education, and develop resilience.
- Increase numbers of countries having national and local disaster risk reduction strategies by 2020.
- Enhance international cooperation to provide sustainable support to complement national implementation plans in industrialising countries.
- Increase availability of and people's access to multi-hazard early warning systems and disaster risk information and assessments.

Its four priorities were to:

- Understand disaster risk.
- Strengthen disaster risk governance to manage disaster risk better.
- Invest in disaster reduction initiatives to build resilience.
- Enhance disaster preparedness for effective responses and 'building back better' expressed as resilience in recovery, rehabilitation, and reconstruction.

The Sendai Framework attempted to learn the lessons of the HFA and engage all member states in its implementation. The mid-term review of the Sendai Framework occurred in May 2023. It identified achievements and gaps to inform future work.

Exercise

Read about the Sendai Framework at this link:

www.undrr.org/publication/sendai-framework-disaster-risk-reduction-2015-2030

Discuss what you think of these priorities. What are their strengths and weaknesses?

The Sendai Framework, the United Nations International Strategy for Disaster Reduction

The United Nations International Strategy for Disaster Reduction (UNISDR), now known as the United Nations Disaster Risk Reduction (UNDRR) is responsible for the strategic frameworks used in guiding member countries to develop their disaster risk reduction strategies. Since 1999, UNISDR's work had been supplemented by the United Nations Office for Disaster Risk Reduction (UNDRR) which assisted it in the implementation of international strategies aimed at reducing risk. The UNDRR acronym brings these two offices together. The current strategic framework is known as the Sendai Framework for Disaster Risk Reduction and runs from 2015–2030. The Sendai Framework promotes disaster risk management globally through seven targets that aim to reduce or mitigate current risks, prevent new ones from arising, support the development of resilience in individuals, communities and state institutions. It also considers natural and 'man-made' hazards alongside environmental, technological, and biological hazards and risks. It also attempts to improve human health and wellbeing. The Sendai Framework also seeks to:

- Enhance understanding of disaster risk, exposure, vulnerability and hazard properties.
- Strengthen disaster risk governance, including in national platforms.
- Hold institutions accountable for their disaster risk management strategies.
- Prepare communities to 'build back better' (or transformatively).
- Acknowledge the diverse roles held by participating stakeholders.
- Mobilise companies in risk-sensitive investments and avoid the formation of new risks.
- Help develop resilient workplaces, health infrastructures, and institutions to protect cultural heritages.
- Promote international cooperation and global partnerships.
- Devise risk-informed donor policies and programmes, including financial support and loans offered by international financial institutions like the IMF (International Monetary Fund) and World Bank (WB).

The Sendai Framework recognises that the Global Platform for Disaster Risk Reduction and regional disaster risk reduction platforms can provide coherence across different agendas to monitor and review achievements. The Sendai Framework replaces the Hyogo Framework for Action (HFA) of 2005–2015. The HFA introduced risk awareness and early warning systems and insisted that humanitarian aid workers became aware of local and cultural sensitivities when working with local residents.

National organisations active in humanitarian aid

The international frameworks have provided the backdrop within which donors and humanitarian workers operate in a disaster-affected nation-state. Many donors fund specific programmes that cover diverse emergency situations and disaster interventions and pay for overseas and local workers to deliver services. Key government-based funders include the Canadian International Development Agency (CIDA), Swedish International Development Agency (SIDA), UKAid and USAid. Additionally, there are a plethora of international charitable agencies, some of which have religious origins, although they provide services to victim-survivors regardless of religious affiliations, and others that are secular. Their derivations can cause confusion if people think that there are inbuilt criteria that they must meet to access services. Some of the better-known agencies active in the international sphere (in no particular order) include, Save the Children, Oxfam, the Red Cross, World Vision, Mercy Corps, Christian Aid, the Red Crescent Societies, Doctors without Borders (Médecins Sans Frontières), which have branches within the UK, USA and other countries, Social Workers Without Borders (in Australia, Hong Kong, the UK and Italy), Plan International and Christian Aid. The UK's national Disaster Emergency Committee (DEC) is an organisation that brings together 14 agencies to raise funds for different emergencies, including COVID-19, and Russia's War Against Ukraine.

Besides Social Work Without Borders, operating in several countries, e.g., the UK, Italy, Hong Kong, there are several social work organisations that operate at international, national, and local levels (usually through branch systems) to support social work education, practice, and policy. These have supported disaster interventions, including COVID-19. The key international organisations are the: International Association of Schools of Social Work (IASSW), International Federation of Social Workers (IFSW) and International Council of Social Welfare (ICSW). First founded in 1928, they are called the three 'sister organisations' which collaborate across a range of activities, including holding joint conferences and sponsoring the journal *International Social Work*, and relate to UN actions through the Global Agenda. The Global Agenda aimed to address international issues and strengthen the voice of social work globally. These organisations were all involved in COVID-19 initiatives which can be found on the relevant website for each one.

There are national associations in each country, many of which are linked to their international bodies in diverse ways according to their structures. For example, in the UK, the Joint Universities Council, Social Work Education Committee (JUC-SWEC) sits on the Board of IASSW to shape policy. Each national association decides whether to join an international association directly. IASSW also has a regional structure, e.g. the European Association of Schools of Social Work for Europe. Similar regional bodies exist for Africa, the Asia-Pacific Region, North America and the Caribbean, and Latin America, mimicking the 5 regions of the UN. IFSW and ICSW have their own slightly different national and regional structures and relationship to individuals. In the UK, social workers join IFSW through the British Association of Social Workers (BASW) or as 'Friends of IFSW', the latter without voting rights. Each nation in the UK, has its own body for social workers affiliated to BASW: BASW Cymri (Wales), BASW England, BASW Northern Ireland and the Scottish Association of Social Workers (SASW). This structure differs from IASSW which has both university (known as schools of social work) and individual membership as well as of national associations. Each of these categories holds voting rights, although an individual has 1/10 of a vote. Social workers cannot join IFSW as individual members with voting rights. ICSW also has organisation-based membership structures. Moreover, each country has its own structures, for example, in the USA, the Council for Social Work Education (CSWE) is an accrediting body as well as the national association representing American academics on the IASSW Board. Its equivalent organisation, the National Association of Social Workers (NASW) is a member of IFSW. Recently, there have been no American organisations on the ICSW Board. Some countries have different structures, and this can complicate representation on international bodies. In China, there is the China Association of Social Work Education (CASWE) which brings social work academics together nationally. The Association of Schools of Social Work in Africa (ASSWA) represents tertiary level institutions in sub-Saharan Africa. The situation differs again elsewhere. For example, there is no national association for academics in India, although there are active city-based associations. In Australia, the accrediting body, is not the Australian Association of Schools of Social Work, but the Australian Association of Social Workers.

Social workers often deliver services in highly stressful situations including in armed conflicts, and many have lost their lives. The lengthy list of casualties covers the bombing of the UN Headquarters at Hotel Canal in Baghdad, Iraq on 19 August 2003. This killed 21 humanitarian aid workers including social workers and Sérgio Vieira de Mello, the UN High Commissioner for Human Rights and UN Special Representative for Iraq. Others have been individual workers, working alone, but vulnerable to people determined to pursue their own agendas. Many anti-humanitarian aid actors ignore aid workers' commitment to impartiality, which has been advocated for a very long time, by one of the first voluntary players in the field, the Red Cross. Those killed have been either embedded within the military and/or accused of taking sides by virtue of providing services in the locales where they were murdered (Hoogvelt, 2007). At the same time, some sexual predators have assumed the humanitarian or social worker mantle to exploit and traffic children during disaster situations as happened in Sri Lanka, Haiti and Nepal, among others. This has led to strong endeavours to institute procedures to check the background of those 'volunteering' to deliver aid or provide services in chaotic disaster situations and ensure that children are based in places of safety and sent to school to acquire a familiar daily routine with trusted adults as quickly as possible.

Conclusions

The governance structures for humanitarian aid and the delivery of disaster interventions are complex, and straddle the local, national, and global levels, with different structures applying at each level. However, there are important pieces of national legislation and UN Conventions and Protocols that contribute to service delivery and coordination. In the UK, a multi-nation country, legislation is both UK-wide and nation-specific. These levels are also responsive to UN-based protocols and treaties. Whether international, national, or local, all levels are inadequately funded. Fund-raising takes much staff time, especially of those allocated to this specific task. Despite this, social workers including humanitarian workers, work hard, often as unacknowledged heroic actors in the background, to deliver services that are human rights based and anti-oppressive, and aimed at meeting the needs of victim-survivors. They often place their own lives at risk, and humanitarian workers have been casualties of war, terrorism, natural disasters and health pandemics, like other members of populations living in disaster-affected areas.

3   COVID-19

A health pandemic that
challenges the social
work profession

Introduction: doing social work during a pandemic

In December 2019, Wuhan, China, experienced a new respiratory ail-
ment that was subsequently identified as caused by a new strain of coronavirus. The virus was subsequently labelled SARS-CoV-2, and the illness
became known as COVID-19. Once the Chinese government realised the
seriousness of the situation, it imposed a lengthy lockdown initially in
Wuhan, but later throughout the country. It cleverly prolonged the lockdown at first by extending the period of the Chinese New Year which
curtailed travel among the many people who had travelled from the cities
into the rural areas to visit family. Eventually, diverse travellers moved
around and took the virus to other countries and hastened its spread.

A pandemic is a specific kind of health disaster that affects large numbers of people across many geographic areas and is likely to overwhelm
the capacity of a national health system to cope unless the spread of the
disease is contained and controlled. Containing the virus to reduce demand upon and protect health services in the short-term became known
as 'flattening the curve'. A pandemic is about the spread of a disease,
not its infectiousness. The World Health Organization (WHO) declared
this new coronavirus a pandemic on 11 March 2020. Doing social work
under these conditions was challenging, fraught with difficulties and
risky. It was also rewarding when people were helped despite the barriers practitioners faced, including insufficient supplies of PPE, remote
working and deaths of colleagues, family, and friends. In many countries, social workers are a formal part of the emergency response system, and legislation guides their roles, responsibilities, and performance
during disasters. These varied according to country and the legislation
adopted (IASSW, 2020). Social work employers should know what these
are and inform their employees. Guidelines were also available online
and disaster-based practice should form part of qualifying education and
in-house training programmes to prepare practitioners for a pandemic.
I argue for their rapid inclusion in the social work curriculum as this is
seldom the case (Dominelli, 2012a).

DOI: 10.4324/9781003105824-4

In the UK, the 2004 Civil Contingencies Act (see Chapter 2), and its variations in the different nations, places social workers and health professionals as key responders. The police, firefighters, ambulance services and sometimes, the military, are on the frontline as First Responders. In a pandemic, the burden of dealing with people who succumb to the disease falls on the medical profession. Public appreciation of medical interventions during COVID-19 was very high. People were less aware of what social workers were doing. Social work's invisibility during the pandemic raises the issue for practitioner and academic engagement with both traditional and social media to promote the valuing of their work.

In this chapter, I consider the nature of COVID-19, the challenges, and opportunities this virus raised for social work theory, practice, policy, and implications for the academy. I conclude with important lessons drawn from this pandemic to mitigate the potential of future health crises to disrupt society.

State actions to reduce the spread of COVID-19

Social workers, as citizens of a nation-state, abide by the regulations applying to themselves and the population as a whole and playing their part in containing and controlling the pandemic professionally. Under COVID-19, they often conducted professional duties remotely. At the beginning of the pandemic when vaccinations were unavailable, the WHO and public health authorities advised people to mitigate or reduce the risk of catching COVID-19 by:

- Not touching the face, including the mouth, nose and eyes.
- Wearing a properly fitted mask with appropriate filtration (preferably N95 or FFP3).
- Washing hands frequently with soap and water (20 seconds) or using alcohol-based hand sanitisers if this were impossible.
- Disinfecting contaminated surfaces.
- Coughing into a tissue and binning it.
- Maintaining social distance (originally 2 metres).
- Testing people suspected of having the virus and if confirmed, tracing those with whom they had come into contact.

Such advice is relevant to various infectious diseases. The burden that COVID-19 imposed on the medical system and health professionals led to 'suppression' strategies to contain and control the spread of this virus. The mitigation instructions remained in place, especially during lockdown, when social and economic activities were disallowed. The key mitigation strategies utilised were:

- Lockdown or staying at home with limited rights to go outside. Going out was restricted to purchasing food and medicine.

- Social and physical distancing – remaining 2 metres away from another person if taking a daily walk or meeting them in public.
- Prohibiting large gatherings including sports fixtures, religious services, and concerts. Some countries defined this as having more than two people together in one space unless they were members of the same family.
- Closure of educational facilities including nursery facilities and schools except for the children of essential workers, and universities.
- Closure of bars, restaurants, and retail outlets except for grocery shops and pharmacies.
- Disallowing visits to care homes, attendance at funerals and weddings (although these were later relaxed somewhat to allow a small number of in-situ participants).
- Working from home except for essential workers.

The aim of a suppression strategy is to 'flatten' the curve, i.e. to reduce a huge upward rise in cases requiring hospitalisation as that could overwhelm the capacity of a medical system to cope. 'Flattening the curve', reduces the potential of transmission occurring and stretches the numbers requiring medical attention over a longer period. The closure of many industrial and commercial enterprises had a substantial economic impact as growth became curtailed and increased the likelihood of causing an economic recession. To reduce this impact, some governments provided financial support to retain people in work, e.g. Britain's furlough scheme, and supporting businesses through grants and no-interest loans. These measures carried implications for service users. Social workers informed them of their rights to assistance and supported mitigation activities, especially around lost income for low paid workers regardless of supportive measures in place.

COVID-19: Its characteristics

COVID-19 is not a seasonal cold or influenza. It is a highly infectious, respiratory virus that attacks mainly the lungs, but also other organs. This coronavirus is known as SARS-CoV-2 or severe acute respiratory syndrome coronavirus. The disease it created was called COVID-19 by the International Committee on Taxonomy of Viruses (ICTV). COVID-19 caused an atypical pneumonia outbreak in China during December 2019 and spread throughout the world later. As mentioned above, it was declared a pandemic by the WHO on 11 March 2020. A pandemic refers to the geographic spread of a disease, not its infectiousness. COVID-19 has several symptoms that occur together. These have varied over time as scientific understanding of how the coronavirus operates has grown. The most frequently cited ones are:

- cough; (and)
- fever over 38°C; (and)
- difficulty breathing (usually affecting the lungs).
- Later, it included the loss of sense of smell and taste.

A person displaying these symptoms is likely to have been in close contact with someone who had tested positive (confirmed) as having COVID-19; travelled to an infected area and acquired the virus there; acquired the virus from an infected person during the incubation period when the person concerned may have been unaware that they were carrying and spreading the virus (when they were asymptomatic); and/or had been exposed to COVID-19 contaminated materials in a laboratory or medical facility. Close contact has been defined as being within 1–2 metres for 10 minutes or longer of a person carrying the virus. In some countries, social workers have been exposed to contaminated surfaces when assisting health professionals dealing with the virus. The dangers of contracting COVID-19 made self-care and wearing personal protection equipment (PPE) essential. PPE consists of an appropriately filtrated and correctly fitted mask (N95 or FFP3), disposable gloves, a coverall, an alcohol-based (over 67%) hand gel sanitiser for use until hands can be washed thoroughly with soap and water for 20 seconds. Some professionals wore a visor above their masks.

Different countries experienced different levels of spread and number of cases and deaths. The UK was among the worst hit due to the shortage of PPE for health professionals, social care workers and population generally. The government of Boris Johnson, himself a victim-survivor of COVID-19, has been severely criticised for its failure to deal adequately with the coronavirus outbreak, although it succeeded in curtailing demand for National Health Service (NHS) services to levels that did not overwhelm provision and bed spaces despite an initial shortage of acute intensive care beds, PPE, and ventilators. Staff shortages were addressed by calling upon retired doctors and nurses, increasing the number of volunteers to undertake non-medical tasks, and bed shortages were addressed by creating 'Nightingale' field hospitals in major cities including London, Birmingham, and Glasgow. Many 'Nightingale' beds proved surplus to requirements and were closed.

According to Worldometer (www.worldometers.info/coronavirus), by 12 June 2020 globally, there were 7,775,661 cases leading to 428,970 deaths. These figures changed daily, and the ordering of countries varied as new cases and deaths were confirmed. On that day, the USA had the largest number of cases (2,121,381) and deaths (116,925). Brazil reported 831,064 cases and 41,952 fatalities. Russia and India also declared significant numbers of cases (520,129 and 310,760 respectively), but with substantially fewer deaths 6,829 and 8,995 respectively). The UK had 292,950 confirmed cases and 41,481 deaths. These figures are difficult to compare as there was no agreed universal system of reportage. The actual picture and bases on which figures were compiled will not be known until the pandemic is over, and these are revealed. Other countries with more robust response systems, especially in testing and tracing infected individuals and other measures to contain the virus, e.g. Taiwan and Hong Kong reported fewer cases and deaths. Taiwan had 443 confirmed cases and 431 deaths; Hong Kong had 1,110 cases and 1,061 fatalities at that time (Worldometer, 2022).

By this date, China, the country which first reported the coronavirus, had declared 83,075 cases and 4,634 fatalities. However, it was dreading a second wave in big cities including Beijing. This fear was made worse when 53 people linked to the Xinfadi market selling seafood, fruit and vegetables in Beijing tested positive for the coronavirus. The market was shut down on 13 June 2020. Five other markets were closed alongside 11 residential districts and 9 schools. All were placed under lockdown. The government also controlled traffic in and out of the capital, and disallowed sports events among other measures. The fear of a second wave was shared by countries across the world.

By 15 May 2022, Worldometer (2022) reported 521,077,873 COVID-19 cases and 6,288,098 deaths. The USA retained the top spot for cases (84,209,473) and deaths (1,026,646). The comparable figures for the UK were 22,159,805 cases and 176,708 deaths. By this time, China had 221,804 cases and 5,209 deaths (data from www.worldometers.info/coronavirus). Despite these relatively low numbers, China was again in the news because its 'zero tolerance' strategy permitted the shutdown of Shanghai, Beijing and other cities to prevent the virus from spreading. Meanwhile, some European nations, including the UK, had removed all mandatory requirements in favour of individual decision-making around public health safety measures, leading to jubilation among the general public. I consider this a form of 'ideological medicine' because the number of coronavirus cases remains high, although those who fall ill have mild symptoms if they have been vaccinated. The discovery and deployment of effective vaccines have been crucial in reducing death rates and cases requiring hospitalisation. However, new variants keep appearing, long COVID-19 remains a worry, and the pandemic is not over (WHO, 2022). On the positive side, the most vulnerable people in the UK have been offered a 4th (booster) vaccine, and various drugs can be used to treat the illness, e.g. remdesivir and other anti-viral medicines. Although the death rates in many low-income countries have been proportionately less than in rich countries, vaccines are poorly distributed across countries due to vaccine nationalism in the West, and limited solidarity was displayed in the international arena (West-Oram and Buyx, 2017). On the 14 August 2022, WHO (2022) reported a downturn in the statistics from the previous week with 587 million confirmed cases and 6.4 million deaths globally. On 26 October 2022, there were 633,547,896 cases and 6,585,019 deaths globally. The USA remained in the number one spot with 99,136,830 cases and 1,093,274 fatalities. The UK's figures were 23,855,522 and 192,682 respectively (data from www.worldometers.info/coronavirus/#countries).

COVID-19 legislation

The British government introduced the Coronavirus Act 2020, rather than using existing legislation. The statement summing up this position was:

> The duties on Local Authorities to meet eligible needs under sections 18, 19 and 20 of the Care Act 2014 (or sections 35 and 40 of the SSWA) would be replaced by a duty to meet needs for care and support where failure to do so would breach an individual's human rights and Local Authorities would have a power to meet other needs.

In keeping with the different legal system in Scotland, the Coronavirus Act focuses on this in Clause 15 which describes the duty of a local authority to assess needs. It states:

> Under this clause the duty on Local Authorities to conduct a needs assessment under the Social Work (Scotland) Act 1968 will be relaxed to allow local authorities the discretion to dispense with the requirement in order to provide services and support for those most in urgent need without delay. It provides that local authorities can dispense with the requirement if conducting an assessment would be impractical or cause undesirable delay.
>
> The clause also amends the duties under the Carers (Scotland) Act 2016 and associated regulations, to convert the duty to prepare an adult carer support plan/young carer statement to a power to do so.
>
> The territorial extent and application of this clause is Scotland. And there is further provision for issuing statutory guidance, charging and protecting authorities against legal action if there are delays in providing assessments when the normal system is switched back on again.

Social workers were very perturbed by the idea that they could ignore the duty to assess those in need, and BASW raised objections. Individual social workers did their utmost to provide services and visit people at home where necessary, including doing so, at great risk to themselves and their families. Although figures are hard to establish, at least 98 social workers died from COVID-19 while simply doing their job during the first year.

Social work under COVID-19: Hindrances and opportunities

Social workers faced many challenges in addressing the COVID-19 pandemic. Training on health pandemics was limited, and the idea of using remote technology to conduct investigations into the abuse of children and older people was frightening, especially as most practitioners were simply thrown into getting on with the job (IASSW, 2020). Social workers have many generic skills for use in any disaster, including a health pandemic. Key among these are: undertaking risk assessments, developing plans of action, evaluating the effectiveness of interventions, conducting interviews and investigations into family dynamics, crisis interventions, family reunifications, and counselling individuals suffering grief, loss and bereavements.

Anti-oppressive principles and practice

Throughout their interventions, social workers have sought to practice anti-oppressively. While many dimensions of anti-oppressive practice (AOP) are familiar (Dominelli, 2002), its principles had to be adapted specifically to COVID-19. Crucial to their considerations were to protect the health of service users, their families and themselves, and keeping well to ensure the delivery of services in risky conditions. The following principles provide relevant guidance for working anti-oppressively in the context of uncertainty around and lack of knowledge of this coronavirus. For social workers, social care workers, and welfare assistants serving the public, these included:

- Treating people with respect, dignity, and sensitivity.
- Doing no harm, either to others or to yourself.
- Staying connected (remotely or with safe physical and social distancing) with colleagues, service users, friends, and extended family.
- Being prepared for ethical dilemmas, including knowing how to improvise on self-care if home visiting without PPE.
- Being kind, compassionate and understanding within existing guidelines for good practice to ensure that important cues were recognised.

- Reducing sources of fear by explaining issues clearly and simply to yourself and others.
- Providing counselling if required, referring people to specialist services as necessary, especially when dealing with mental ill health, grief and loss which can include fatalities, loss of liberties and unfamiliar routines.
- Active listening and understanding the local situation on physical and social distancing and resourcing.
- Engaging service users in improvising and coproducing new locally viable solutions to their problems.
- Tailoring your responses to be locality specific and culturally relevant, including acknowledging language differences and the importance of your own cultural standpoint in how you view the world and others.
- Looking for strengths and capabilities to build upon, without ignoring problematic issues.
- Being critically reflective and aware of the impact of social issues embedded in structural inequalities such as poor health, low incomes, poverty in its wider aspects, discrimination, and oppression.
- Knowing what resources are available among individuals, families, and communities and how to refer service users onwards to access additional resources, and obtaining training for yourself and others, particularly the volunteers supporting your work.
- Supporting others including colleagues and the volunteers who back-up your interventions.
- Looking after yourself, securing regular support and supervision informally among your peer group and formally from your line manager.

Other guidance for COVID-19 included how to protect others when delivering services and self-care. Both concerns are relevant in other disaster situations, so a helpful, if unexpected positive outcome of practising under COVID-19, was that social workers acquired skills and confidence in working in a disaster situation. Some social workers have continued to deliver services in a form of *blended working* which meant sometimes working from the office, at other times, working remotely from home, as opportunities and barriers dictated.

Protecting yourself and others when delivering services

Supplementing official guidance

Various government departments issued advice for practising under COVID-19. In the UK, this has included the Department of Education (DfE), Department of Health (DH), local authorities and professional websites. The general suggestions given below complement these as points to be considered vis-à-vis protecting others under COVID-19:

- Maintaining physical and social distancing (keeping 2 metres distance; some suggest 1 metre is sufficient, but this is very context specific and needs adaptation when space is unavailable, limited or poorly ventilated), and mitigating risk by wearing a properly fitted N95 (FFP3) mask, overall and disposable gloves, staying home, working from home wherever possible, not attending public gatherings, gigs or other social events.
- Following safety precautions as advised by health authorities: wearing properly fitted suitable masks (filtration, type of mask and correct fit with no spaces left around the face, nose and chin), using protective clothing; not touching your face, eyes, nose and mouth even when removing PPE; washing hands with soap and water often; throwing away used tissues or paper products properly; and disinfecting hard surfaces in your office, car and home.
- Giving service users advance warning (electronically or by post) if visiting that you will be wearing PPE.
- Being vigilant in spotting safeguarding issues because living in the same space can intensify tensions and stress within relationships and lead to higher levels of child abuse, elder abuse, and intimate partner violence.
- Finding additional resources for those in need, e.g. counselling, for those who feel socially isolated and/or are mentally ill.
- Encouraging those staying at home to stay connected with others remotely, and undertaking activities, exercises, and digital games, safely.

Working in the office

Questions of how to maintain safety while working from the office exercised many practitioners. Responses depended on the physical layout of the building and office. Key queries included:

1 How do I address issues about working around colleagues, hot-desking, and having a 'coronavirus-free' environment?
2 How do I remain professional including sticking to ethical behaviour and maintaining confidentiality?

Keeping the building and office 'coronavirus free' could be challenging in situations where open-plan offices and 'hot-desking' constituted the norm. In these, more than one person had to share desks, computers, keyboards, and other equipment. These had to be disinfected after each use, but this was not always possible. Thus, practitioners had to wear PPE at all times - mask, disposable gloves and removable overall to protect their clothes which had to be washed at hot temperatures with detergent once reaching home and showering before doing anything else. These measures were to protect themselves and others and avoid spreading the virus or becoming sick. Other important elements of safety in the office included physical and social distancing and working in a bubble such as having a plastic screen like Perspex around a desk to separate one person from another and disinfecting this space after each use. In China, some factory workers were separated by wooden screens around desks outside as these were more readily available. But like a plastic separator, these needed to be physically distanced from others – 2 metres all around if possible and disinfected after use.

Working from home

Working from home posed different challenges. These included the issue of blurring the boundaries between work and family life. Responding to this critical issue satisfactorily was problematic for those with caring responsibilities ranging from home-schooling for children to caring for older family members who might be shielding or self-isolating within the home alongside carrying out household duties like cooking, cleaning, and doing laundry. These concerns became intensified if the home were small with space at a premium for finding somewhere for an 'office' in which to work.

Furthermore, when working from home, those with pre-existing conditions required specific attention. These included diabetes, asthma, and obesity, all of which could exacerbate vulnerability to the coronavirus. Social distancing, wearing PPE to protect yourself and others from the virus, especially if you were asymptomatic (and vice versa) after coming into close contact with someone carrying the virus were critical. If someone were ill, that person had to self-isolate, preferably in another room, for 14 days (later reduced to 5). Items like food and books were left and collected at the door using disposable gloves. Hands were washed frequently with soap and water.

Working from home became the norm under lockdown. The issue of when it could be eased was controversial. Nonetheless, those considering a home visit, had to undertake a risk assessment which could be discussed with their line manager and peer support group. Crucial questions covered:

1 Is a home visit necessary? Why?
2 What is its purpose?
3 Can it be done safely? What steps could be taken to ensure it is safe?
4 What could be done if it is not?

Completing a risk assessment helps you decide what you ought to do. There would be procedures to follow if a home visit were assessed as unsafe. Under these circumstances, you would have to initiate a remote discussion within your team and consult your line manager regarding the next steps. You would also have to be prepared to 'escalate' or pass the issue upwards to a higher level of decision-making if you continued to feel concerned.

General guidance to cover working from home includes:

- What training is required? This should include putting on, wearing, and taking off PPE safely and training in using remote technology appropriately to replace face-to-face visits.
- Identify IT (technology) needs and where support can be accessed when problems arise.
- Make your workspace ergonomic to minimise damaging your spine, back and eyesight, and take frequent breaks from your computer.
- Have you got the correct technology to support you in your working from home? Check the speed of your broadband and what support the IT experts from work can offer you when your computer fails. Check these out as soon as you can and keep these details easily accessible.
- Can you define the strengths and weaknesses of the families and each individual that you work with? Identifying these can assist in enthusing families to take your advice seriously and feel less threatened when in contact with you.
- How can the family protect itself? What advice or resources can you provide? In these circumstances, protecting yourself, others including service users and family members is essential. If you do not have the answers, do you know whom to approach to get them? You can also search government websites for legislation and advice.
- How can service users maintain connections with others? Maintaining connections and links with others, whether families, neighbours, service providers or other professionals is essential, so explore how they can develop safe links and remain mindful of the COVID-19 restrictions on socialising or entering another's personal space in the office or at home.
- How can emotional wellbeing be supported among service users, family members, and for yourself?

Emotional work is not a luxury, but necessary to maintain good mental health. You may wish to talk to colleagues and organise a regular, virtual check-in or contact meeting to touch base and enjoy a virtual coffee together to discuss anything informally or have a social chat.

If considering service user needs, you could consult with your peers and supervisor, reflect on your practice, share concerns, pool knowledge and experiences of COVID-19 with all the technological means at your disposal. These could include laptops with Skype, Zoom and Teams, smartphones, landlines, or old-fashioned mail, and you might wish to explore the provision of laptops to families that cannot afford such equipment. Also, look up and familiarise yourself with mental health resources online, including materials on emotional first aid like those on the WHO website.

How can you manage your workload and the cases that you have? It may be challenging to maintain a work–life balance and protect spaces for work when the home is a family space that must be shared with others whose needs also have to be addressed.

Remember, you are not immune from the stresses of the strange new world humanity is in. Self-care, relaxation, exercises, mindfulness exercises, yoga and other forms of indoor exercise can help you relax. Some, like yoga can be done remotely with others, and with your family, providing you keep physical distancing between you.

Self-care

Every social worker meeting the public should wear PPE. However, a shortage of PPE locally, nationally, and globally for substantial periods of time necessitated prioritisation for access to these scarce resources. In these circumstances, social workers had to explore how to access and evaluate alternative possibilities for masks, protective gowns or coveralls, disposable gloves, and disinfectant materials using the precautionary principle to mitigate risk. These alternatives were not ideal but were justified through the precautionary principle on the grounds that some protection for themselves and others was better than none.

Self-care will require a cultural shift for those social workers who typically neglect to look after themselves in their eagerness to serve others. Self-care is essential in disaster situations to protect social workers from burnout, and not undermine continuity in service provision. Below are principles that endorse self-care. To look after yourself, a risk assessment is undertaken to ascertain what you need and what self-care means to you. Self-care covers:

- Accessing support and supervision among peers and managers, including debriefing regularly, preferably daily.
- Forming and using your peer-support group to create a safe space for considering different scenarios and ethical dilemmas encountered when doing home visits, agency visits, or delivering services and exploring various solutions to problems.
- Obtaining appropriate psychosocial support if you become traumatised by your experiences, speaking to your manager, and ensuring

that support will remain available for as long as necessary, which may be a while.

- Learning from other people's personal and professional experiences, including those from overseas sources.
- Being prepared to improvise safely and seek information that will enable you to do so.
- Trusting your reflective, critical and innovative capacities to evaluate what you hear, say or do.
- Planning for contingencies and looking after yourself when outside your safe space, e.g. taking a thermos flask of tea or coffee or water with you; wearing disposable gloves; disinfecting surfaces like those in your home, office, and car regularly; and disposing of PPE carefully by keeping a disposal bag handy and washing hands with disinfectant and/or soap and water asap.
- Looking after your physical wellbeing by eating healthy food, getting plenty of rest, and taking exercise as often as allowed by local lockdown restrictions. These originally emphasised indoor exercise and outdoor exercise once a day when walking the dog or going for a walk while maintaining physical and social distancing (initially 2 metres throughout).
- Staying at home and self-isolating if you feel ill to avoid spreading the coronavirus to others.
- Discussing your situation with your line manager, obtaining the best possible online advice and support initially, and seeking health care in a safe manner if required.
- Keeping and making available a record of where you have been and whom you have contacted in case follow-up is necessary.
- Staying calm, staying safe, and staying connected while keeping your social and physical distance!
- Remembering that social workers are essential, if sometimes undervalued, professionals!

Despite such guidance, practitioners had to address additional concerns daily. Shortly after the pandemic began, guidance descended upon practitioners like a blizzard, making it difficult for them to read and understand it all. Sometimes, advice from different sources was contradictory, an issue exacerbated by the lack of unanimity among the scientists who provided the research on which such guidance was predicated. Thus, it is crucial that practitioners become well-informed to assess and mitigate their own risks, according to a well-informed understanding of these.

Among other issues worrying social workers were those relating to the loss of relationship-based practice: What was happening on the other side of the screen? What aspects of a relationship was the abuser – known or potential, hiding? What would happen if a key factor were missed during remote conversations? Many social workers spent sleepless nights thinking about what they might not have noticed. Others utilised remote-working effectively, using broadband technologies to have one-to-one sessions with service users, engage children in internet-based games and other activities. At the same time, they ensured that children became familiar with internet-based scammers and sexual predators. Similarly, with older people, social workers had to discuss self-protection from unwanted online attention and ensuring that older people and their carers became aware of the clever ways financial predators could utilise to gain access to their bank accounts. Such discussions also raised questions about the ethical dimensions of online communication with service users as another space for potential exploitation (Boddy and Dominelli, 2017). This space became wider under COVID-19.

Protecting the community

The community becomes both a source of support, resources and infection – called community transmission, during the coronavirus pandemic. There are many different groups with high levels of 'vulnerability' living in every community – people with compromised immune systems, at-risk groups including those with existing conditions such as asthma, coronary disease, cancer. To protect them from an accidental spreading of the virus, not going to see them face-to-face but maintaining phone, email or internet contact is critical to preserving their wellbeing and reducing social isolation. In this context, valuing remote connections as meaningful acts, rather than extras is crucial to sustaining emotional wellbeing. Even if delivering services, upholding social and physical distancing, including by remaining on the doorstep and leaving items there are important protective measures. If you feel unwell, self-isolate for 14 days to prevent community-transmission (note that in the UK, the periods of isolation varied, and was reduced to 5 days just before all restrictions were lifted). In the UK, those feeling unwell were initially asked to consult the NHS website for advice. If this action failed to answer people's queries, they were asked to contact NHS 111 or their GP. Some GPs also provided online advice and/or someone a service user could talk to on the phone.

Social workers can consider helping young people to challenge the assumption that they cannot catch the virus as raising awareness. Young people can catch a mild version of the virus and may be unaware of being ill. However, they can pass the virus on, even if asymptomatic, i.e. not showing signs of the disease, particularly before they begin to feel unwell. To be safe, young people who feel unwell should self-isolate, preferably for 14 days. Wearing masks can reduce viral spread if you are not tested. Mask availability became problematic in many countries including the UK. Priority use was reserved for essential workers providing health services. Those in social services including the social care sector may have had to improvise. This could include making their own face covering or mask using 3–6 layers of cloth; and using a plastic bin bag with holes for the head and arms as a coverall.

An environmental or nature deficit

Experiencing nature became indispensable for many people during the pandemic. Some people were caught breaking lockdown restrictions to walk in various national parks. For others, this restriction created a 'nature deficit'. Cunsolo and Ellis (2018) call the grief emanating from ecological losses produced by climate change 'eco-grief'. Environmental loss became more visible during the summer of 2022 during heatwaves and floods. Despite this, sustainability of the environment and demands being made of it were often ignored during COVID-19. The use of countless disposable items loaded landfill sites with garbage that would take a long time to decompose and being constantly online using servers consumed significant amounts of fossil fuels.

Exercise – Ecological sustainability

Public gardens and parks are an invaluable natural resource. Individuals and families often take the availability of 'natural surroundings' for granted.

In pairs, consider the following questions:

- How might this indifference be offset when lockdown ends?
- How might you encourage those living in high rise flats to become aware of nature?
- How might ecological sustainability be maintained by those living in urban environments, particularly in high-rise flats?

Planting trees is often used to offset greenhouse gas emissions. Those in houses with gardens could plant shrubs and grow vegetables to mitigate demands for energy. Shrubs can be grown from cuttings of those already in the garden; vegetables can be grown in a yard, balcony, pot, or window ledge. Such endeavours can be shared with children while maintaining physical and social distancing if they are ill.

Media expertise

Social workers are skilled communicators. They constantly exercise these skills when communicating with service users, colleagues, managers, family members, and friends. They are less familiar in contacting the traditional media for professional purposes. Most social workers tend to avoid the media. However, the wonderful work that social workers are doing with people under COVID-19 provides an opportunity to show the public the positive side of social work and highlight its impact on people's health and wellbeing. Like doctors and nurses and other essential workers including bus drivers, social workers, and care workers also risked their lives to serve others and became casualties of COVID-19. The media can be a powerful ally, but also a dangerous one if broadcasters do not share control of what they say you said with you. Always ask to approve of what they communicate about you or how they quote you. Their agenda can be quite different from yours, so clarify such issues before you give them your story/quotes. Role-play an interview with a peer group to prepare yourself beforehand, if this would give you confidence in giving a live interview.

Responses to COVID-19 challenges and opportunities for social workers

Professional values are those principles that guide professional behaviour. These may coincide with or diverge from personal values. Professional ethics involve the codification of values into a code of practice used to regulate professional behaviour and sanction professional misconduct. Values may be universal, although identifying which these are can be controversial. Ethical codes tend to be national. An ethical dilemma is a situation that arises when one value or ethical principle is contradicted by another, creating a situation that a practitioner seeks to solve by using professional judgment and adherence to the ethical code. Personal and professional dilemmas may be difficult to resolve and can induce emotional turmoil. Ethics applying to COVID-19 are like those described in practising anti-oppressively. Additional ones for child protection and welfare cover:

- Exercising professional discretion to ease hardship when appropriate.
- Reducing fear by explaining issues clearly and simply.
- Upholding social justice including human rights and entitlements to services.
- Controlling unreasonable or unacceptable adult behaviour.

Key ethical dilemmas can occur in any situation and are resolved anti-oppressively within a human-rights, social justice framework, and locality-specific, culturally relevant settings. Common ethical dilemmas involve

marginalisation, structural inequalities, limited resources including fi-
nances, and inadequate opportunities for groups deemed 'vulnerable',
e.g. people who are homeless, misuse substances, are unemployed. Their
existing medical pre-conditions complicate susceptibility to COVID-19.
Vulnerabilities or lack of protective factors are used to identify groups
requiring additional interventions to keep them safe, without giving any
guarantee of safety. The lack of certainty in what can be done can create
an ethical dilemma, and these can be discussed with other professionals,
line managers and service users.

**Case study – Child protection and welfare under
COVID-19: Roles and responsibilities**

The normal standards of high quality, professional practice should
be observed whether working remotely or conducting face-to-face
visits in the office or service user's home. Seek help from your line
manager and/or supervisor, if discharging your duties is impossible, regardless of reason. No social worker should feel ashamed or
inadequate if they ask for help. All team members and managers
should work to make this is possible for everyone regardless of experience, qualification, or other attribute. The UK's Coronavirus
Act 2020 loosened some general responsibilities by stating:

> The duties on Local Authorities to meet eligible needs ... would
> be replaced by a duty to meet needs for care and support where
> failure to do so would breach an individual's human rights and
> Local Authorities would have a power to meet other needs.

In small groups, choose a chair and a notetaker to record and
report-back on your discussion. In it, consider how you feel about
this change to practice. Then consider the following questions:

- How would you safeguard children (or older people) remotely?
- Consider what supplementary information you would seek,
  what, where, from whom, and how?
- Following your discussion, do you feel as you did earlier?

No guidelines can encompass every eventuality. Below are general points
that social workers should consider when making decisions about what
to do if preparing for a home visit. Guidelines should be used with cau-
tion, adapted to the nuances of each specific case, and draw upon your
professional judgement and experience. No toolkit can replace careful

professional thought and investigation of the issues involved. Useful questions to consider are:

1 What should social workers do during a pandemic to support children at risk of emotional, physical, sexual and other forms of abuse? What signs should be looked for? Checking your risk assessment with others may help your decision-making.

2 How should social workers investigate concerns, face-to-face or remotely? How can community members, especially family, neighbours, friends, and other professionals including community nurses and teachers assist in this assessment? Use the internet including Facebook and other social media but acknowledge their limitations.

3 How do social workers obtain the PPE necessary to do home visits when necessary? What should be done in its absence? Who can help? Is it appropriate for social workers to improvise on PPE? How do practitioners decide what is safe? Asking others what they have done may help take appropriate action. Ultimately, you will have to follow your professional judgment based on your risk assessment and listening to other workers' experiences. If in doubt, consult your line manager. If your line manager is unable to respond, s/he should seek support up the chain of command by 'escalating the issue'.

4 How do social workers handle multi-agency working – in virtual interventions, virtual case conferences, virtual family group conferences, using technology to support home visiting? Where do practitioners get the technological support and advice that they need to do this effectively? Having a trial run and exploring possible scenarios with colleagues may help you become technologically proficient. Your peer support group may create a safe space in which to test out your capabilities.

5 How do social workers stay in touch with changing policy and practice when working from home, and internet connections let them down? How do practitioners achieve a work–life balance when they are looking after their children/older parents/or other dependents? What do you do when you feel stressed by these demands? Having peer support in place and taking time out to respond to your own needs including having time alone, doing something you enjoy (even late at night when everyone is asleep) is crucial. Some practitioners found mindfulness, yoga, dance exercises, walking, reduced stress. Keep a safe distance (2 m) as much as possible when encountering others.

6 How do social workers meet their own child's/children's needs under lockdown? Can they use new technology, to facilitate connective relationships remotely to avoid social isolation, undertake home schooling and meet leisure needs? What lessons learnt from your work–life

balance can you share with service users and vice-versa? What can you learn from them? Some TV channels offer home schooling classes. You can also get family and friends to connect virtually with Skype or Zoom to play games. For example, I devised a *virtual hide and seek* game that asks the seeker to keep their eyes shut or close their screen while others hide around a room in their different homes. The seeker then tries to guess where each individual is hiding. They come out when they are 'found', and the last one found becomes the next seeker. Disabled people lacking mobility can play by thinking of where they would hide, and the seeker must guess where this is. Virtual reality was also used to hold a virtual Easter Egg Hunt with children discovering the clues that led to the eggs, some hidden in their own homes. Cooperation from their parents enabled chocolate to work its wonders.

7 How can social workers encourage strengths and resilience among service users without ignoring the weaknesses in their behaviour and strategies? How do practitioners suggest alternatives respectfully? You could role-play different scenarios for handling difficult situations with your peer support group beforehand.

8 How do social workers support children and families requiring food if they cannot obtain any from a local food bank? What other resources exist? Will a local charity, super-market or other organisation help? Get this information from your support group or the internet before you contact service users remotely or otherwise, so that you can provide useful advice about how to obtain food.

9 What should social workers do to support children with medical requirements, or complex health and social care needs if there are no social care workers or health professionals including GPs available? Should practitioners use volunteers, and what conditions are appropriate for doing so? What precautions should the volunteers take? Check that they are prepared and trained for their tasks and have adequate PPE.

10 How do social workers address children's heightened emotional and mental health needs? Where can practitioners refer children to? Is there a counsellor or approved mental health practitioner available to do this work? Can counselling be undertaken remotely? Is anyone offering such a service? Is there a COVID-19 specific helpline they can use? WHO's website has emergency psychosocial guidelines for practitioners.

11 What records should social workers keep? Record-keeping is crucial not only for professional reasons, but also for follow-up. There will be office policies and guidelines available, so use these. Also, keep track of where you have been, whom you have seen, what you have done, to facilitate contact tracing in case you catch COVID-19.

Although a community might not have the resources to do contact tracing, this information is crucial to containing the spread of the virus. Should you fall ill, this information could be passed on to your line manager for action. This would facilitate phone calls to alert those you met to self-isolate for 14 days, as a safety precaution. Some experts argue this is unnecessary as it enables a community to acquire 'herd' immunity. However, this can be very dangerous for people with existing health conditions and other fragilities that could lead to their becoming a fatality. You should not assume that age is always a protective factor. Other variables are also relevant, and can interact unpredictably to cause death among babies, children, young people, and adults. Other variables include gender, ethnicity, deprivation, and structural oppression.

These guidelines may facilitate your becoming vigilant in identifying cases of violence against the person including physical, emotional, sexual, and financial abuse. These usually increase when people are experiencing 'natural' or human-made disasters. COVID-19 places additional stresses on individual and family lives, so be alert for signs indicating that violence could be occurring among those you have contacted and ask probing questions and talk to the victim-survivor independently of other household members. Do a home visit if necessary. Anecdotal evidence from social workers and data from helplines like Childline suggest that domestic violence and child abuse have risen under COVID-19. Social workers ought to be on guard for signs of additional tensions from being locked down inside a home with perpetrators – past, present, and alleged, as tempers fray and space and other resources become prized commodities. Understanding power dynamics and resource disparities within households can help make the required judgment calls. Using your usual knowledge and skills and being vigilant are key to making these decisions. If in doubt about what is going on, discuss your concerns with your peer support group and line manager. Know what resources you can refer the individual/family to for help, e.g. Women's Aid, police.

The biggest challenge in reaching a judgment in specific situations when working remotely is that of being unable to observe all interactions during contact with those concerned - abuser or abused. Working remotely and making real time videos (having obtained permission to record your video on Teams or Zoom beforehand) where you can observe what is going on, studying the dynamics, making a risk assessment and (re)playing these later can help identify subtle signs of abuse. However, not all people will have access to such remote technologies, and even with these, you may have to do a home visit to achieve peace of mind regarding the family dynamics in situations where people are confined together. In such situations, you will want to maximise your protective gear including wearing an adequate mask (N95/FFP3 with filtration for small particles like viruses) and do your homework, i.e. preparation, beforehand.

Case study – An ethical dilemma concerning child abuse

This case study illustrates concerns involving a face-to-face investigation in a case of alleged child sexual abuse. The woman social worker that investigated this referral was aware of the need to work from home as much as possible, the urgent need to see the child and speak face-to-face, and fear of taking COVID-19 to their family. This social worker's home circumstances included an older mother recovering from breast cancer (and thus belonging to a 'vulnerable' group), a three-year-old daughter, and a twelve-year-old son. Conducting a home visit would be ideal, but the social worker was fearful of bringing COVID-19 into her home and jeopardising the health and wellbeing of her family, especially her aged mother. Her husband is not at home as he is self-isolating overseas where he went for a job interview and caught COVID-19.

The social worker can undertake initial explorations with this family electronically, but dreads missing crucial details that might further endanger the child. The mother has neglected her eight-year-old son previously but had been managing to cope before COVID-19 struck. Ella (the mother) had phoned the social worker to say that the child had a high fever and was poorly. The social worker completes a risk assessment that shows that a home visit is not advisable. Ella's family usually lives hand-to-mouth because both parents have a poor employment record, and the father is rarely home when the practitioner visits. The family is known to social workers and other professionals as constantly needing financial support. The boy is generally withdrawn. Having been bullied at school prior to COVID-19, he is pleased that he does not have to attend. Ella cannot provide home-schooling. The practitioner raises the problem with her peer support group, but opinion is divided on what she should do, so she raises her concerns with her line manager.

The line manager decides that notwithstanding the risks entailed, the social worker must do a home visit, sooner rather than later. The social worker remains worried and discusses the issue with her trade union whose officer promises full support if she decides not to do the visit. This response does not satisfy the social worker. She agonises over what to do for the remainder of the day, but uses the time to contact the family's GP, community nurse and headteacher at the child's school to deepen the picture already available about the family. Ultimately, the social worker decides to visit the family. She rings Ella to prepare her for a visit the next day as she intends to explore how they are coping with lockdown and other issues. The social worker explains that she will be wearing a mask, goggles, and disposable gloves as precautions necessary to protect her family and those she will meet. Fortunately, she finds no evidence of neglect. Both children seem well-fed and cared-for as did Ella, following self-isolation procedures. However, the social worker noted that a neighbour was concerned that the daughter aged three had been sleeping in Ella's bed due to regularly occurring nightmares. These, the mother described as the little girl missing her father, and the social worker decided to phone regularly to see whether this situation changes. As the family could not afford a computer, the social worker thought that she would try to obtain funds to purchase one for the family so that they could download a free version of either Skype or Zoom to enable the children to talk to their father and her. The social worker also noted the need for a referral to charities for fresh food, vegetables, clothes, and toys. These would be left outside the door by properly trained volunteers wearing PPE. Before leaving the home, the social worker tells Ella that she will explore the possibility of obtaining an iPad so that they can have regular Zoom meetings. However, she worries about the time spent on meeting needs that the welfare state should have been providing automatically.

The social worker has a plastic rubbish bag to dispose of unwanted items, hand sanitiser to wash her hands and disinfectant wipes in her car to ensure that she disinfects its surfaces before reaching her own home. Before leaving for home, she removes her goggles, mask, coverall and disposable gloves and places them in an empty plastic rubbish bag and puts them into 'quarantine' for 72 hours so that she can reuse them. Once inside the house, she takes a shower. The clothes she removes go straight into the washing machine for a hot soapy wash. After showering, she dons on clean clothes, before meeting her family. She is happy that she has a house large enough for her to take these precautions. However, she worries about colleagues who do not, and spends a restless night worrying about signs of abuse that she might have missed in her eagerness to help and desire to reduce the stresses being experienced by Ella. She also wonders how she will obtain funding for the iPad. She falls asleep while dreaming her support group is offering advice on arguments essential in convincing her line manager to over-ride tight financial constraints and fund the iPad.

This case study indicates the multi-layered nature of professional anxieties that social workers had to juggle in their practice. These were intensified by the constraints placed upon relational social work during the pandemic. Read Martin (2015) for a deeper understanding of the psychological impact of a disaster on health and wellbeing.

Exercise

What did you think of the social worker's responses? Discuss.

Case study – Juggling issues to provide adequate social care for elders

Sally is a social care worker who loves her job. She is on a zero-hour contract, and in any one day, she may be required to visit two care homes for older people and provide services to four services users living in their own homes in the community. Sally is apprehensive about what she is being asked to do because there is no PPE to do her job safely and minimise the danger of either catching or passing on the virus. She is also not given travel time, and so she juggles by pinching a few minutes from the time allocated to each service user so that she can get from one service user to another without causing undue distress. However, she remains extremely concerned about the lack of PPE. She has raised this with her manager, the owner of the home. He maintains that he has asked for this, but it has not materialised.

The guidance provided for social workers focuses largely on working with children and families. Nonetheless, much of it applies to social care workers whether working in residential establishments or providing care for older people in the community. The importance of using PPE, cannot be over-emphasised whether doing a visit in someone's home, a public care home or a private one. Many elders have died because visitors and/or carers may have been asymptomatic and were unable to take precautions when visiting. This passed the virus onto those with fragile immune systems and greater vulnerabilities due to age. Residents discharged from hospitals into care homes without testing and adequate safeguards to prevent the spread of COVID-19 also increased risk. Similar issues were faced by care workers working in both these spaces. Care workers and visitors can carry the virus, so PPE must be worn as a matter of course. This PPE should be changed as workers move from one room to another to work with/attend to another bed-bound older person. They should also change their PPE every time they go from a care home to a private dwelling to provide care, and also when delivering services to different residential establishments, or from one private house to another. Care homes have been sites of disproportionate numbers of deaths under this health pandemic. Ideally, workers should be restricted to working in one establishment for the same number of overall hours. Care workers in the community have to take PPE precautions to protect themselves and others by changing PPE every time a worker goes into a different house. Also, they need enough supplies for each service user (sometimes called clients). They should remove used outer clothing protection outdoors or in the car where possible, put on another clean coverall and use another pair of clean disposable gloves before going into a different house. Adhering to this regime can be challenging, and frustrating when care workers have workloads that ignore the time needed to travel or change, face a shortage of protective supplies, and must improvise. Also, they are on time-limited contracts, and given inadequate travelling time, so undertaking all these additional steps to undertake precautionary measures to maintain safety is not counted in the workload of most, especially those on zero-hour contracts. At such points, contacting your line manager, a union or professional association official, elected members and the media can be useful in encouraging colleagues to become allies in getting the protective gear that you need to do your job safely. Without PPE, you risk your health and that of others with whom you come into contact and may result in vulnerable people losing their lives.

Dr Bonnie Henry is Provincial Medical Health Officer in British Columbia, Canada leading the response to COVID-19 in that province. She realised the importance of adequate PPE and ending the revolving door of carers in and out of care homes and into homes in the community and introduced many of the safeguards in this case study during her response to the COVID-19 crisis in care homes early in the pandemic (Henry and Henry, 2021). I had the privilege of listening to her daily broadcasts from January to March 2020.

Exercise

What do you think of the social worker's responses? How could you improve her work–life balance?

Case Study: Contextualising Older People's Care

Care home residents exemplify a vulnerable but insufficiently protected group in the absence of PPE, hospital beds, and residential
home beds. This raises another factor critical in assessing susceptibilities to COVID-19 – geopolitical and socio-economic contexts.
The lack of PPE and equipment for testing can be attributed to
nation-state failure in undertaking adequate preparatory measures including stockpiling masks, disposable gloves, goggles, and
coveralls. Kerasidou and Kingori (2019) has attributed these to
extensive austerity programmes that reduced public expenditures
in health and social care including bed numbers, staffing, trainees
among health professionals, social workers and social care assistants and infrastructural developments.

A hospital requires a social worker to return to a care home
a resident admitted to hospital for suspected COVID-19 due to a
lack of ventilators. The social worker, aware of the potential danger of cross-infection among other residents and care staff faces
an ethical dilemma of protecting others in an environment lacking PPE. She attempts to reduce harm utilising the precautionary
principle by shielding or isolating the returnee in a separate room
with its own disinfected toilet and shower facilities, TV, radio,
books, table, easy chair, personal effects, and artefacts such as
photos, pictures; preventing visits by other residents, family, and
others; excluding care staff working with other residents or caring for people in the community and health professionals lacking PPE. Having to resort to such actions places the burden of
preventing the spread of COVID-19 onto individual practitioners
and could subject them to intolerable stress, especially if other
residents catch COVID-19. A further outbreak could be caused
by inadequate PPE among other care staff, insufficient disinfection
of infected surfaces throughout the care home and asymptomatic
visitors. This response exemplifies the inadequacy of dealing with
COVID-19 one resident at a time.

Exercise

Imagine that you are the manager of this residential home.
Working in small groups, consider what steps you might take
to protect residents, staff, and visitors from further transmission
of the virus. Also, think about how you might influence policy
changes to cope with this scenario. Report your discussions to
your plenary group.

A holistic approach that bars all visitors to residential care homes until adequate PPE is provided for all care and health workers, service users, visitors; and disinfecting all surfaces within the home could be another way of proceeding. This could put unbearable stress on family members and friends as well as the service user given the importance of social relationships with others. Maintaining connectivities between residents, external family and friends is essential. Remote means like giving each resident an iPad and disinfecting it after each use would be another strategy for protecting residents while maintaining contact with others and might mitigate the risk of spreading COVID-19 in the short-term, but it is not a long-term solution. The COVID-19 Bereaved Families for Justice (see https://covidfamiliesforjustice.org/) have made this view clear.

Conclusions

COVID-19 presented an unprecedented challenge for everyone. Practising ethically and appropriately under COVID-19 requires sensitive, holistic, and imaginative approaches to provide locality-specific, culturally relevant services and solve ethical dilemmas. Skills in using remote technologies to work from home, advocating for user entitlements, and devising environmentally friendly policies to protect vulnerable individuals and groups in a post-COVID-19 world, are critical.

Social workers must work together to move beyond the current pandemic, learn from each other to control and contain the coronavirus. Meanwhile, social workers focus on behaving ethically, exercising their professional judgment wisely and when unsure, seeking support and advice from their peers and line managers. Ensuring that people's human rights are upheld is key to endorsing social justice and bringing an end to the environmental degradation that undermines the resilience of fragile individuals, communities and eco-systems. Showing solidarity and accepting the interdependencies between countries, nature, individuals, and families are crucial underpinnings of such an approach, and advocated by green social work.

4 Climate change
Social work responds to political failures nationally and internationally

Introduction

Climate change knows no borders and has become a major socio-economic problem that must be addressed as a global issue. However, national reluctance amongst the major emitters to make these changes has been a key hindrance to making progress on this front. Climate change is central to widening the agenda of social work theory and practice in the twenty-first century. Although hotly debated, climate change is deemed primarily a human-based, not a natural, phenomenon, caused by burning fossil fuels that discharge toxic greenhouse gas emissions into Earth's air, water and soils; and land use changes to meet the needs of industry and agribusiness (WWF, 2020). Both purposes exploit natural resources for profit and degrade the environment. Climate change is partially expressed through warmer climates that give rise to extreme weather events that result in damaging floods, droughts, heatwaves, cold-snaps, storm surges and hurricanes. Burning fossil fuels also increases acidity in the ocean, causes glaciers and permafrost to melt, and pollutes water, soils and air which also create problems identified as environmental degradation, loss of biodiversity, ill health, food insecurity and loss of livelihoods or income insecurity. Each of these events have profound impacts on human health and wellbeing and environmental degradation. Climate change is among today's top ten drivers of poor health. Another of its critical consequences is illustrated by the melting ice in the Chukchi Sea and Baring Sea. This is creating a navigable channel along the Baring Strait that separates Alaska from Russia. This is encouraging freight traffic along a new route, all of which is stressing even further the Arctic Region which is warming more quickly than elsewhere. It has also initiated a scramble for oil in the Arctic Region (WWF, 2020).

In this chapter, I discuss what climate change is, the damage it causes to the physical environment, biodiversity, food security, livelihood stability, and energy insecurity. Floods and droughts damage food production and create not only food shortages, but also famine

DOI: 10.4324/9781003105824-5

and destroy socio-economic activities in both traditional agriculture and agribusiness as adaptation measures fail to provide much needed water security, crops, and livelihoods. Fossil fuel-driven activities also simultaneously undermine sustainability in physical environments. This chapter argues that social workers have a responsibility to look beyond their concern with micro-level practices involved in providing food aid, and temporary financial or humanitarian relief because these provide little more than an inadequate bandage to bind a gaping socio-environmental wound. Transformative action requires transdisciplinary working, an understanding of what climate change is and how it needs to be addressed politically, socially and economically in global collective co-produced endeavours in which solidarity secures the resources and goodwill that will enable humanity as a whole and planet Earth to survive and thrive. To achieve this aim, this chapter discusses the transdisciplinary approaches that social workers can use to promote action among a wide range of community-based and other stakeholders to find ways of coproducing innovative solutions. Bottom-up coproduction processes have been avoided by national ruling elites who favour expert-led, top-down approaches. Case studies are used to portray transformative practices. This chapter also argues for social work training to facilitate practice that tackles climate change.

What is climate change?

Climate changes refers to varying climatic behaviours driven by greenhouse gases (GHGs) produced by modern industrialisation, agricultural production, and deforestation initiatives. GHGs consist of water vapour (H_2O), carbon dioxide (CO_2), methane (CH_4), nitrous oxide (N_2O) and chlorofluorocarbons (CFCs). The more carbon dioxide held by the atmosphere, the more the Earth will heat up. This dynamic was identified as contributing to climate change by Eunice Foote in 1856 (Foote, 1856), John Tyndall in 1859 (Jackson, 2020). In 1884, Savante Arrhenius of Sweden made similar claims. Foote's work was neglected because she was a woman in a man's world. Tyndall was given credit for the discovery and Arrhenius won a Nobel Prize for his work. These findings were unpalatable to the ruling and manufacturing elites of the time and ignored. Although the impact of burning of fossil fuels on climate was identified in the late nineteenth century, politicians and the general populace ignored it until the 1960s. The impact of daily human activities on the environment were highlighted by the shocking analysis provided by Rachel Carson in her path-breaking book, *Silent Spring* (1962). This exposed the devastating effects of chemicals upon the environment, including routinely used household items like detergents that left toxic chemical residues in water and soil.

Greenhouse gases trap infrared radiation in the Earth's atmosphere, thereby increasing air temperatures. This will enable the atmosphere to hold more moisture and contribute to more intense rainfall (Hajat et al., 2005). By 2018, anthropomorphic greenhouse emissions had risen from 280 parts per million (ppm) before the industrial revolution to nearly 408 ppm 9IPCC 2014, 2015, 2018). According to the World Meteorological Organization (WMO), this dramatic rise is causing unprecedented changes in climate systems and impacting significantly on all aspects of human life. This dynamic has been discussed in numerous United Nations led conferences since the 1970s.

The *Special Report on Global Warming of 1.5°C* by the Intergovernmental Panel on Climate Change (IPCC, 2018) delivered a warning to the United Nations Framework Convention on Climate Change (UNFCCC) Conference of the Parties (COP) 21 meeting held in Paris in 2015. Its clarion call claimed that to save planet Earth, anthropomorphic predations had to be contained within a temperature rise of 1.5°C, not 2°C as previously believed. Addressing this threat required immediate attention. To achieve this goal, the Paris Agreement reached on 12 December 2015 at COP21 required each UN member-state to develop a National Action Plan (NAP) to reduce greenhouse gas emissions and report regularly on its achievements. However, the Agreement lacked teeth. No penalties were proposed for those not complying. Without urgent, substantial mitigating action on climate change, the risks to health, livelihoods, food security, water supply, human security, biodiversity, and economic growth will be horrendous (WWF, 2020; IPCC, 2018). To emphasise this point, the naturalist Sir David Attenborough warned at COP 24, 'Right now, we are facing a man-made disaster of global scale. Our greatest threat in thousands of years'. Subsequent COPs, including that of COP26 in Glasgow in 2021, failed to deliver on the ambitions for *radical action, now*! In the summer of 2022, much of the Northern Hemisphere suffered from extreme weather events, including heatwaves, droughts, and wildfires. Yet, COP27 in Egypt in November 2022 achieved little on this front.

Research on the 'lived-experience' of those already affected by climate impacts, reveals that the world's poorest people, and those living in small island states are the most adversely affected by the existing temperature rises (Pernetta, 1992; Abbott and Wilson, 2015). Moreover, the World Health Organisation (WHO) declared that climate change will result in 250,000 additional deaths yearly in the years 2030–2050 (WHO, 2018). Additionally, already vulnerable environments and landscapes will be subjected to extreme stress and pressures (Barrett, 2014). Flood plains, wetlands, and peatlands, exemplify already endangered fragile environments. If left undeveloped, these terrains can store carbon and water, control flows of storm water, and enhance resilience to climate change. Their development under hyper-urbanisation undermines this capacity and contributes to the unpredictability of extreme weather events caused by climate change. These would intensify water, food and energy insecurities and pose problems for global peace as different nations would engage in struggles to obtain these life-supporting resources. Meanwhile, climate change would continue to cause injuries, illnesses, post-traumatic stress disorders, mental ill health, and deaths (Kolbert, 2006). Others would experience compassion fatigue (Västfjäll et al., 2014), recovery fatigue, eco-grief or solastalgia (Cunsolo and Ellis, 2018), survivor guilt and/or commit suicide (Cianconi et al., 2020).

Migrating populations escaping climate change pose new challenges. Receiving countries, whether reluctant hosts or welcoming them as settlers are currently inadequately prepared for the newcomers. The patchy delivery of the Homes for Ukraine Scheme initiated by the Home Office in the UK highlighted the serious gaps which exist in relation to housing availability, safeguarding concerns for children, young people and elders, and lack of matching between sponsors and Ukrainian people who have agreed to become 'guests' in their homes. Ironically, the word 'guests' says it all. It implies an asymmetrical relationship that depends on the goodwill of the sponsors doing the inviting and suggests a charitable impulse over a rights-based one. In Scotland, housing shortages led to a proposal to house new arrivals from Ukraine on a cruise ship and caused outrage locally. A few weeks later, the reception of new arrivals without housing or sponsorships arranged beforehand was halted in both Scotland and Wales due to housing shortages. Migration raises questions about whether these people are climate migrants or not. I argue that climate change cannot be detached from war due to discharge of military ordinance into the air, soil, and waters of our planet. The impact of Putin's War Against Ukraine is a case in point. His military's environmental degradation is compounded through the destruction of Ukraine's housing, farmlands, and built infrastructures. Here, the resources consumed to build these in the first instance required the burning of fossil fuels. Their destruction required the burning of even more fossil fuels. Rebuilding these once the war ends will consume even more of Earth's valuable resources, and discharge copious amounts of toxic gases and other substances into the planet's environment. Should Putin pay? My answer to this question is a resounding yes! This environmental damage stands as testament to why Putin should be tried not only for crimes against humanity, but also for crimes against the environment.

Climate change migrants currently have no legal recourse to help and support as they leave for other climes, mainly in cooler regions of the globe. They cannot rely on the 1951 Geneva Convention for asylum seekers and refugees as that was created largely for those fleeing political persecution. Choosing appropriate places and ensuring that the numbers received are compatible with the environmental capacity to support them is essential in assisting migrants to make the transition from refugee to settler status an acceptable and manageable experience. Otherwise, difficulties for both parties will mount. For example, indifference to environmental capacity to meet long-term demands made Kenya's Dadaab refugee camp, among the largest in the world, a degraded locale. Founded in 1992, Dadaab was constructed for 90,000 refugees. The UNHCR claimed that by 2011 it housed nearly 500,000 migrants who had fled climate change and armed conflict. Their numbers have halved since then as some refugees were returned to their original homelands. Some armed struggles begin as battles over scarce resources that sustain human life, e.g. water. The demands of environmentally induced migration have led to resettlement capacity assessments to identify potential destinations for climate migrants. Completing these assessments is useful in identifying appropriate locations and enhancing resettlement outcomes. However, conceptual frameworks embedded within resettlement capacity assessments are inadequate for climate-induced displacements due to competition over resources as the environment becomes further degraded by the climate crisis affecting all locations.

Today, the deleterious impacts of climate change are exacerbated by rising population numbers and hyper-urbanisation, both of which are proceeding rapidly (Satterthwaite, 2009). The Environmental Performance Index includes 24 indicators across ten dimensions of environmental health and ecosystem resilience and vitality. These can be used to determine what progress has been made in reducing environmental degradation and promoting healthier physical environments.

Additionally, WHO asserts that the burden of climate-sensitive health outcomes will increase with each additional unit of warming. No one and nothing will escape the impact of climate change on the environment, but it will be experienced differentially. This statement is controversial. Giddens (2009) encapsulates the two opposing positions adopted on climate change by referring to those who think that it is predominantly a 'natural' phenomenon as the *sceptics* and those who acknowledge its anthropocentric origins and the urgency of changing human behaviour in this regard as the *greens*. Green social workers are amongst the 'greens' and have a key role to play in raising climate consciousness among community residents and work with them to devise climate mitigation and adaptation measures. Moreover, green social workers are now describing climate change as a climate crisis or climate breakdown, to emphasise its degradation and the importance of taking urgent action to mitigate and prevent adding to it. Furthermore, green social workers are promoting the right of planet Earth to be cared for and treated as an end in and of itself instead of a means to a few entrepreneurs exploiting its resources to generate profits (Dominelli, 2012a). WHO calculated that children will suffer disproportionately from climate change, claiming that 88 per cent of the 150,000 deaths attributed to climate change so far this century have involved children. Climate change affects human beings throughout the lifespan, from the womb to birth, childhood, adolescence, adulthood, and death. Children, adolescents, and young people are ignored in decisions that affect them because adults have appropriated that prerogative. However, inspired by Sweden's Greta Thunberg, young people are beginning to assert their agency by taking strike action, not attending school and demanding that adults, especially politicians, take immediate action to 'Save the planet!' and end the climate crisis. This action gave a huge impetus to public interest in the climate crisis. Consequently, some countries including the UK have declared a public health emergency and undertaken some activities in response. Yet, despite such activism, sustained, and significant global action has not been forthcoming from politicians (Cohen, 2019). Even COP26 in November 2021 did not become pivotal in promoting such change as many had hoped. No such ambitions were proposed for COP27. Prime Minister Rishi Sunak planned not to attend COP27 but did. King Charles III, long-time environmentalist and COP attendee, was prohibited from going.

The 2009 'Copenhagen Flop' or failed negotiations during COP15 in Denmark initiated the EU's shift to post-colonial understandings of justice based on mutual recognition and non-domination. Climate change debates have moved from considering risk to examining threats posed by those refusing to: assume responsibility for historic greenhouse gas emissions; and action to reduce current emissions. Reluctant responses are unlikely to keep temperature increases below 2°C above pre-industrial levels because these do not compel those with historical debts listed in Appendix 1 of the Kyoto Protocol and the newly emerging ones, especially China, India, Russia – the three biggest polluters excluding the USA at number two, being added to the tally. Moreover, none of the Big 4 are planning to reach 'net zero' before 2050, with India aiming for 2070. Nation-state reluctance to act is occurring alongside well-publicised disastrous extreme weather events as the window for a step change closes. The IPCC (2018) limited this to a 12-year timeframe, of which nearly half has already elapsed without substantial change. Time to act is disappearing rapidly. The current largest polluters must accept responsibility for action now. Their development cannot continue to pollute Earth for hundreds of years because the technology to develop in non-polluting ways is available. Still, politicians must enact global solidarity and encourage less greed among wealthy corporations to build and share renewable technologies everywhere (Smith and Sorrell, 2014). Green social workers must lobby for this.

Global inaction has spawned direct action movements like Greta Thunberg's school strikes and Extinction Rebellion, a civil disobedience campaign demanding environmental justice now. Extinction Rebellion seeks to implement a new politics by engaging in non-violent direct action and civil disobedience (Engler and Engler, 2016; Latour, 2017). Such environmentalists have initiated new discourses that have crossed borders and encouraged people across all walks of life, age groups, and ethnicities to engage in setting a 'new narrative for climate change' (Du Cann, 2019). Direct action has turned people into 'everyday environmentalists' (McTeer Toney, 2019). On the flip side, despite growing environmental degradation, inaction has become normalised, particularly among those most responsible for raising greenhouse gas levels and who shift blame and liability to the victim-survivors of floods, droughts, wildfires, storm surges, hurricanes, and other extreme weather events. These are the marginalised peoples who have contributed least to the climate crisis, but who endure most of the hardships (Monbiot, 2019). Discourses by climate change deniers spread responsibility globally by referring to the impact of the planet's geological forces and the Anthropocene to implicate everyone and ascribe the duty to reduce greenhouse gas emissions to all humanity. This strategy lets major polluters off the hook. Another sleight of hand is to endorse initiatives focusing on bottom-up approaches so that adaptation and mitigation measures become the responsibility of those with fewest resources and lowest carbon emission rates. Thus, poor people experiencing environmental degradation carry the heaviest burden for changing this situation and finding the funds to do so, e.g. the people of Kiribati, whose island state has already partially sunk into the sea. However, their request for an uninhabited Australian island to save their culture was denied.

Solutions to reducing carbon emissions are scarce. One of them focuses on making polluters pay. Under this scheme, the social cost of carbon (SCC) attempts to calculate the economic damages caused by emitting an additional ton of greenhouse gas emissions. Whether charging for emissions will reduce them is disputed. Nordhaus (2018) argued that setting an SCC of $49 per ton of carbon dioxide by 2030 would result in a 3.5°C warming by 2100, and damage the environment disastrously. The IPCC (2018) suggested that a carbon tax rising from $135 to $5500 in 2030 would enable the global community to achieve the Paris Agreement target of holding global warming at 1.5°C, a target currently receding into the distance.

Exercise – What to do about climate change?

Climate change has become an existential crisis with eco-grief becoming normalised in many countries as the time available for urgent action evaporates.

Working in small groups, choose a chair and a notetaker to record the discussion and present the key points of the deliberations to the plenary group. Then, discuss the following questions:

• What can social workers do to overcome political inaction over climate change?
• What can social workers do to address eco-grief at individual and community levels?
• What can you do personally to promote climate action and how would you do it?

Taking action at individual, community, national, regional and international levels simultaneously, even if undertaken by different social actors is essential to stemming increases in greenhouse gas emissions (Yamada and Galat, 2014).

Transitioning to a low carbon economy by reducing carbon emissions through carbon trading schemes can turn this development into a normative commodity that can create new injustices and vulnerabilities because these ignore existing structural drivers of injustice in energy markets and wider society. This danger was evident in several European low-carbon transitions, and inequitable distribution of energy prices on domestic consumers in the summer of 2022. An energy justice perspective asks not what co-benefits renewable energy produces, but reframes the question around various injustices incurred because nations fail to initiate low-carbon transitions and exacerbate social risks and vulnerabilities. Thus, Dominelli (2012a) argues against all carbon trading.

Carbon trading raises queries about what policies can produce just transitions. An energy justice approach focuses on: (a) distributive justice including costs to people and the environment, not only benefits; (b) procedural justice by undertaking inclusive processes in decision-making and governance; (c) a cosmopolitan justice that includes global externalities; and (d) recognition justice, i.e. one that identifies and includes vulnerable groups (Sovacool et al., 2019). These authors examine various low-carbon transitions in Europe, each being challenged to implement social justice including nuclear power in France, smart meters in Great Britain, electric vehicles in Norway, and solar energy in Germany. Viewed through a critical social and environmental justice lens indicated in Figure 4.1 below, these initiatives remain governed and managed through hierarchical and unaccountable structures, with cost burdens falling more on poor and marginalised groups than those with high status and high incomes (Sovacool et al., 2019). Additionally, energy transitions need sensitive handling to protect the interests of those likely to suffer most because considerable job losses can occur, and whole lifestyles and communities are undermined when public subsidies are transferred from the public sector to the private one. Although more than energy matters preoccupied Margaret Thatcher, she ruthlessly destroyed the highly unionised, publicly owned British coal mining industry in the 1980s. Thatcher's actions devastated mining communities to such an extent that many have not fully recovered yet, despite breathing cleaner air, e.g. Northeast England. Then, there are the waste disposal costs of the debris generated by the destruction of power plants, meters, and other equipment. These rarely acknowledged costs of environmental degradation are usually carried by poor communities (Bullard, 1990). Additionally, energy sources are publicly subsidised in inequitable ways, e.g. in the UK, nuclear power receives higher levels of subsidy than renewable energy. Also, smart meters might reduce consumption, but unit costs for energy remain expensive and continue to rise despite energy suppliers making significant profits. Before the current rise in fuel prices attributed to Putin's war Against Ukraine, high energy costs resulted in fuel poverty which affected 20 per cent of the European population (Thomson et al., 2017; Mutascu et al., 2022). Green social workers can initiate cross-stakeholder dialogue to hear marginalised communities and act upon their suggestions.

Another initiative is the UN programme, *Reducing Emissions from Deforestation and Forest Degradation in Developing Countries (REDDS+)*. It seeks to reduce greenhouse gas emissions caused by deforestation in the Global South. Under this scheme, industrialising countries that desist from destroying forests in accordance with the REDD+ criteria are remunerated according to results achieved (UN-REDD, 2016), e.g. Norway's agreement with Brazil. Sadly, some REDDS+ programmes cause damage through illegal 'development creep' into protected areas, destruction of community habitats, and generalised insecurity (Agrawal et al., 2011). Emphasising reductions in current deforestation rates REDDS+ can inadvertently promote the eradication of ancient forests to replant them rather than facilitating forest-dependent, indigenous communities to preserve them (Stern, 2007). Deforestation activities have accelerated economic growth, substantial urbanisation and rapid population increases, thereby undermining local ecologies and energy sources in the Global South. Changes in land use often displace precarious indigenous communities (Borras et al., 2016). Market-based mechanisms monetise environmental services with few benefits for local livelihoods,

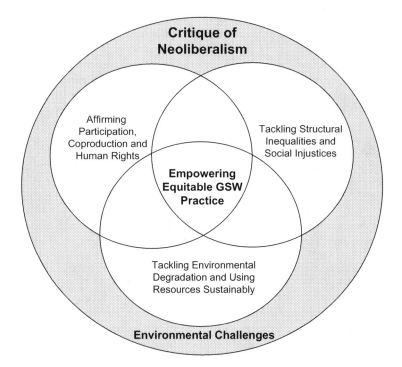

Figure 4.1 Green social work model for intervening in the climate crisis.

income security, food sources and biodiversity (Bayrak et al., 2014). These deleterious results are particularly evident in Pakistan which incurred the worst floods in its history in 2022 (British Red Cross, 2022). Pakistan exemplifies local and global interdependencies and the importance of tackling both simultaneously.

The *Green Climate Fund (GCF)* seeks to mobilise and disperse funds to facilitate industrialising countries' responses to climate change. Eco-activists support the Green New Deal that calls for massive public investments in efficient, renewable energy, jobs for all to maintain social stability and social justice. Green New Deal measures are anticipated to support resilience among vulnerable communities as these measures aim to endorse the public, collective good and eschew neo-liberalism. Poor communities require relevant resources and knowledge to complement their lived-experience and indigenous knowledges to promote climate change mitigation endeavours (Nyong et al., 2007; Makondo and Thomas, 2018). Corporate multinationals that argue for the deregulation of finance pose a threat to Green New Deal programmes, as financial mitigation and adaptation assistance remains elusive (Winston, 2019). Yet, the Green New Deal seeks to promote funding mechanisms to make carbon reduction a reality. These attempt to:

- Encourage governments to provide finance for public borrowing.
- Value future benefits so that these become multipliers that increase value.
- Increase taxes for those responsible for creating the most greenhouse gas emissions.
- Redirect subsidies given to dirty energy sources such as coal to clean, renewable ones.
- Transform financial institutions to give them more responsibility for responding to the climate change challenge, e.g. the Bank of England in the UK.

People are more conscious than ever that climate change is caused by human action. Some expect that becoming aware of the impact of climate change would facilitate agreement on its harmful effects and promote action to reduce it (Bøhlerengen and Wiium, 2022). However, unless the roles of neoliberalism and capitalist forms of production and consumption are linked to climate change and growing inequalities, and these mechanisms are transformed, little will change. Without such connections becoming overt, neoliberal captains of industry will pursue their interests through strong lobbying and representation within political structures to secure policies that favour them and stymie climate action. Trump in the USA and Bolsonaro in Brazil illustrated how climate change deniers can hold the levers of power to subvert caring for indigenous peoples and planet Earth through policies that deny that climate change to endanger further the lives of precarious groups. The IPCC has advocated against delaying tactics on climate change to avoid global catastrophe. Their Report (IPCC, 2015) provides evidence to enhance the global community's endeavours on climate change knowledge and coproduction. By acting together, communities can find innovative solutions and combine scientific expertise and local knowledge based upon direct experience of the severity, frequency, and scope of global environmental destruction (Beck and Forsyth, 2015) to end this crisis.

Social workers, climate change, and social and environmental justice

Social workers have engaged in arguments about environmental justice since the 1990s. At that point, environmental social workers, especially those endorsing the deep ecology movement argued for a role in which social workers protected the physical environment as part of adhering to the slogan of practice with the 'person-in-their environment'. The deep ecology movement thereby incorporated the physical environment in Bronfenbrenner's (1979) social system approach to providing services for service users (called clients then). This was a major step forward. However, twenty-first-century challenges highlighted the inadequacy of this amendment because it failed to integrate structural inequalities into social work's commitment to social justice and include environmental justice within that. Additionally, the deep ecology movement was seen as failing to critique industrial methods of production in using land, producing, and consuming commodities, and not engaging in holistic transformations of social relations to achieve social change. Green social work (Dominelli, 2012a) made this step-change and raised debates within social work to a new level. Green social work 'respects and values the physical environment as a socially constructed entity, with the right to exist in its own right' and makes the relationship between people and their sense of 'place and space interdependent and symbiotic' (Dominelli 2012a: 25) and acknowledges the differentiated experience of climate change among different groups of people, including the most disadvantaged and the most privileged.

Green social workers affirm a specific right to a healthy environment within a human rights and social and environmental justice framework that enhances people's wellbeing alongside physical environmental sustainability and underpins their rationale for supporting environmental justice while responding to environmental disasters. They also acknowledge the interdependencies between people, their physical, social, political, economic, and cultural environments and have devised holistic responses to social problems that have linked local, national, and global actions. Local, traditional, and indigenous knowledges are appreciated for topical, local geographically based information about biosystems and innovations for moving forward together. These premises are embedded within an ethic of care that integrates the duty to care for planet Earth within a feminist ethic of care that involves caring for others while being cared for by others. Green social workers combined the need for structural change on all counts by arguing for the use of green, renewable energy in manufacturing and other production processes, a move away from consumer-driven lifestyles, an equitable distribution of goods and resources and an end to structural inequalities like poverty, racism, sexism, and other forms of oppression within a people and planet-centred approach. Green practitioners would work within partnerships that use co-productive processes to co-create solutions to jointly identified problems that are devastating local environments. Coproduction includes considering expert perspectives alongside those portrayed by local, indigenous knowledge-holders and deems all knowledges as of equal worth in working across disciplines, professions, and communities to understand the contexts, risks, and challenges for policymakers, practitioners, and residents and seek consensual solutions. Green social workers' social critique of inequality and injustice encourages their opponents to see themselves as 'political' by asking them not to ignore the 'political' dimensions of their own standpoint which favours the status quo.

Feminist researchers (Enarson and Morrow, 1998; Dominelli, 2019b) highlight the precariousness of women's lives, especially women from indigenous communities across the world, and of black, Asian, and other ethnic minorities (BME's) in majority white societies. Women's work remains invisible, and women under-represented in the managerial ranks of disaster interventions (Islam and Winkel, 2017). The Gender Inequality Index and Gender Development Index cover life expectancy, schooling, income, health, political participation, labour market involvement, urbanisation, industrialisation, militarisation, age dependency ratio, democracy, GDP, income inequality and population growth. These items expose existing inequalities between men and women and are utilised to assess progress in fostering gender equality, a crucial aspect of Social Development Goal (SDG) 5 (SDGs, 2015). The gender income and status gaps identified in a report by the World Economic Forum (2020: 15) reveal that at today's rate of progress the global struggle to achieve gender equality will require another century.

Patriarchal gender inequality dominates relationships between men and women, thereby upholding unequal political, social and economic opportunities for women. Social and cultural gender norms and high levels of poverty disadvantage women in the Global South, thereby increasing their vulnerability to climate change. Although women are targeted in development projects, the intersectional and complex nature of their oppression means that gendered socio-economic marginalisation, inequality, and power imbalances become obstacles to change. Market-based ventures and solutions are often imposed upon them through projects linked to agriculture and income generation schemes that lack women's involvement. Thus, overcoming gender inequalities turns women's empowerment into an important tool in reducing global warming. Moreover, men and women perceive risks differently. While women are generally deemed more risk averse, engaging them in coproduction and addressing their interests can produce better outcomes. For example, women have endorsed small-scale renewable energy projects which reduce household energy bills and residential greenhouse gas emissions. Policies and practices that support low-income women's engagement in small-scale renewable energy sources, enable them to access technological innovations that can improve their lives while reducing greenhouse gas emissions and encouraging behavioural and societal change.

These can include providing solar panels and solar powered stoves to women to reduce the burdens they carry in walking long distances to fetch water and firewood (Dominelli, 2012a). Progressive changes encourage women to:

- Engage in social movements that support climate justice.
- Encourage young people's involvement in climate change mitigation and prevention strategies.
- Demand jobs that promote environmentally sustainable initiatives.
- Promote collaborative solutions that engage people locally, nationally, and internationally.

Women have taken legal action to protect their interests. Their endeavours have initiated legal suits against governments and multinational corporations to protect their human rights and ask for the implementation of social justice legislation to reduce oppressive actions against them (Abbott and Wilson, 2015). However, women who become climate change refugees are seriously disadvantaged. They have no recourse to international laws because none exist to compel nation-states to accept them into their countries (Nishimura, 2015). Social workers have a role to play in lobbying for their rights.

People living in informal settlements, townships or slums endure high levels of poverty and overcrowding. Their inhabitants live within informal economies, face housing insecurity, poor basic utilities, and susceptibility to infectious diseases. They are socially excluded by government policies which fail to acknowledge their human rights and need for services. Their habitations are highly vulnerable to extreme weather events, particularly storms and heatwaves due to inadequate built-infrastructures and geographic layouts. Despite these drawbacks, many migrant groups are attracted to these areas as they have nowhere else to go, even if they are migrating to escape climate change. In some cities, gentrification of city centres where such populations congregated earlier are displaced by wealthier groups and organised criminals who use coercive methods of eviction. Such deplorable action was exemplified by the removal of Roma people from Gianturco in Naples (Goddard and Sturrock, 2017), and predatory gentrification where poor people were offered enormous sums of money for their property as occurred in Red Hook in New York City following Storm Sandy (Berner, 2018). These tactics are not new. For example, New York City removed poor African Americans and Irish settlers from Seneca Village to make way for Central Park as a recreational site for its wealthy elite in the mid-nineteenth century (Wang, 2015).

Climate change also occurs through the trafficking of modern-day slaves for exploitation. People are coerced into working in illegal mines, fishing, capturing wildlife, agribusiness, activities that intensify the deforestation of virgin tropical and temperate forests, degrade the environment, and undermine biodiversity. These production activities create excessive contributions to human-generated CO_2 emissions, destroy the environment and increase the precariousness of life.

Working with people following disasters to recognise their losses and support them through personal sufferings including the eco-grief associated with environmental and habitat losses (Comtesse et al., 2021) can lead to vicarious trauma among young people, the public, and environmental practitioners. Helping people deal with the issues raised by environmental degradation also highlights the importance of self-care and recognition of trauma-induced stresses that may require professional interventions, possibly for years. These feelings may be compounded if the practitioners are victim-survivors coping with their own losses, compassion fatigue or other issues. Informal peer support groups can validate and assist practitioners to address their own grief.

What roles do social workers undertake in climate change scenarios?

Social workers have important roles to play in climate change. However, engaging in ventures to eliminate greenhouse gas emissions may require them to move out of their comfort zone of dealing with children, families, and older people. Within the workplace, climate change issues are not normally considered social work concerns. This attitude must change because those most affected by climate change are poor, marginalised peoples who rarely benefit from burning fossil fuels, although they often reside in the environments degraded through their exploitation. Social worker involvement in climate change disasters would need the support of their managers, who could rely on emergency legislation to prepare practitioners for new tasks. These could involve consciousness raising activities, projects linked to green socio-economic development and income generation, lobbying for policy changes, advocating for resource redistribution and research, and training. Moving into new territory could involve practitioners in engaging with interdisciplinary, multi-agency community-based partnerships that focus on reducing greenhouse gas emissions while allowing low-income countries to develop using green technologies. This requires major advocacy initiatives to secure agreement on transferring green technologies freely to those people who do not have them. This is a huge task, given the reluctance of those who own the patents to make them available without making substantial profits from such moves (Veleva, 2020). Social workers could mobilise to lobby for such changes locally, nationally, and internationally.

Social workers seeking to innovate through transformative social change and community engagement should understand key issues that are associated with mitigating the impact of climate change. These include:

* Acknowledging the differentiated and unequal experiences and consequences of extreme weather events.
* Arguing for industrialised countries to accept their responsibility in reducing their consumption of fossil fuels and paying to readdress the disproportionate suffering experienced by the poorest people in the world.
* Promoting the right to development within a more equitable climate change regime.
* Supporting emerging economies and low-income countries to exercise their right to development within green, renewable, sustainable energy infrastructures and technologies.
* Sharing green technological knowledge and undertaking and seeking funding for collaborative research.
* Encouraging the consumption of equal shares of greenhouse gas emissions by agreeing a per capita allowance which will require those currently personally emitting a lot of greenhouse gases to reduce their consumption of goods, services, and energy.
* Recognising and upholding human rights for all peoples, including indigenous rights to traditional resources including land.
* Promoting social and environmental justice within social policies and practices.
* Encouraging the use of renewable energies and providing funds for poor people to switch.

Changing people's attitudes towards climate change is difficult, especially for people struggling to survive. Social workers need to develop strategies at the local, national, and international levels to change policies and practice, especially in a world of competing demands on scarce resources. These strategies could cover, public health issues, economic stability, resources, and compliance with guidance to keep climate change within the safer limit of 1.5°C. Such guidance ought to address change at the local, national, and international levels. Local difficulties may prevent change from occurring. For example, an older interviewee in the UK-based BIOPICC climate change research project said, 'I wouldn't mind it being a few degrees warmer'. Such people are keen to explore alternatives that focus on choices available to them. These include explaining the problem of fuel poverty and housing structures which indicate that some homes cannot be heated properly without insulation, double glazing, a green energy solution (e.g. solar panels) and obtaining funding for these. When this was offered through another development project, this person felt empowered by 'being able to see a way of doing something about the problem'. Social workers working in communities should remember this point when working on energy transitions.

Social workers also need to consider how they can influence opinion formers, policymakers, and entrepreneurs to take seriously action on eliminating climate change. Key to their ability to influence such groups is the ability to hold them accountable to the community for the decisions they make. This is critical to protecting the environment and ensuring that the carbon footprint they leave is minimal while providing sustainable, well-paid jobs, capacity building and other projects promoting sustainable, inclusive, egalitarian social relations. In endorsing accountability, social workers will have to work to alter behaviour that induces climate change among the following groups and individuals within them:

- Large corporations, especially technological giants, multination firms and banks.
- Elites including ruling elites, economic elites, political elites, social elites, and their decision-making capacities over many areas of life affecting communities and residents.
- Governments at all levels, especially around their policymaking and resource allocations to ensure climate change becomes an integral part of their agendas.
- International organisations including the UN and its agencies such as UNDP, FAO, UNICEF; UNWomen, the IMF; and World Bank to ensure green, sustainable developments.
- Other actors, including charitable organisations, NGOs, CSOs, community groups, individuals, and families to ensure that they support reductions in greenhouse gas emissions.

By demanding such accountability, social workers can form alliances with poor people who endure the greatest impact of disasters, partly due to poverty, lack of access to resources, opportunities, governance mechanisms and poorly built infrastructures. They can also advocate for their interests and voices to be heard. This task will not be easy because governments are reluctant to control global corporations offering to invest in and bring jobs to their country. Media 'wars' between business and a critical public also often define who and what is the problem, and how to address it.

Resilience is an important feature of rebuilding societies in transformative directions –'build back better' (Manyena, 2006) or transformatively (Dominelli, 2012b). I reject 'build back better' because it can reinforce existing inequitable power relations, especially for women, disabled people, and other marginalised groups. Resilience exists on a coping continuum ranging from failure to cope and surviving to thriving. Most individuals and communities hover around the survival point. Failure to thrive or being unable to reach the apex of resilience in fully developing one's talents following a disaster can be attributed to various causes. These include:

• Political failure, which can include poor governance structures and corruption.
• Institutional failure that often means poor structures, faulty decision-making processes, and lack of institutional infrastructures.
• Failure to engage community groups in decision-making.
• Financial failure either in the banking system and financial institutions, or the lack of funds for purchasing additional resources, expertise and personnel.
• Human failure regarding the lack of expertise, inability to act, and in extreme cases, loss of life.
• Individual failure, particularly in lacking the skills, knowledge, and resources necessary for adapting to change.
• Cultural expectations that privilege one group over another, particularly those situated around accepted societal norms.

All these factors matter during climate change. A good example of multi-faceted institutional and human failure is that of not reaching a legally binding and enforceable international agreements to replace the Kyoto Protocol.

Case study – Addressing climate change

Angelo was concerned about the impact of climate change on poor communities. Flooding, a common occurrence, involved the movement of toxic wastes that created daily risks in his community. He was aware of the need to influence government policies and thought he should organise his community to take the lead on this. He looked for allies in the task, as it was an enormous undertaking.

Exercise

If you are a community worker working with Angelo, how would you advise and assist him to find allies at the local, national, and international levels, and why? Discuss.

Communities require material support and encouragement to take climate action seriously. And they need allies among all stakeholders with an interest in addressing this serious social issue (Dominelli and Vickers, 2014). Carefully building alliances and acquiring resources to build sustainable, resilient communities is part of the community development mix (Parker, 2020).

Conclusions

Climate change is a contentious topic with major emitters failing to live up to their obligations to reduce greenhouse gas emissions to keep to the 1.5°C target articulated by the IPCC (2015) and agreed through the Paris Accord 2015. Global warming is already set to transcend this target to the detriment of poor, marginalised people living primarily in SIDS and the Global South. They experience the worst impacts of the climate crisis having contributed least to it. Funding their resilience is a critical but neglected goal. Neither must society overlook low fossil fuel consumption among disadvantaged people in the Global North, e.g. among homeless people.

Ending the climate crisis presents huge agendas and choices that face the largest emitters of greenhouse gases. Those concerned about their inaction must dialogue with and convince them that they are undermining their own self-interests alongside those of others. The planet does not care whether the carbon burden it is carrying is historical or comes from the USA or China today. Reductions are possible and both countries have the technical knowledge and resources to take immediate action and still meet the needs of their people. But it requires political will, collaboration, and green technology transfers. Social workers must contribute to initiatives aimed at eliminating the climate crisis through their daily practice. The GSW model of practice can help them do this.

Appendix
Climate Change Statement for Social Work, 2009

Introduction

Energy consumption and industrial pollution today contributes substantially to climate change. The impact of climate change is already affecting low-income countries and poor people drastically. And, according to scientific research the earth's biodiversity and climate stability is seriously threatened. Avoiding this damage requires that global pollution is reduced drastically so that atmospheric warming does not exceed 2°C.

The Kyoto Agreement that expires in 2012 has attempted to get nation-states to agree to reduce their carbon emissions. The Kyoto Agreement was, however, weak and did not include major players other than the USA in the production of industrial pollutants, particularly of carbon dioxide like China and increasingly India and Russia.

Another problem was the issue of equity between industrialised countries in the Global North and industrialising ones in the Global South. Although the per capita emissions of people living in the Global South are substantially lower than those in the Global North, they are the ones who will suffer most from climate change. This has occurred already in countries like Ethiopia that are experiencing unprecedented levels of drought; and Bangladesh where flooding is a regular occurrence. The legitimate aspirations of those in low-income countries to acquire higher standards of living will change this ratio in time. However, it can no longer mean the adoption of consumeristic lifestyles as the earth cannot sustain these either for those in the West who have them already, or for the growing populations that aspire to these globally, particularly in emerging countries like India and China where significant numbers of middle-class people already seek these. Moreover, the world's inhabitants are set to exceed 9 billion by 2050. Meeting their demands for energy alone carries profound implications for the climate. Finding new, sustainable ways of meeting people's aspirations and needs are urgent priorities if the goal of each one of the earth's inhabitants having a decent standard of living and dignified lifestyle is to be met.

These problems indicate the importance of promoting social justice in solutions to them. All nation-states must work together both to reduce global pollution and raise the standards of living of the world's poorest peoples. In this scenario, an equitable sharing of resources, substantial reductions in pollution levels and the urgent sharing of clean technologies and renewable energy sources are imperatives. The talks following Copenhagen must succeed in achieving these aims if humanity and the physical environment of planet earth are to flourish rather than perish.

Social work educators and practitioners are the group of professionals concerned about people's wellbeing. Their relationship with their physical, spiritual, and social environments are similar to those of social welfare NGO's and other bodies interested in climate change. They are well-placed to advocate for policies that promote social justice, equity and human rights rooted in notions of collaboration, reciprocity, mutuality and solidarity. Thus, we propose the following actions to safeguard the interests of those who have the least voice in raising their concerns about the cost they will have to bear if nation-states fail to agree to take the necessary actions immediately.

Principles

We affirm the following principles in seeking to get nation-states to reach agreement about substantially reducing global pollution:

1 *Interdependence.* We live in an interdependent world, thus what happens in one location affects people in all others and makes us responsible for one another.
2 *Equity.* The inequalities that allow rich or powerful nation-states to dictate terms to low-income ones are unacceptable. Enshrining equity in any agreement facilitates the transfer of clean technologies and sharing of endeavours that will ease the threat of climate change.
3 *Collaboration.* Nation-states must collaborate with each other to find solutions to the profound problems raised by continuing climate change.
4 *Reciprocity.* Reciprocity requires all peoples to contribute to the wellbeing of others and is essential in recognising interdependence and promoting solidarity.
5 *Solidarity.* Solidarity between peoples promotes a sharing of resources, skills and knowledge that are needed to address the problems that humanity faces, regardless of whether or not an individual is personally experiencing the problem.
6 *Sustainability.* Sustainable development on a global scale requires co-ordinated action amongst nation states to share clean technologies and resources equitably and eliminate inequalities.
7 *Holistic approaches.* Each nation-state faces different problems in relation to climate change and countries and peoples have contributed differentially to the problem. The current position of any one

country is likely to change as low-income countries industrialise and raise their low standards of living. As Western lifestyles are physically, spiritually and environmentally unsustainable, they cannot be promoted as the way forward for all. Consequently, all nations of the world must work together to find sustainable lifestyles for everyone now living on earth and for the generations to come. This will mean transferring knowledge, skills, and resources more equitably across the world and a holistic approach that encompasses the physical, spiritual and social domains.

Actions

Individual social work educators and practitioners will have to find their own way of reducing their personal carbon footprints, but as a profession, it can together with social welfare organisations commit to the following actions:

1   *Raise awareness* of the issues linked to climate change locally, nationally and globally.
2   *Lobby* the United Nations and national governments for the affirmation of the above principles; the adoption of the social policies necessary for their implementation; and the commitment to undertake urgent action that will: reduce global pollution; encourage the equitable sharing of clean technologies and the world's resources; and create dignified sustainable lifestyles for all.
3   *Mobilise* people to raise their concerns and promote solutions at the local, national and international levels.
4   *Research* the subject of climate change to develop social work perspectives on the issues raised and provide the evidence that is needed to support people and proposed plans of action in reducing global pollution and its impact on local, national and international communities.
5   *Train* people in understanding the issues linked to climate change and ensuring that these are covered in the social work curriculum. This should include undertaking placements that address climate change in local communities.

(Drafted by and submitted by Lena Dominelli to IASSW, IFSW and ICSW during the Copenhagen Climate Change Conference in 2009 and accepted by the IASSW Board at its January 2010 Meeting in Copenhagen, Denmark.)

5 Extreme weather events

Flooding and wildfires, disasters frequently calling upon social workers' contributions

Introduction

Extreme weather events are wreaking havoc everywhere as the climate crisis exacerbates and intensifies their occurrence. Floods, droughts, heatwaves, and wildfires are encompassing places that have not experienced these before. Their arrival can be surprising, as happened during July 2021. Floods then killed 243 people in Europe and, floods in China, inundated parts of the Zhengzhou Metro. Floods are the commonest source of disasters globally. They are responsible for more deaths and damages than other types of disasters. Moreover, flood frequency is likely to increase. Currently, floods impact 42 per cent of lands across the world and affect between 27 and 93 million people. Most floods occur in low-income, densely populated countries that are poorly equipped to tackle them. Also, the American states of Florida, Georgia, and Virginia, South America, Africa and Asia are predicted to experience extreme flooding every 2 to 50 years (Polka, 2018). Given projected increases in the world population by 2050, the consequences of extreme weather events linked to the contemporary climate crisis will be disastrous, especially for those forced to migrate elsewhere. This potential calamity must be avoided. Compelling all governments to take the climate crisis seriously, adhere to the Paris Accord and restrict greenhouse gas emissions to achieve 1.5°C temperature rise over pre-industrialisation levels by severely curtailing fossil fuel consumption, is critical in avoiding this dire situation (IPCC, 2018).

Storm surges are increasing in frequency and the height of waves, and sea levels are rising. Sea defences for floods and coastal erosion are becoming contentious given the vested interests involved in either maintaining the status quo or demanding change as a matter of urgency. In England, the development of shoreline management plans is the responsibility of DEFRA (Department of the Environment, Food and Rural Affairs) which replaced MAFF (Ministry of Agriculture, Fisheries and Food). The flood measures adopted depend on assessments of overall

DOI: 10.4324/9781003105824-6

safety, risk, and cost (Jongman, 2017). The Environment Agency (EA) has detailed plans of flood risks for England, and the Scottish Environment Protection Agency (SEPA) determines these for Scotland. The Environment Agency Wales separated from the English one in 2013 and became Natural Resources Wales. In Northern Ireland, the Northern Ireland Environment Agency (NIEA) is situated within DEFRA.

Flooding has also increased because human behaviour has degraded the environment to meet human needs on a market-basis that requires profit generation. Urbanisation has increased flooding risk enormously through population growth in large cities, house construction in unsuitable areas, and covering land in concrete instead of ground cover and plants. Flood risk can be reduced with 'hard' engineering solutions such as structural flood protection measures, early warning systems, risk-informed land planning, and 'soft' engineering or nature-based solutions like planting mangrove trees in low lying areas subject to flooding, especially in the tropics, and drawing upon social protection and risk-financing instruments. Social workers can inform communities of these issues and mobilise them into taking action to lessen the climate crisis such as reducing fossil fuel consumption and encouraging diverse mitigation measures.

Nation-states are encouraged to respect, protect, and fulfil the human rights of people vulnerable to disasters, including climate change and follow four key principles in their duty to protect. These are:

• accountability
• information-sharing
• participation
• non-discrimination.

However, the principle of sovereignty trumps the duty to protect. Thus, a nation-state's responsibility to protect does not include the victim-survivor's independent right to assistance. Nonetheless, human-rights based approaches to flooding are expected to reduce social and individual vulnerabilities by enhancing resilience, or people's capacity to cope with adversity. They can also promote: the empowerment of service users (Dominelli, 2012c), their capacity to hold service providers to account for their actions, and advocacy for disaster risk reduction initiatives.

The obligations of the territorial nation-state are both long-term and short-term. These aim to:

• Prevent a disaster like a flood from occurring.
• Send out public warnings of impending natural disasters like floods or earthquakes. The UK first tested its national warning system on 21 April 2023.

- Respond to a flood which may include accepting disaster assistance offered by other states and cooperating with the UN to ensure that humanitarian aid reaches flood victim-survivors.
- Rebuild the flood-affected areas and collaborate with those affected in actions that mitigate risk throughout the disaster cycle.

The international community has the duty to offer humanitarian aid to disaster-affected areas. Social workers often provide practical assistance in such situations. They also support reconstruction endeavours and assist in mobilising communities to discuss the reconstruction projects they want.

Floods can be rapid rise or slow rise. There are three types of floods: fluvial floods, pluvial floods including flash floods and surface water floods which can occur without a body of water being nearby, and coastal floods. A fluvial flood occurs when rivers overflow their banks including on floodplains, particularly around housing built on water meadows. Dams that break can also cause floods. Definitions of flash floods are varied, and refer to lag time, rapidity of onset, peak flow, volume, and impact upon life and property. Heavy rainfall in a short period of time can trigger a flash flood but it depends on the topography, channel characteristics of a river and its previous condition. Flash floods can be extremely dangerous and arise quickly, even in areas not prone to flooding. River flash floods can occur along a riverbed as occurred on the River Rye near Helmsley, North Yorkshire on 19 June 2005. Pluvial flash floods can cause flooding in places faraway from rivers, e.g. Newcastle's 'Toon Monsoon' of 28 June 2012 (Archer and Fowler, 2018). Moreover, floods can disrupt power supplies, traffic as the transportation infrastructure can fail, and thus adversely affect economic activity and social life.

Coastal flooding is an area of concern in the UK, with the number of places being flooded rising in recent years (Haigh et al., 2017). The Shoreline Management Plans (SMPs) are used strategically to mitigate flood risk in coastal areas. The SMPs are of three types: managed retreat, accommodation, and holding the line. Recently, land loss on the coasts of the UK has become of lesser concern than raising agricultural productivity substantially, and, consequently, land has been allowed to fall into the sea. Climate change will increase the risk of flooding in low-lying coastal areas. Research into appropriate forms of coastal engineering for coastal defences is required. This could include the Thames Barrier, which was constructed to protect London through to 2030 and is being upgraded for use until 2060–2070. An important precaution involves warning people to take action to protect themselves from known flood risks. Early warning systems should be in place to alert people to potential flood sites, place emergency services on alert, and evacuate people.

Local flood wardens can also alert residents easily and quickly. Social workers are normally waiting to provide practical aid and ensure people are taking their prescribed medications at the evacuation centre(s). People throughout the UK can now receive adverse weather alerts, and many do on their smart phones. Rainfall forecast alarm thresholds used by the UK Flood Forecasting Centre can now occur at 1-hour, 3-hour, and 6-hour intervals to enable people to take preventative actions including evacuating to safer places. 'SurgeWatch' was created to record systematically flood events in the UK from 1915 to the present. No national database existed before this. Flood events are scored from 1 ('nuisance') to 6 ('disaster'). These data are used for flood management purposes.

Insurance is used by middle class families to mitigate flood risk. However, insurance companies are charging huge premiums for houses that have been flooded more than once and seeking to renew coverage. They can also refuse to insure these. PM David Cameron introduced FloodRe to spread the risks of flood insurance among the entire population, rather than restrict it to those facing flood risk. This has resulted in a £1 surcharge on insurance premiums for everyone, i.e. a pooling of risks. Calculating risk relies on the equation:

Risk = hazard (probability of event) x exposure (which can impact on value) x vulnerability

Floods have been occurring in the UK for millennia. However, records for early ones are scarce, e.g. data on those that incurred along the east coast in 1099, 1421 and 1446 are limited. Severe flood damage was also caused by later flooding. For example, in 1607, the Bristol Channel Floods killed 2,000 people. In 1703, the 'Great Storm' washed away the lower streets of Brighton. The Central London Flood of 1928 drowned 14 people. The 'Big Flood' or East Coast Floods of 31 January–1 February 1953 covered 1000 miles of coastline from Spurnhead to Kent. The 1953 floods were among the most serious to hit the UK. These breached seawalls, causing extensive damage to 24,000 homes, the evacuation of 32,000 people and 307 deaths. The terrible floods of 1953 reshaped the UK's approach to flood risk management, and encouraged scientific research to improve forecasts, warnings, and sea defences.

Endorsing human rights-based service delivery

Human rights are key to strengthening the capacities of flood victim-survivors to carry on with their lives (Pyles, 2006). Human rights also facilitate the transition from victim-survivor to exercising agency as decision-makers capable of regaining control over their lives and becoming resilient (Mathias and Nahri, 2017). Emergency plans that uphold these rights are urgently needed. The Universal Declaration of Human Rights (UDHR) was adopted on 10 December 1948 and set the human rights standards for all peoples/nation-states. Nineteen social workers participated in these deliberations under the auspices of IASSW (International Association of Schools of Social Work). These rights consisted of:

• Civil and political rights, e.g. the right to life, equality before the law, and freedom of expression.
• Economic, social, and cultural rights, e.g. the right to work, social security, health, and education.
• Collective rights, e.g. the right to development and self-determination of people.

Nation-states are responsible for upholding human rights among their populations. Some authoritarian regimes flout these. However, the empowerment process in upholding human rights involves participation, information sharing, and non-discrimination (Dominelli, 2012c).

The United Nations (UN) has highlighted the importance of human rights in disasters through the following instruments:

• The 13 May 1971 Report by the Secretary-General on Assistance in Cases of Natural Disaster which emphasised the state's duty to protect the right to life, health, and property of victims. This did not challenge state sovereignty.
• General Assembly Resolution 36/225 of 17 Dec 1981 reaffirmed these views about sovereignty by rejecting the right of others to interfere in a nation-state's internal affairs.
• Resolution 43/131 of 8 Dec 1988 asserted that the agreement of the nation-state concerned was required for other actors to provide humanitarian aid.
• The UN Secretary-General's report of 12 January 2009, *Implementing the Responsibility to Protect*, confirmed the nation-state's duty to protect within the sovereignty principle which had been adopted in the 2005 Hyogo Framework for Action (HFA).

The HFA required nation-states to prioritise the following strategic activities. These were to:

• Ensure that disaster risk reduction became a national and local priority underpinned by a strong institutional base for implementation.
• Identify, assess, and monitor disaster risks and strengthen early warning systems to protect lives.
• Promote knowledge management capable of building a culture of safety and resilience.

- Reduce or mitigate underlying risk factors associated with specific hazards.
- Enhance preparedness for effective, sustainable responses.

With regards to human rights, people are the rights-holders. The nation-state is the duty-bearer and is accountable for providing the core necessities of life following a disaster. It undertakes action to avoid a disaster in the first place by following disaster risk reduction strategies to mitigate vulnerabilities. Vulnerable sectors of the population, e.g. women, children, people with disabilities, older people, indigenous communities, and minorities, are more exposed to risk, and experience the worst impact of disasters, especially in loss of life, property, and livelihoods (Costa and Pospieszna, 2015). Other factors that exacerbate vulnerabilities include: deleterious 'legacies' resulting from colonialism, and imperialism, careless exploitation of natural resources, dictatorship, persistent poverty, extensive levels of income disparities, mass migration, uncontrolled urbanisation as well as settlements located in areas prone to landslides, floods, and other disasters, destructive land usage, environmental degradation, and the climate crisis. The health impact of floods must be assessed and the risks have to be reduced through comprehensive, risk-based emergency management programs enshrined within a human-rights framework. It should cover all key stages of the disaster cycle - preparedness, response, recovery, and reconstruction. Social workers play key roles in implementing disaster action plans, reformulating them for the future, and planning to reconstruct communities, all within a human rights framework.

The right to health is a human right that the nation-state is required to uphold. Health issues are a major concern for those helping flood victim-survivors due to the likelihood of increased rates of diarrhoea, cholera, dysentery, respiratory infections, hepatitis Types A and E, typhoid fever, leptospirosis, and various diseases borne by insects, e.g. malaria, dengue fever, Zika, chikungunya. Medical issues to be addressed following serious flooding include:

- Identifying and recovering corpses.
- Evacuating sick people and older people to safe facilities.
- Ensuring general practitioners receive routine supplies and medicines.
- Setting up emergency hospitals to take care of evacuated people if necessary.
- Quickly restoring hygienic services, particularly of food, water, sanitation.
- Taking measures to reduce the spread of disease.
- Preventing epidemics or dealing with those that arise. This is critical in low-income countries to avoid the rapid spread of dysentery and cholera.

- Preventing toxic substances from hazardous chemical sites contaminating water supplies and ensuring that people are not exposed to these.
- Addressing mental health issues, especially those associated with grief and loss, and stress.
- Acknowledging that emotional recovery from floods can take a long time.
- Social workers usually support such endeavours, provide psychosocial support, and become involved in raising consciousness about self-care and self-help.

Examples of serious flooding events in the UK

Lynmouth, Devon

The Lynmouth flood is one of the worst river floods in British history. On 15–16 August 1952, a severe storm in North Devon dumped 9 inches (229 mm) of rain onto a sodden terrain that had already endured 12 days of heavy rain. Water levels rose throughout the Chains, as the Exmoor catchment area was called, and the water in the West Lyn River rose 60 feet above normal at its highest point. The swollen tributaries and the East and West Lyn rivers collected debris consisting of large boulders and trees enroute and rushed down the Chains to create a flood that killed 34 people, damaged 28 of 31 bridges, and caused 39 buildings to collapse. Cars, crops, and livestock were damaged or destroyed by the force of water rushing through Lynmouth and surrounding areas. The hydroelectric power station nearby had to be evacuated (Kidson, 1953).

The Lynmouth flood was unexpected. Lynmouth had 250 times the normal rainfall during 15–16 August 1952, when 90 million tons of water swept the through the narrow valley into the village during that night. The flood became more complicated when a tidal surge breached sea defences and added to the damage caused by the torrential river coming down the main street. The actual cause of the Lynmouth disaster remains contentious. Some argue that there are other issues that remain shrouded in mystery, e.g. the 'seeding' of clouds to produce rain in the area. Operation Cumulus, an experimental attempt to create rain under the auspices of the RAF is one of these examples. Records have gone missing, and the RAF does not acknowledge these experiments. People in Lynmouth claim that they smelt sulphur dioxide and that falling rain hurt their faces. The BBC claims that Alan Yates was a pilot on such flights (BBC News, 2002). Kidson (1953) does not speculate about the cause of the flood but acknowledges instability in the weather.

The flood began during the night, so it was difficult for people to see what was happening. As hotels and houses collapsed, people were screaming while desperately trying to save their families. Most of the dead were from Lynmouth (27/34), with the others from Parracombe, Filleigh, Simonsbath, Withypool, Exford, Winsford and Dulverton. Disaster intervention knowledge was scarce, and self-help was the main way in which people helped each other survive. The army assisted in clearing the debris. The Red Cross helped victim survivors by providing practical assistance and psychosocial (not called that then) support through counselling. The rebuilding of Lynmouth took 6 years and the Flood Memorial Hall was built near the harbour on the site where the lifeboat station originally stood. The Memorial Hall, Memorial Gardens and a 10-foot Cross have been created to honour those who lost their lives. The flood overflow area above the Maybridge was (re)designed to hold 1.5 times the water that flooded Lynmouth. Yet, Middleham, a hamlet that was completely destroyed, was never rebuilt. A policeman, Derek Harper, received a George Medal for his rescue work during the disaster. See the flood video at www.youtube.com/watch?v=ak9_2PopSU4

Doncaster's Toll Bar floods of 2007

The 2007 Toll Bar floods affected 1,400 residents in a part of Doncaster that had been devasted by the closure of coal mines in the 1980s. To retain their sense of community, the flood-affected residents asked to be kept together in temporary housing which included a laundry area. They were placed in 50 mobile homes in a farmer's field. Local responders joined the residents on the site in a temporary building called the Neighbourhood Support Centre. It was staffed round-the-clock and facilitated a new relationship between the local council (Doncaster) and victim-survivors to address known complaints about the formulaic way in which emergency planners normally conducted meetings with residents. These procedures were considered alienating and offering little opportunity to engage residents. According to Haraway (1988: 585), this approach 'privileges contestation, deconstruction, passionate construction, webbed connections, and hope[s] for transformation of systems for knowledge and ways of seeing'. Such responses, termed the 'technologies of recovery' include the templates, checklists and guidance produced to help victim-survivors recover (Easthope, 2022).

Past events are utilised by emergency planners to formulate these instruments. Thus, what matters greatly to those currently affected may be missed. Residents and responders refashioned local bureaucratic guidelines to suit their needs. Artefacts reminding people of their previous life, are normally thrown into skips by council employees despite being crucial in preserving significant memories. These should not be discarded without the owner's permission. Easthope and Mort (2014) writing about the Toll Bar Floods argue that the loss of home, sense of security, space and possessions following a flood is a traumatic event that the nation-state fails to support adequately. This may be particularly relevant for children who will display symptoms of mental distress (Gaffney, 2006). Ignoring basic needs including not saving artefacts, however soiled, can create mental health issues that can overwhelm the UK's already over-stretched mental health services. Uninsured residents were linked with voluntary organisations for funds to replace building contents. These Toll Bar residents empowered themselves through collective self-help initiatives and challenged emergency planners to engage with them to find solutions to the problems they faced as they identified them. Some were served badly by insurers and tradespeople who did not repair houses quickly, as indicated in this video at www.youtube.com/watch?v=NJILmSlA178

Social work interventions

Social workers play various significant roles in disaster interventions. These vary from assessing needs to coordinating and delivering services. Much of what they do depends on the stage in the disaster cycle, although readers must be cautioned against the idea that people and organisations move smoothly from one stage to another. To begin with, there is no agreement about the number of stages there are in a disaster, although the most common one depicts a disaster as having four stages: the immediate response, the relief response, the recovery phase, and the reconstruction phase. There are often overlaps between these different stages.

The immediate response phase which usually occurs once victim-survivors have been evacuated to a place of safety has social workers delivering food, clothing, water, temporary shelter, family reunification and ensuring that people take their medication. They undertake a needs assessment to ensure that people can access the resources they require to resume their lives as quickly as possible (Pyles et al., 2008). Another evacuation issue is finding and making provisions for pets if they cannot be kept with their owners. The challenges presented by pets were evidenced during Hurricane Katrina.

During the recovery stage, finding permanent housing or repairing and returning to an original habitation are key interventions. This can involve social workers liaising with the housing department and planners and compiling lists of tradespeople that could assist residents to repair their homes.

During the reconstruction phase, social workers will facilitate discussions about the kind of community residents want, link them with experts in civil engineering and those rebuilding communities after similar disasters (Ku and Ma, 2015). This can be critical in rebuilding their built infrastructures including hospitals, health clinics and surgeries, power supplies, communications systems and so on. Below, there is a case study indicating lessons that can be learnt from recent experiences of floods in jurisdictions other than those in the UK. This is intended to show that in a world committed to decolonisation, much can be learnt by engaging in dialogues in which those in the Global North can demonstrate appreciation of the knowledge and experiences derived from countries located in the Global South. The case study below is taken from practice during a disaster and depicts such a possibility.

Case Study – Reflecting upon the KwaZulu Natal (KZN) floods: Climate change and the 'infrapolitics of power'

Reproduced with kind permission of Vishanthie Sewpaul, activist, thinker and scholar, Emeritus Professor of Social Work at the University of KwaZulu Natal, Durban, South Africa

It is heart-breaking, 395 dead and human suffering that cannot be quantified.

The horrific flooding, and disastrous consequences we have witnessed in KwaZulu Natal is no freak of nature. The Intergovernmental Panel on Climate Change in 2022 concluded, what has been known for decades that, beyond doubt, there is the human contribution to global warming and climate change. Across the globe, we see the effects – cyclones, hurricanes, tornadoes, droughts, floods, fires, mudslides, and earthquakes. A 2020 United Nations Development Programme report draws the links between social and planetary imbalances, concluding that:

> Humans have achieved incredible things, but we have taken the Earth to the brink. Climate change, rupturing inequalities, record numbers of people forced from their homes by conflict and crisis – these are the results of societies that value what they measure instead of measuring what they value.

We are, indeed, experiencing a crisis of values. Neoliberal capitalism, that puts profit and greed above people and planet, has become so normalised and naturalised that we do not question it.

Neoliberal capitalism is so entrenched that South African climate activist, Kumi Naidoo, said that it might be easier for people to conceive of the end of the world than the end of capitalism. It is the over-consumptive world, fuelled largely by media advertising, that slowly and insidiously gets people to define their worth by their purchasing choices and purchasing power, so we all become complicit in the destruction of the planet.

Neoliberalism, with its overarching emphasis on individualism and self-reliance, precludes consideration of structural constraints on people's lives. It constitutes a key ideological barrier to South Africa considering a basic income grant, which will help minimise poverty. Under conditions of extreme poverty and inequality, it is easy to manipulate identities, which lay fertile grounds for rioting, violent protests, and xenophobia. With fuel and food prices increasing with Russia's invasion of Ukraine, things are bound to get worse.

Given its colonial and apartheid legacy, and regrettable post-apartheid neoliberal capitalist choices, combined with rampant corruption and self-serving politicians, South Africa is in the unenviable position of being one of the most unequal countries in the world. The fissures of the social fault-lines based on race, class, gender, and nationality run exceptionally deep. While the floods in KZN show the vulnerability of all of humanity, it is the poor who bear the worse brunt, particularly those in informal settlements. But the fates of the poor and the rich are inter-twined in many ways. The encroachment of informal settlements into natural habitats de-stabilises the eco-system with the destruction of flora and fauna and life under water. With [most] informal settlements and traditional rural households lacking sanitation, effluents degrade the quality of water, which the flooding is worsening.

In a 2016 Report, the World Bank highlighted that the eThekwini Municipality has institutional capacity and has been a leader in conservation planning in Africa with the inventory of greenhouse gas emissions to baseline climate change mitigation strategies, and resiliency planning for climate change adaptation. However, environmental objectives are severely compromised by failure to implement and enforce regulations. Agreements between environmental activists and government fall through and the interests of big business prevail. As is the pattern across the globe, those who contribute least to carbon emissions, suffer the most.

The World Bank concluded that the Municipality's Integrated Development Plan is the product of very little cross-sectoral dialogue and coordination, with a scathing indictment that the plan is integrated in name only. The gaps limit the ability of any sector, or the municipality as a whole to pursue more environmentally sustainable development plans and policies. Projections show a 1.5–2.5°C increase in mean annual temperature by 2065 and a 3–5°C increase in mean annual temperature by 2100, and that the future sea level in eThekwini is expected to rise at a rate of 2.5 cm per decade, which if not taken seriously is only going to increase the frequency and intensity of environmental disasters.

For some, witnessing the human suffering engendered by this environmental disaster in KZN is converting their anger and despair into what is now termed eco-grief – a deep sense of mourning for loss of Earth. We visited some of the sites where people died in collapsed homes. I spoke to a grandmother who lost her seven- and nine-year-old grandsons whose parents are in hospital. Watching the family trying to salvage what they could from the wreckage was heartbreaking. The house was completely flattened, but they were looking for memories. They found cards and notes from the boys. Although soiled it means so much to them. For others, unfortunately, the deaths, destruction and losses are yet another opportunity for party political engineering and promotion of self-interests.

It is time to fully acknowledge the 'infrapolitics of power' (Kleinman, 1999) at global, regional, national and local levels within which environmental crises occur, listen to the incontrovertible scientific evidence, and respond to the desperate calls of environmentalists to save people and planet.

This case study demonstrates how climate change wreaks havoc everywhere, but especially among poor communities, and the indignities that poor people endure to salvage meaningful artefacts from the wreckage. Their stories emphasise the importance of a critique of neoliberalism and climate change as advocated by GSW, and the centrality of those in the Global North taking action to keep global warming within 1.5°C to 2°C before 2030. Also, acknowledging that climate change can adversely affect everyone, including those in the middle classes whose lifestyles contribute significantly to the accumulation of greenhouse gases is critical. Jenny Boddy, Professor of Social Work at the University of Queensland, Brisbane, Australia when speaking of the 2022 Lismore Floods on 26 August 2022 said:

Things have returned to normal in some parts of the northern Rivers, but others are still struggling with the devastation. Big decisions are needing to be made about what to do with whole towns that have now gone under twice in five years. It's terrible. I just hope government has both sensitivity and the willpower to address the issues, but I don't hold out much hope.

The analysis is strong and highlights Kleinman's (1999) 'infrapolitics of power' wherein even articulate people feel disempowered. I now turn to wildfires which are also increasing in ferocity.

Wildfires

Wildfires, another type of extreme weather event, arise during periods of drought through both human activity and carelessness such as throwing cigarette butts out of a car window, and naturally through lightning strikes. Wildfires are increasing in frequency and intensity due to climate change including heatwaves in temperate regions of the world. Population growth and extensive urbanisation also affect the numbers of wildfires as people's activities encroach on forests for industrial and recreational purposes and increase already heightened fire risks. In 2017, high-profile fire events occurred in Canada's Northwest Territories, British Columbia, Alberta, Saskatchewan, and Manitoba. In the USA, wildfires included the huge 'Mendocino Complex' and 'Tubbs' fires in California. Wildfires in Chile; Portugal; Spain; South Africa; Ireland; and Greenland added to the toll. In 2018, there were noteworthy fires in Greece, England, Sweden, and North America, including Ontario and back-to-back fires in British Columbia which were among the worst in Canadian history and huge ones in California in the USA.

In 2019, there were 137 wildfires larger than 25 hectares (250,000 m²) recorded in the UK, up from 79 a year earlier, and rising. In 2021, there were 237, and by May 2022, there were already 221 (Cuff, 2022). Wildfires are increasing in frequency and severity. Scotland has the highest number of wildfires in the UK, largely occurring in fragile peatlands (Seton, 2022). Some people are concerned that rewilding can increase fire risk if debris is left on the forest floor, for example, through poor management (Cuff, 2022). Poor forest and peatland management, i.e. leaving debris in these habitats provides fuel once a fire commences, and makes the heat more intense and the flames spread more rapidly. The Scottish Fire and Rescue Service advises everyone to bear in mind the risks that wildfires pose and respond appropriately. It says: 'Wildfires are very dangerous, spreading fast, changing direction, jumping to and from other areas potentially threatening life. If you see a fire, however small, call 999 immediately' (Scottish Fire and Rescue Service, n.d.).

Most fires in the UK are caused by humans. The UK is poorly equipped for wildfires, and if climate change is not reversed, all fire services will be unable to cope with extensive and severe wildfires. For example, a typical fire engine holds only 10 minutes' worth of water. Also, engines used to fight housefires are not equipped for off-road terrain, and the gear that firefighters wear is too heavy for the agility and speed with which they must move during a wildfire.

Gendered dynamics are also important in wildfires. There is a more extensive literature around violence and wildfires that have occurred overseas. The feminist literature from Australia, especially during the Black Saturday (7 February 2009) Wildfires discuss patriarchal relations. These highlight the different roles that men and women played during the fire. Women focused on evacuating with the children early during the outbreak, considering what should be done once a wildfire starts, dealing with it when it is a nearby threat, escaping, and rebuilding communities when it is over (Parkinson and Zara, 2013).

Additionally, fire risk is different for black and minority ethnic groups. Davies et al. (2018) argue that 29 million Americans live in areas of extreme wildfire risk. Of these, the majority are white and 'socioeconomically secure'. However, there are 12 million Americans who are socially vulnerable and unable to cope should they be subject to a wildfire event. Moreover, these risks are higher among Black, Hispanic or Native American populations whose vulnerability is 50 per cent greater than the majority population.

Wildfires are also traumatic events for disabled children and young people and their parents. A study by Ducy and Stough (2021) found that children and young people who had survived wildfires in 2017 in California experienced mental ill health, stress, grief, and other emotional and behavioural issues during evacuation, in the immediate aftermath, and after the disaster. Parents also endured stressful situations when seeking to meet their families' needs, especially for housing, and mitigating the impact of disabilities upon children and young people. These authors also claim that school and community-based mental health endeavours must be sensitive to the impact of disasters on children with developmental disabilities. They argue that both preparedness and response efforts must support children with disabilities and their families, post-disaster.

Wildfires in Scotland

The Scottish Fire and Rescue Service (SFRS) is the key responder in controlling wildfires in Scotland. Many of these occur in its peatlands. Peatlands are fragile ecosystems that require protection, not least because they encompass roughly 12 per cent of the UK. They are also a significant carbon storage instrument, holding 3 billion tonnes of carbon. This is equivalent to the carbon storage capacity of all the forests in the UK, Germany and France combined (Rowlatt, 2022).

Peatlands are a special type of wetlands that cover 3 per cent of the world's land mass. They have four important environmental functions. These are: being a huge carbon storage facility, maintaining biodiversity, reducing flood risk, and providing a source of safe drinking water. Conserving peatlands is essential in any strategy of reducing environmental degradation. Those that have been damaged already should be restored and conserved. This would be one way of reducing the 5 per cent contribution to carbon dioxide emissions when peatlands are destroyed (IUCN, 2021).

On 2 April 2013, BBC News reported that 80 wildfires in the Highlands had lasted for 5 consecutive days. One of the largest near Fort William stretched over three miles. In March 2022, a wildfire near Mallaig and on the sides of Ben Lomond was extinguished by fire crews drawn from nearby areas. The blaze extended over 80 acres between the A830 and B8008, south of Mallaig. The fire prevented walkers from using the Ptarmigan Path. Also in April 2022, a wildfire began in Erbusaig, in the moorlands near the hills of the Kyle of Lochalsh in the west Highlands. Water bombers were used to control that fire which stretched over 3 miles. Another fire started on the Isle of Lewis at Bayble because relatively hot, dry, windy weather prevailed at the time. It required the SFRS, the airport fire service and the coastguard working together over several days to bring it under control. Hot, dry weather exacerbates the likelihood of more such incidents occurring. This is due to wind quickly drying dead grass, leaves, twigs, and heather, which if ignited, burn speedily and with high intensity. Thus, people using the hills need to ensure that they heed the fire warnings that are in place during their visits. An extreme wildfire warning for west and northeast Scotland had been issued before these fires started.

Wildfires have other negative impacts on the environment and society. Wildfires in peatlands and forests also impact upon water sources, especially if ash (from whatever type of fire) reaches water in reservoirs. It will then adversely affect water quality. Also, peatland fires lose their carbon storage capacity and can burn for a very long time. Wildfires can release large amounts of GHGs when trees and peatlands burn (Wiltshire, 2019). Peatlands can also release large amounts of carbon dioxide and methane when they dry out (IUCN, 2021). Keeping peatlands wet is crucial to keeping them healthy.

Developing a new wildfire strategy for Scotland

The Scottish Fire and Rescue Service is developing a new strategy to enhance its wildfire capability under the leadership of Area Commander Bruce Farquharson, the SFRS Scottish Wildfire Lead. It is taking on board the increased risk of wildfire and changing climate in Scotland;

considering the latest developments in wildfire management, training, and operational procedures; and technological advances in PPE (personal protective equipment) and specialist fire appliances and equipment. This will be supplemented by a reorganisation of fire stations. Based on a 4-tiered classification of fire stations, this has Tier One composed of first responders. Tier Two will comprise of 15 strategically located stations composed of specialist teams. They will be supported by 10 Tier Three fire stations, and a Tier Four team of tactical advisors.

Wildfires in England

The Saddleworth Moor and Winter Hill wildfires near Manchester in June 2018 lasted for three weeks and may have accelerated nine deaths. Some people had to be evacuated. Firefighters from nearby areas, 100 soldiers and water bombers also assisted in fighting these blazes. At one point, a trench had to be built to protect a house at the top of Winter Hill. The wildfires polluted the air for millions and required miles of hosing to bring water up to the hills to douse the fire. People affected by the polluted air were advised to keep their windows closed and remain indoors if possible. The loss of water security and ill health caused by fine particulate matter (PM of 2.5) are major concerns following wildfires (Albertson et al., 2010). Some firefighters thought sparks from portable barbeques had started the constellation of wildfires throughout the affected moorlands during this period. There are discussions about banning their use alongside the smoking of cigarettes, another source of human-caused wildfires and arson. Another cause of wildfires occurring across the UK is that of controlled burning that goes out of control.

Controlled burning of heather and gorse that are rich in oils that burn readily is intended to remove debris that could feed moorland fires. Such burning is used to allow fresh shoots of heather to grow for grouse to feed on before being shot by hunters. The 'season' for controlled burning on shooting estates runs from 1 October to 15 April. This may be too long given the changes in climate which has resulted in drier periods during the autumn and spring. In 2021, controlled burning was banned from peatlands in England that were unlicensed, contained a depth of more than 40 cm of peat, were sites of special scientific interest or too steep and rocky to mow. This ban was also considered a way of protecting 'blanket bogs' which are areas of deep peat soil. Action is required as a matter of urgency because damaged peatlands across the UK discharge 3.7 million tonnes of CO_2 annually. This equals the amount of GHGs from 660,000 households, or the combined populations living in Edinburgh, Cardiff and Leeds (Rowlatt, 2022). Campaigning groups like *Wild Moors* have sought to record and report sites where they believe 'illegal burning' has occurred on what have been termed the UK's 'national rainforests'. *Unearthed*, another campaigning organisation, found 251 sites of potentially illegal sites of burnt peatlands following the ban. Also, fires that penetrate the peat can burn for some while. Peatland wildfires in Yorkshire following the drought of 1976 took a year to extinguish.

Wildfires in Wales

Wildfires are a significant problem in Wales. There were 55,000 recorded grassfires and nearly 550 forest fires in South Wales between 2000 and 2008 (Jollands et al., 2011). In March 2022, firefighters in Wales battled with a blaze at Cefn Rhigos in the northern Cynon Valley. Later, there were 70 grassfires that were deliberately started for the South Wales Fire and Rescue Service crews to tackle on a weekend in June 2022. Large wildfires occurred in Garn Wen in Maesteg, Fox Hill in Rhiwderin, Trealaw area of Tonypandy, and Penrhys in Ferndale. These constituted a considerable rise from previous periods. Fighting these blazes stretched existing firefighting resources because their scale necessitated the use of multiple appliances. Critical equipment such as multiple fire engines, specialist wildfire vehicles, a helicopter, and other resources had to be brought into the area. Those tackling these fires also included the police, Natural Resources Wales, and relevant local authorities. When emergency services are fighting such wildfires, their services become unavailable to others who may require their assistance. This places undue pressures on emergency workers to respond to everyone within a given length of time. Those involved in fighting the Cefn Rhigos wildfire had formed a partnership linked to Operation Dawns Glaw earlier. This was a taskforce established to reduce the number of deliberate fires in this nation and provide effective and efficient emergency responses. However, deliberate fires constitute a drain on emergency service resources and could put lives at unnecessary risk. Air pollution is an important hazard, and as elsewhere, residents were asked to keep their doors and windows closed.

Jollands et al. (2011) found that most of the wildfires in South Wales occurred in the most deprived areas. Most of these fires were caused by young people. Additionally, the public was unaware of wildfires or their economic, environmental, or social costs. These authors argued that strategic thinking was required to come up with long-term solutions to the lack of awareness and proactive thinking about how to avoid arson-based wildfires. Concerns covered the lack of care for the environment that everyone relies upon for survival, and the significant proportion of fires caused by young people who were 'bored' or looking for 'fun'. Like other parts of the UK, the resourcing available for the emergency services to deal with wildfires alongside other tasks in their remit, were seriously inadequate (Jollands et al., 2011). Social workers, community workers, and youth workers can play crucial roles in consciousness-raising endeavours to discuss wildfires with young people and alert the public to the seriousness of wildfires and their destructive potential.

Wildfires in Northern Ireland

Wildfires occur regularly in the gorse lands and mountains of Northern Ireland, including those in Cave Hill and Black Mountain around Belfast, and Slieve Donard in the Mourne Mountains of County Down. Some of these sites are home to ground-nesting birds such as meadow pipits and skylarks. They also need protection along with other wildlife including lizards and frogs (Stewart, 2022) The Northern Ireland Fire and Rescue Service (NIFRS) sent crews to fight 1,872 gorse fires between 1 April 2021 and 24 March 2022, and their numbers are rising (Stewart, 2022). Like the fire services in other nations, these blazes stretched the resources available to the NIFRS. Consequently, other service users may have not been able to access emergency services when they needed them to attend to their needs. Also, as many of these fires had been started deliberately, there is an urgent need to engage the public in attending educational courses and consciousness raising workshops about the health and economic costs and destruction of wildlife, biodiversity and physical terrain of wildfires.

Lessons from abroad: Wildfire in Fort McMurray, Canada

Canada in no stranger to wildfires. Their impact on the economy, environment and people is substantial and costly. A horrendous one involving thousands of people occurred in Fort McMurray, a town located in North-eastern Alberta in the Regional Municipality of Wood Buffalo (RMWB), near the oil sand production areas (Landis et al., 2018). The Fort McMurray Wildfire led to the evacuation of 88,000 people for one month, the loss of 2,579 homes and commercial structures, and 5,890,552 hectares of burnt forest. It started as a two-hectare wildfire, called the Horse River Fire on 1 May 2016, and burnt until 13 June 2016. It cost \$3.6 billion. It also released large amounts of CO_2 and deposited other toxic contaminants, e.g. heavy metals and PAHs (polycyclic aromatic hydrocarbons or chemicals released by coal, gas, crude oil), on trees and soils. The Wood Buffalo Environmental Association

(WBEA) monitored air quality for firefighters to protect their health in difficult conditions.

The fire was linked to climate change. The hottest temperatures on record globally occurred in April. This caused drought, earlier snowmelt, and high fuel loading, especially the undergrowth and tree density which promoted an aggressive fire. Moreover, cuts in fire and forest management budgets also affected prevention and mitigation endeavours, e.g. tree thinning was reduced and increased the fuel available for the fire. Moreover, lobbying by oil sand exploitation companies led to a disregard of environmental concerns and risks associated with oil extraction.

Canada's management of wildfires focuses on five emergency management phases. These are:

- prevention
- mitigation
- preparedness
- response (most of the money is spent on efforts that occur here; and it forms the critical management phase)
- recovery.

Firefighters' recommendations regarding future expenditures often focus on prevention and mitigation. Moreover, increased fire management planning at the landscape level can include fuel management (e.g. thinning debris on the forest floor); prescribed burns to proactively protect communities at risk; harvesting; and silvicultural regimes to reduce wildfire hazards. Canada's FireSmart Program was developed to provide citizens with information related to fuel management, planning, fire-awareness education, cooperation, training, and development (FireSmart Canada, 2019). As British Columbia, Alberta and Saskatchewan all had forest fires at the time of the Fort McMurray fire (and since), calls for the development of a national forest fire plan for Canada ensued.

Like many other disasters, this wildfire had a negative impact on mental health and wellbeing Brown et al., 2019). For example, young people. Fort McMurray students in grades 7–12 had higher levels of mental ill health following the fire than control groups who had not been involved in the fire. Their mental states indicated that they had higher rates of:

- depression (31% versus 17%)
- moderately severe depression (17% versus 9%)
- suicidal thinking (16% versus 4%)
- tobacco use (13% versus 10%) (Drolet et al., 2021).

These figures highlight the need for programs to avoid mental ill health among adolescents affected by wildfires. However, such facilities are scarce. A shortage of such resources is relevant to the position in the UK as well. Training in addressing eco-grief and ensuring that mental health social workers are supported are necessary.

Evacuations

Evacuations are essential in taking victim-survivors of disasters including wildfires to places of safety (McGee, 2019). Evacuations can be mandatory or voluntary. Prior consideration of issues that promote smooth evacuations include:

- What would you take with you and where you would go?
- Dealing with evacuees who may be in denial about the nature of the threat (people carried on as usual).
- When the evacuation can take place can be crucial, e.g. if people are at work or in school, they may be unable to return home to get belongings and important documents.
- The social, cultural and health problems, financial problems and accommodation needs that may be encountered can be mitigated by pre-evacuation planning.
- Finding spaces for pets could be another challenge as they are not accepted in all accommodation sites.
- Considering traffic flow during evacuation planning as congestion can occur. This happened on Highway 63 because it was the only road in or out of Fort McMurray.
- Evacuation processes during wildfires are stressful events causing stress and anxiety due to:
  - disruptions in daily routines;
  - loss of control;
  - uncertainty about personal safety;
  - worries about the safety of their homes;
  - fear of being close to the danger; and
  - inadequate communication.

Social supports can reduce this negative impact, and so keeping families together is a good strategy. Communities can get to know one another and provide support before, during and after an evacuation. People's perceptions of risk, situational factors and other barriers may affect their willingness to prepare in advance of a disaster. Preparation involves becoming aware of the potential disaster, making an action plan including evacuation arrangements, copying important documents and obtaining emergency supplies.

The Protective Action Decision Model (PADM) (Lindell and Perry, 2012) has the following stages:

- A pre-decision stage which includes receiving, paying attention to, and comprehending warnings; exposure to the warnings; attention to and interpretation of environmental and social cues, especially those that they can see, hear, or smell.
- A stage of activating core perceptions to acknowledge threats, protective actions, all stakeholders, and a willingness to act upon this knowledge.
- The risk identification stage which involves conducting a risk assessment, searching out protective actions, making a protective action assessment, and implementing protective action.

Exercise – Wildfires

Working in small groups, choose someone to chair your discussion, and another person to report back to the larger group at the end. Then proceed with the exercise. It involves reading the Gordezky case study linked to the Fort McMurray Wildfire (Gordezky, 2017). You will find it at https://ymcawun.files. wordpress.com/2015/04/fort-mcmurray-wildfire-case-study-final-jan-6-2017.pdf

Consider the following questions:

- What did you learn about preparing an organisation before a disaster like a wildfire (Note: the YMCA in Fort McMurray had child-care and other resources that social workers could use)?
- What criteria matter most in making decisions about how to respond to a disaster like this one?
- What did you think of the communication strategy used in the Gordezky case study, and how could it be improved?

Wildfires can be handled better if there is advance preparation to ensure that if you are at home, you know where your 'grab and go bag' is located and that it is replenished regularly to ensure that foods and medicines are not out of day, contact details and important documents are copied and originals readily available. If at work, your employer will have made arrangements for evacuation, and if at school, your teachers will guide you in getting evacuated. The guidelines below may assist you in this.

Guidelines for responding to extreme weather events: Wildfires

Preparing for the eventuality of a wildfire for people living in areas where the wildfire risk is high is central to protecting individuals and families and merits consideration before disaster strikes. Such preparation requires the formulation of a family action plan. Discussing the issues, including what you need to prepare before such an event occurs, what to do when it happens, and how you maintain contact in case you are separated are among these. Also, you should consider what documents you need to take with you including taking photocopies (that can be left with a trusted person outside the area) and artefacts that are of crucial sentimental value. You will probably be limited to one rucksack or one suitcase that doesn't require enormous amounts of space that you can take with you, so think of this when you prepare. Below are guidelines to help you plan.

Before the wildfire strikes

Think about your home in its environment and think about how you might keep your home safe. Take steps to ensure that you:

- Keep flammable items and debris as far away from your home as possible.
- Have a water hose available so that you can 'water' your home and keep it damp and cool during hot dry weather, especially if it is made of timber.
- Have a 'fire-break area' or a bare area of land or closely cropped lawn if you live near a forest. Some experts advise a strip 10 metres wide around your home if in wooded areas.
- Keep the area around the house free of debris including old cars, firewood, timber.
- Site your fuel tanks away from this area if you can and maintain the area around fuel tanks free of debris.
- Ensure that containers for storing fuel are fire-resistant and store such containers in a shed that cannot burn easily.
- Know where you and family members can meet up if you must evacuate separately from places other than your home, e.g. if the adults are at work and children at school.
- Organise a 'grab and go bag' for each member of the family, considering what specific needs each person has and how to meet these. Some items that go in the 'go bag' may need replacing regularly according to expiry dates on the products, e.g. milk formula for babies, insulin for diabetes. Also, make sure that the insulin is always kept cool.

- Discuss any community issues that need to be covered with your neighbours.
- Make sure that your children are 'fire aware' and appreciate that playing with fire is unacceptable.
- Compost dead leaves and other debris where possible, and do not light outdoor fires when winds are high.
- Check to see whether you can burn debris on your property as a permit may be required.
- Have a water hose and shovel ready and make sure that a fire is totally out before leaving it.
- If you are building a fire for a barbeque, make sure this is allowed, and that you have it in a container or fire-pit where you can contain and control the fire easily and ensure that it is totally extinguished when you no longer require it.
- Ensure that the emergency services can find your home easily by having easy-to-see signs at the entrance(s) to the property.

Exercise – Engaging young people in wildfire prevention

Andy was a bored teenager and was looking for something to do. He got talking to some other bored young people on the Estate, and one person said, 'I love fires. Let's go a have a barbeque on the hills nearby'. They bought some sausages and went up the hill, picking up sticks lying on the ground as they went along. They eventually started a fire and roasted their sausages on sticks. When they finished, they stomped on the fire and left. A short while later, a wind began to blow, and some of the logs that had remained hot produced sparks that lit the dry grass nearby. Before long, a wild grass fire was blazing away.

Discussion

You are in a group of youth workers, considering how you might engage young people in protecting their precious environment from destruction. What would you do to attract a group of 'bored' teenagers to join you in fire-awareness activities?

Young people are often not fire aware and may be careless around it. Discuss with your local fire department if they might provide interesting fire safety training that includes 'hands-on' training.

Conclusion

Extreme weather events, whether floods, droughts, wildfires or other hazard, will challenge all people, including the emergency services who must respond to calls for help when disaster strikes. Preventing a disaster is preferable to having to intervene when it occurs. People need help to cope with the devastation of the environment. Immense losses including loss of life, economic and livelihood disruption, and loss of important, intangible cultural heritages at individual and community levels produce hardship and grief alongside lifelong challenges for those involved (de Silva et al., 2023).

Social workers have important roles to play in raising consciousness about the severe damage that wildfires can do to people, the environment and economy. They can also advocate for better conservation measures and explain these and their necessity to community residents. Engaging community members is crucial to their taking mitigating action in relation to extreme weather events. Community members are likely to be among those who support people who are evacuated during wildfires or help them deal with the grief and loss that they experience when fire strikes close to home. Social workers have a major task in making people aware of their roles as disaster responders. In the UK, according to the Civil Contingencies Act 2004, social workers are first tier responders under the local authority with specific tasks to undertake. They are not volunteers drawn from the general public.

6 The Grenfell fire disaster

Introduction

The Grenfell Tower Fire in the Royal Borough of Kensington and Chelsea in London, England on 14 June 2017, represents one of the UK's most tragic fire disasters of modern times. In it, 72 people died, 70 were injured and 223 escaped from the 24-storey tower block. Property damage is estimated between £200 million and £1 billion. The Borough is home to some of the richest people in the UK as well as some of its poorest. The Grenfell Tower was built during a council housing building programme in 1974. However, the residualisation of council housing during the Thatcher era when much of it was sold off, meant that their assignation as social housing tenants associated with disadvantaged households subjected them to austerity measures through curtailed public expenditures on housing. Cuts resulted in severe shortages and under-funding for the sector (McLeod, 2018). Over time, their wealthy neighbours convinced the Royal Borough of Kensington and Chelsea Council (RB-KCC) to make this old building less of an eyesore. This ultimately led to the addition of flammable cladding that was a major contributor to the disaster. These policies were significant factors in the Grenfell Disaster. This chapter considers the issues these policies raise for personal health and wellbeing and fire safety in the refurbishment of people's homes. It then turns to the issues confronting social workers' involvement in such disasters.

Background to the Grenfell Fire

The Lancaster West Estate, in which Grenfell Tower is located, is a sprawling, inner-city social housing complex. It contains around a thousand dwellings inhabited mainly by working class, multi-cultural and multi-ethnic communities. The Lancaster West Estate, located in North Kensington in the Royal Borough of Kensington and Chelsea, is owned by the RBKCC. However, during the years 1994 and 2017, this Estate

DOI: 10.4324/9781003105824-7

was managed on behalf of RBKCC by the Kensington and Chelsea Tenant Management Organisation (KCTMO). The residents had spent years complaining about the fire risks and inadequacies of Grenfell Tower, including the fire danger posed by the cladding, but the KCTMO constantly ignored their complaints (McLeod, 2018; Moore-Bick, 2021).

The Royal Borough of Kensington and Chelsea is a locale of contrasts. Residents living on the World's End Estate have an average income of £15,000 annually while those on the other side of King's Road average £100,000 yearly. Life expectancy for those who live in its more affluent parts is the highest in the country. For example, a man living near Harrods in Knightsbridge is likely to reach the age of 94; a man living on the nearby estate is likely to live to 72 years of age. Child poverty levels average 27 per cent across the borough, rising to 58 per cent in its poorest areas, while the wealthy area around Hyde Park has 6 per cent (Shildrick, 2018).

Former MP for Kensington and Chelsea, Emma Dent Coad, highlighted these gross inequalities in that part of London when she commented in the *After Grenfell: Inequality Report*:

> Kensington and Chelsea, where I was born and bred, is a microcosm of everything that has gone wrong in our country in the past few years … It is a place where inequality has become a gross spectacle. Where childhood poverty, overcrowding and homelessness live cheek by jowl with opulent second homes, palatial apartments for the mega-rich and vast outflows of rent to corporate landlords … The entirely preventable atrocity at Grenfell Tower has revealed the extent of inequality in Kensington and Chelsea, and the years of poor political decision-making and financial mismanagement.

The Grenfell Fire began as a small domestic fire with an electrical fault in a fridge-freezer in Flat 16 on the Fourth Floor of the Tower. On 14 June 2017, at 00:54, Behailu Kebede, a resident of Flat 16, dialled 999 to call the London Fire Service (FBS). The first firefighter arrived 5 minutes later at 00:59. At that point, firefighters followed a policy of advising the inhabitants of high tower blocks to shut the windows and doors and 'stay put' until firefighters arrived to evacuate the person(s) in the event of a fire, a practice known as 'compartmentalisation'. However, 'staying put' was not feasible as a response once the fire broke out of the space in which it had started. Once compartmentalisation is shown to be failing because the fire is spreading elsewhere, 'staying put' advice should be changed to helping people escape in an orderly manner. The policy for 'staying put' in high-rise buildings, known as PN633, proved a danger to the people who refused to leave unless a firefighter told them to do that. This policy was not reversed until it was too late for many residents.

Although the firefighters at Grenfell had plenty of time to examine the policy and reverse it given that they had over an hour before the fire escaped out of Flat 16 at 01:09. However, they did not do this because poor communications between the police, firefighters, and helicopter flying overhead, meant that no one person had a clear picture of what was happening to the building as a whole. Revoking the compartmentalisation advice did not occur until Assistant Chief Fire Officer Andrew Roe did so at 02:47. By that time lives had already been lost.

Another part of the tragedy in the case of Grenfell, was that the cladding used to 'modernise' the building included panels made of aluminium composite material (ACM) that was illegal to use because it had been found to be highly combustible. Moreover, it was difficult to control fires fuelled by this material (Parker, 2017), as London's 2009 Lakanal House Fire had shown earlier.

Sir Martin Moore-Bick (2019: 5) who presided over Inquiry into the Grenfell Tower Fire commented in the *Report into the Grenfell Inquiry*, that the material used to refurbish the 'external walls of the building failed to comply with Requirement B4(1) of Schedule 1 to the Building Regulations 2010'. This restricted the ability of firefighters to hold back the spread of a fire in such a tower. The material in question included aluminium composite material (ACM) for the rainscreen panels. These contained polyethylene cores, which further fuelled the fire. Added to this was the fuel source provided by the polyisocyanurate (PIR) and phenolic foam insulation boards which lay behind the ACM panels and which could also be found in parts of the window surrounds. These sources of fuel explain the speedy spread of the fire vertically and horizontally along the Tower, thus destroying the relevance of the 'stay put' approach. A quick, orderly evacuation would have been the best option in those circumstances.

The tragedy of Grenfell had an antecedent that should have provided strong lessons about the inadequacies of the 'staying put' policy once compartmentalisation had failed. This was the Lakanal House Fire in Southwark, London which occurred on 3 July 2009 when a faulty television set started a fire in a flat on the ninth floor of a 14-floor building. Originally built in 1959, this building had recently been refurbished with cladding that had proved unfit for purpose. The fire and the acrid smoke that engulfed the other parts of the Lakanal Building caused the deaths of six people and injured others. The coroner recommended various changes following the Lakanal House Fire which were directed at the London Fire Brigade (LFB). The LFB undertook a detailed internal review of its practices and policies relating to the handling of 999 calls in general and those calls requiring potentially life-saving fire survival guidance (FSG calls). The review questioned whether the control room should assume that fire crews would reach FSG callers quickly and whether those in charge of the control room correctly balanced the risk of 'staying put' against that of attempting to escape or evacuate. Having missed the correct balance in the case of Grenfell, the reversal of the compartmentalisation policy came when many avoidable deaths had occurred.

As these injunctions were not observed correctly in Grenfell (Moore-Bick, 2019: 7), 72 people, mainly from black and minority ethnic communities died in this conflagration. The LFB has an operational risk database (ORD) for buildings in London and a risk assessment policy (PN800). This information is made available to all operational firefighters at an incident. However, that pertaining to Grenfell was out of date. Additionally, the Inquiry revealed that those attending the Grenfell Fire had not been adequately trained for what they found on the ground. Their preparation and previous planning had not equipped them properly for the eventualities they faced, and so precious time was lost because there was lack of clarity regarding the best action forward. The control room operators (CROs) were also overwhelmed by the number of FSG calls reaching them and so were not able to stay with callers until they were safely evacuated as stipulated by policy and their training. The Grenfell Inquiry had this worrying conclusion about the CROs:

> CROs had not been trained to handle numerous simultaneous FSG calls, on the implications of a decision to evacuate, or on the circumstances in which a caller should be advised to leave the building or stay put. They were not aware of the danger of assuming that crews would always reach callers, which was one of the important lessons that should have been learnt from the Lakanal House Fire. As a result, they gave assurances which were not well founded.
>
> (Moore-Bick, 2019: 7)

Moreover, there was lack of communication and coordination between the other responders – the RBKCC, and the LAS (London Ambulance Service). Also, no single contact point in each control room had been agreed to act as the link between the other emergency services. Consequently, there was no direct contact between the supervisors in each control room. Moreover, the Declaration of a Major Incident by the MPS (Metropolitan Police Service) at 01:46 and LFB at 02:06 and the Declaration of a Major Incident by LAS at 02:26 were not communicated effectively to each other or the RBKCC. The latter did not learn of these three separate declarations until 02:42. Moreover, the hele-teli downlink or video connection between the emergency services on the ground, especially the LFB with the police helicopter flying overhead malfunctioned, so information was not flowing from that source either. Importantly, these failures in communication prevented compliance with the protocols in place for handling emergencies in London. This delayed discussions on joint responses to a complex situation. For example, the Fire Brigade Union argued in its submission to the Inquiry that had they been able to view these videos, they would have realised that compartmentalisation had failed much earlier and been able to change the 'stay put' advice earlier.

The RBKCC has responsibilities under the Civil Contingencies Act 2004 to prepare a Contingency Management Plan. This contained no specific role for the tenant management organisation responsible for the tenants in the Tower (i.e. the KCTMO). The KCTMO had an emergency plan that was 15 years out of date. The inadequacies in both these plans meant that there was a serious delay in obtaining a Dangerous Structures Engineer (DSE) who could have understood the details of the structures in the Tower and passed this information to the LFB. Sadly, this did not happen until 08:00 on 15 June 2017. Moreover, the gas supply was not switched off until a gas engineer from Cadent Gas Ltd arrived unprompted and used his knowledge of the area to cut off the pipes supplying gas after many hours of work under the streets nearby, a task achieved at 23:40 on that date.

Grenfell tenants defend their homes and demand accountability from the RBKCC and KCTMO

Grenfell residents had a history of raising objections to what was happening in their neighbourhood and opposing developments that were depriving them of important amenities, especially leisure ones that had been once been publicly owned. In 2010, they opposed the Kensington Academy and Leisure Centre development which they deemed a gross overdevelopment of an inappropriate site. Moreover, they were concerned that this development would involve the destruction of Lancaster Green, one of the few local green spaces available to residents of the Lancaster West Estate and provided play areas for children. Developments such as these sought to squeeze more and more people into high density social housing blocks and contrasted sharply with the green spaces surrounding the palatial mansions nearby. Some of these action groups are described below.

The Grenfell Action Group was started in 2010 by Edward (Ed) Daffarn of Grenfell Tower and Francis O'Connor who lived in Verity Close to promote the interests of tenants in social housing and object to the construction of the Kensington Academy and Leisure Centre. Francis O'Connor had to leave her home due to chronic illness brought about by the constant stress of struggling with the impact of the demolition and construction work being undertaken to create the Kensington Academy and Leisure Centre. She returned to Ireland and worked with Ed to produce a blog until the night of the Grenfell Fire. Ed, a victim-survivor of the fire, nearly lost his life when he had to escape without his possessions. He also had to seek emergency accommodation and find suitable permanent alternative accommodation. This disruption to Ed's life led to the demise of their partnership.

Grenfell United was a new activist group begun by Ed Daffarn, one of its founder members, following discussions with some bereaved and other survivors of Grenfell. Those in Grenfell United were a group composed of survivors and bereaved families from the Grenfell Tower Fire. They organised collectively to demand justice and change the disregard of fire safety evident in the Grenfell Tower, despite endless complaints (McLeod, 2018). The group wanted to honour the memories of the 72 residents who perished in the fire and demand that everyone became assured that their homes were safe to live in and insisted on justice for the loss of lives and devastation they had suffered.

Grenfell United also engaged in direct action. For example, on Monday 14 December 2020, the group went to the French Embassy in Knightsbridge to deliver a letter to Catherine Colonna, the French Ambassador to the UK. The letter asked the French government to compel three former employees of a French cladding company living in France to give evidence about the fire. Speaking outside the building, Karim Mussilhy, whose uncle Hesham Rahman had died in the fire declared, 'We need these people to come to the country [UK] and tell the truth'.

The Arconic Corporation, an American industrial company specialising in lightweight metal engineering and manufacturing, produced the plastic-filled aluminium cladding panels that caused the fire to spread. Its employees refused to answer questions or appear at the Grenfell Fire Inquiry. Three of its key witnesses, including Claude Wehrle, the Head of Technical Sales Support at Arconic, hid behind a 51-year-old statute that prohibited people from disclosing commercial or industrial information in foreign judicial and administrative proceedings. The Inquiry had already been told that Wehrle knew years before Arconic's panels were sold for use on the Grenfell Tower that they were 'dangerous' if 'exposed to fire'. On 14 June 2017, the fire spread from the fourth to the 24th floor in under 30 minutes due to this cladding and deprived 72 people of their lives.

The Justice 4 Grenfell group, formed on 19 June 2017, was launched with a silent walk for truth, accountability, and change. It aimed to prevent another similar fire disaster from occurring. It has also stepped into the breach caused by inadequate state support left by the authorities including the RBKCC and KCTMO. Justice 4 Grenfell aimed to support those people from the Tower who survived, were bereaved, evacuated, and lived nearby. Justice 4 Grenfell also sought to bring to court those individuals and organisations who failed to provide safe homes for those who lived in Grenfell Tower and link up with other organisations and individuals sharing their aims.

Exercise – Holding decision-makers accountable

The Grenfell Fire highlighted the dangers of using ACM cladding on buildings higher than 18 metres. These were estimated to total 486 buildings across the UK and affected thousands of people. Many of these were leaseholders, and they were initially held liable for removing and replacing this cladding which would have been beyond the financial means of most.

This approach also ignored millions of people in medium-rise blocks (buildings between 11 and 18 metres) with ACM cladding. They have little clarity on the dangers they face or who is responsible for making their buildings fireproof. Imagine you are a resident in one of these buildings. You know that many people are anxious about their safety and have set up groups to watch the buildings during the night on a shift basis to ensure that everyone is involved in ensuring the safety of everyone else should a fire break out. You realise that this is a short-term and unsustainable solution and want to address the problem differently. You are thinking about creating an action group to lobby government and developers to tackle the issue and repair all the houses with ACM cladding at their expense. By doing this, you intend to hold the 'culprits', as you consider them, accountable for their decisions.

Discussion

Working in a small group, choose a chair and a notetaker. Then consider the following questions and prepare to report-back to the plenary group:

- How would you organise an action group to lobby for government and developers to act on fireproofing these dwellings? Consider a constitution, group membership, terms of reference, and officers for your action group.
- Whom would you target for your actions?
- What would you aim to achieve?
- How would you raise funds?
- Which people and organisations would you seek to attract as allies? Consider various community groups, trade unions, businesses, elected local representatives, and so on.
- What would you define as successful outcomes?
- How long would you expect the group to run and how would you maintain morale and funding for its activities over this period?

You may seek guidance in Dominelli (2019b) regarding how to form and mobilise groups, handle the media, disseminate publicity and other practical instructions relevant to community engagement and coproduction.

Health risks from fire and chemical contaminants

The discharge of large quantities of toxic materials into the air, soil and water can carry serious health implications for those affected (Parker, 2017). In the Grenfell Fire, one of these effects was the so-called 'Grenfell cough'. Other health concerns included vomiting, coughing up blood, skin complaints and various breathing difficulties reported by victim-survivors. Professor Anna Stec undertook research into these issues because she believed that the air had been contaminated through chemicals such as the polycyclic aromatic hydrocarbons (PAHs) which are potentially carcinogenic. She found that the soil samples that were collected within 140 metres of the Tower contained six key PAHs. Moreover, they were present at significantly higher levels than those occurring in the reference soil samples taken from other urban areas. That is, the Grenfell ones were around 160 times higher, and a source of concern. Her research also revealed that charred samples taken from balconies of between 50 to 100 metres away from the Tower also contained cancer-causing PAHs. The soil samples also had phosphorous flame retardants. These contained chemicals from materials commonly used in insulation foams and upholstered furniture. These toxins affect the nervous system. Looking for contaminants in the soil, as well as in fallen debris and charred samples, Stec and her team identified various synthetic vitreous fibres matching those present in products used in the Grenfell Tower refurbishment. Additionally, analyses of soil, fire debris and charred samples were tested about six months later and taken from 6 locations around 1.2 kilometres away from the Tower. Stec and her colleagues found that the samples still contained PAHs at dangerous levels.

Halogen-based flame retardants used in domestic and other consumer products can produce carbon monoxide and hydrogen cyanide gases which are major causes of deaths resulting from fires because they are released in significant quantities during combustion. Benzene, another carcinogenic substance, was found in noteworthy quantities in soils 140 metres away from Grenfell Tower. These reached levels 25–40 times higher than those in other urban soils. Furthermore, dust deposits and a yellow oily deposit obtained from a window blind inside a flat 160 metres from the Tower 17 months later also contained isocyanates which were strong enough to cause respiratory problems including asthma after one exposure. These substances were also attributed to the burning of specific materials utilised during the 2016 refurbishment of Grenfell Tower. Moreover, these substances can last in the soil and atmosphere for months or years after a disastrous event.

As toxins can be absorbed through the skin, testing air and soil samples is insufficient in determining the risks to health posed by these carcinogenic substances. The most dangerous period of exposure is usually immediately during the event and in the short-term after it. Those most exposed to these substances, e.g. victim-survivors, evacuees, those in the immediate vicinity, firefighters attending the blaze, social workers and volunteers helping at the scene, and workers doing the clearing up could experience serious long-term health complications. Their risks are currently unknown and monitoring of their health for any ill-effects was recommended. Anna Stec's research in 2018 indicated that fire fighters were 3 times more likely to contract cancer because the toxic substances entered through their skin. Even the methods used to wash firefighters' protective gear pushed these substances into the fibres and turned them into carcinogenic stores because this equipment would be reused. Stec's findings (Stec et al, 2018) were contradicted by research conducted by AECOM, consultants to RBKCC. AECOM claimed that its research found that 'immediate action' was not needed because the levels of toxic substances exposed by their studies fell within acceptable levels for urban areas. Such controversies highlight the politics of research that make it difficult for non-experts to determine whose data merits credibility, especially in complex situations where poor health may have a variety of causes.

The politics surrounding the different experts appointed by government meant that there was no consensus possible around the accuracy or otherwise of the data proffered by the different groups, especially those appointed by the political processes that were controlled by the authorities. As a result, Anna Stec resigned. In her resignation letter, Anna Stec asserted that:

> There are still a significant number of people suffering physically and mentally following the Grenfell Tower Fire, and yet, there is still nothing in place to properly evaluate all the adverse health effects of the fire, and specifically exposure to fire effluents.

People who had survived the fire were treated for cyanide poisoning. And yet, according to the then local MP, Dent Coad, local officials ignored those experts who had warned them about the toxic fumes that would have impacted people on the night. Moreover, the authorities did little to protect the children in the schools located within the endangered areas around Grenfell Tower.

Exercise – Health concerns

You are a teacher in a primary school in West London. You have recently arrived to work at the school and note that about a third of the class has serious asthma and other respiratory problems. You ask the parents what they think of their children's health. They reply that they were born in the area and have lived there all their lives and aren't worried as most of their friends' children have similar issues. You wonder what the cause of this is. You ask colleagues, but no one knows. There is a social worker associated with the school, so you talk about your concerns with her. She says she has observed the same issues and this is particularly relevant for several families that are on her books for child neglect considerations. You promise the teacher you will raise it at a case conference meeting for one of these children. It is being called for child neglect reasons in two weeks' time. You think about the issue on your way home that night and resolve to discuss it with one of your friends, Tom, in the health department at your local university. Following that conversation, Tom highlights the school's location near a major road with constant traffic. The air in London is known to have 'pollution hotspots' and this could be contributing to the children's respiratory issues. He also says there might be other sources of contaminants including industries nearby, air traffic overhead, major fires in the surrounding area. He suggests that you raise the issues in relation to the child whose health you are discussing at your case conference and let him know what its decision might be. In the meantime, he sends you several articles to help you prepare for your meeting and consider possible questions you might ask at it.

Discussion

Working in small groups, choose a chair and a notetaker before you begin your discussion so that you can contribute your insights to the plenary group feedback. Consider the following questions:

- How important are pollutants in the air, water, and soil in undermining children's health?
- What information do you need from GPs, teachers, and parents, to understand the child's poor respiratory health and the possible treatments that are available?

- Can these pollutants also affect the health of adults, and thus the parental care given to the child?
- Given the poverty in the household, can the child's food intake be enhanced and made more nutritious, who will pay for it, and will it improve health and performance at school?
- What can be done about improving air quality?
- What balance can be achieved in considering the impact of both personal and structural issues on this problem?
- Can you convince some of the biochemists at the local university to join you in finding out what pollutants are in the air and what can be done to mitigate these?
- Could working on this specific case benefit other children with similar health issues?

You need to persuade those at the case conference that there is merit in finding the answers to these questions so that you can intervene in this child's life more effectively and efficiently and support a mother who comes across as harassed by the stresses of everyday living despite loving all her children.

Social work interventions in the Grenfell Tower Fire disaster

The Grenfell Fire Response Team was created to support residents affected by the Grenfell Fire. This team was composed of representatives from London-wide local government, regional government, central government, the British Red Cross, Metropolitan Police and London Fire Brigade. Additional support offered by others came in the form of a range of volunteers including professionals offering bereavement counselling and people from all walks of life working alongside the community to listen and offer whatever help they could. People quickly gave generously to organisations providing practical aid to victim-survivors.

The RBKCC asked its social workers to volunteer to support the victim-survivors of this horrendous tragedy. They formed part of the 130-strong group acting as key workers to provide 'wraparound care' that included housing, financial and counselling support. They were joined by social workers from other London boroughs, and resilience team members from other parts of the UK. The social workers took their roles seriously even though most were not trained in disaster interventions (Bartoli et al., 2022). However, using skills gained during their generic training, especially communication skills, crisis intervention skills, interviewing skills, loss and bereavement skills, they supported the victim-survivors to acquire needed services They also drew upon their anti-oppressive practice skills and commitment to human rights to conduct needs assessments, talk to the victim-survivors, formulate individual plans of action and deliver appropriate services. However, this way of working proved too time-consuming and expensive for the political masters holding the purse strings at the time, and the social workers were pulled out in favour of more actuarily minded workers based in Price-Waterhouse Cooper's accountancy-oriented offices and those in KPMG, a global accountancy organisation that provides financial audit, tax advice and other advisory services. Social work practice was intense, but it 'was for the community, powered by the community', and stood in contrast to the pressures of working in the RBKCC on a normal workday. Also, its social justice-based approach contrasted with the more actuarially oriented and bureaucratic approaches offered by the accounting agencies.

Mariam Raja and I attended a disaster social work short course on social work during disasters in 2018. She was an adult social worker in the RBKCC when she volunteered to support the Grenfell victim-survivors. Her deployment lasted seven months. The beginning was difficult as there was lack of clarity about what was needed and who the social workers were to serve – victim-survivors, or those already using services or both. Eventually the needs became clearer, and housing was a key one of these. Helping people obtain replacement documents for those lost in the fire was another. Eventually more emotional needs relating to the trauma and bereavements victim-survivors had suffered rose to the surface. Accessing appropriate facilities was to be free from the stigma associated with receiving mental health services. The victim-survivors rejected stigmatisation of their needs which required a holistic and immediate response to address their issues, especially that of being rehoused. Mariam also highlighted the emotional toll of doing social work during times of disaster. Supervision and support from others are important sources of assistance for those doing this work. Mariam's stories are now accessible in print. *Out of the Shadows* (Bartoli et al., 2022) has a chapter devoted to Grenfell.

The failure of central government to understand the nature of the issues at stake in a social disaster were compounded when it appointed KPMG to advise the Grenfell Tower Inquiry, despite opposition to it doing so. Later, the firm was accused of having a conflict of interests regarding this role and its involvement in auditing several key players in the Grenfell saga. These included auditing the accounts of the parent company of Celotex, which produced the insulation for the building; the Royal Borough of Kensington and Chelsea (RBKC); and the Rydon Group, or the contractor that refurbished Grenfell Tower (Taylor, 2018). KPMG insisted there was no conflict of interest as its role did not extend to carrying out investigations or making decisions about evidence submitted to the Inquiry. Those expressing their concerns and opposing the appointment of KPMG in favour of a representative advisory panel to ask questions and ensure accountability at the Inquiry took the government's decision to proceed with KPMG as a signal that it had little understanding of the importance of a transparent Inquiry with the resources to conduct its work properly. They also doubted that including such stakeholders in the Inquiry could ensure that the victim-survivors would receive justice and a rectification of the errors that had killed so many of their community members. Moreover, they wanted assurances that another Grenfell would not happen in future. KPMG eventually resigned its role.

Guidelines for social workers supporting victim-survivors

Social workers are involved in supporting victim-survivors in both (hu) man-made disasters like Grenfell, and 'natural' hazard-induced ones like earthquakes. Having a safe, friendly, and familiar location in which to meet and greet victim-survivors, listening to them, helping to calm them down, providing immediate practical relief including addressing their housing needs are at the top of their agenda. From the Moore-Bick (2019) *Interim Report on Grenfell*, the following issues should also be on a social worker's radar:

- Being prepared to address the trauma and emotionality of disasters in both the short- and long-terms. This requires extensive investment in mental health services.
- Facilitating self-care and supervision (peer group and line management) and debriefing before, during, and after a disaster.
- Demanding proper training and preparation for supporting people in any disaster, including an incendiary one.
- Getting the correct information about what happened before, during, and after the disaster. This may be problematic because the information may be contested, but social workers should be able to explain why their views differ from those going around (if they are) to uphold transparency in and accountability of their responses.
- Empowering residents to express their understandings and voice and build up their evidence about inadequate policies including long-term austerity and political decisions made when ignoring residents' expressions of concern and agitation before, during, and after the disaster. Ignoring their views endangered the lives not only of those living in Grenfell before and during the fire, but also those of firefighters who lacked the necessary equipment within the building to support their fire-fighting efforts and endeavours to save lives.

- Enabling residents to ask questions about the disparities in wealth that hindered the resources and services that should have been available but were not, including those concerning recreational facilities open to children from low-income families. These disparities in wealth also applied to the emergency professionals. For example, the firefighters risking their lives to save people earned 500 times less than the CEO responsible for the company that manufactured the claddings (Hansard, 2019).
- Helping the victim-survivors to hold accountable those responsible for the decision to cut costs in housing expenditures and fire services. Such actions would include Boris Johnson as the Mayor of London who encouraged these cuts, and the RBKCC which endorsed them despite long-standing complaints from residents.
- Helping policymakers and victim-survivors to dialogue over, formulate policies for safe buildings and implement those fit for purpose in ensuring fire safety in high-rise blocks.
- Enabling local community groups to maintain pressure on government officials to make resources available to ensure that all preventable fires did not occur.

Five years after the fire, Grenfell groups continue to demand justice and an end to the use of inflammable cladding in high rise apartment buildings. The groups formed to meet these objectives may have to struggle for some time, as occurred in the Hillsborough disaster.

Preparing for a long struggle for justice following a disaster: the Hillsborough disaster

The Hillsborough disaster showed the significance of establishing a family support group as a peer support group to sustain the commitment to find out what happened in Hillsborough and maintain the strength of all those families who had lost someone during the collapse at Hillsborough Stadium and the responses over the long haul. The Hillsborough disaster occurred on 15 April 1989 in the Hillsborough Stadium in Sheffield where Liverpool and Nottingham Forest were playing their semi-final game for the FA (Football Association) Cup and looking forward to getting a place in the final. During that day, 96 Liverpool fans lost their lives (another died of his injuries years later) and 760 others were injured. But the truth about what happened to those who died and were injured on that day proved hard to extract from the system, and justice was a long time coming, despite inquiries, coroners' inquests and court cases.

The Taylor Interim Report into the Hillsborough Disaster, published on 1 August 1989, did not meet the families' demands for justice, although it acknowledged that the police were responsible for many of the failures in the responses occurring on the day. A. J. Taylor's Final Report, published on 19 January 1990, made suggestions about safety at football stadia. Public pressure for a proper inquiry continued. One was finally granted in 2010. It had the Right Reverend Bishop of Liverpool, James Jones, as chair. The independent report this panel produced, *Hillsborough: The Report of the Hillsborough Independent Panel*, was published on 12 September 2012 (Jones, 2012). Despite being produced many years after the disaster, it makes difficult reading and various issues progressed slowly through the legal processes. Legal challenges continued for more than 30 years after the disaster before the football fans were fully absolved of responsibility for the disaster.

Margaret Aspinall, whose son James lost his life that day, was a leading member of the Hillsborough Family Support Group. Aspinall initially resisted social worker intervention. But, in a speech in Durham on 18 June 2018, she told those of us attending the short course I organised on social work during times of disasters that she was glad the social worker persevered because her help became invaluable in the many dark days that followed as she came to accept that her son, though never forgotten, would not be walking through the door to say 'Hi, Mom, I am back', ever again. The injustice of the situation that she and the many other families faced in getting the information they needed about precisely how and why their loved ones had died, spurred them into forming the Hillsborough Family Support Group and to persist in demanding an Independent Inquiry which finally reported in September 2012 and exonerated the fans who had been blamed by the media and others for the collapse of the pens in the Leppings Lane area of the Stadium (Jones, 2012). The trial of three people charged with perverting the course of justice following the disaster was scheduled for 19 April 2021. Other people including the Chief Constable of South Yorkshire had been charged earlier. After 32 years, the Hillsborough Family Support Group was wound up on 15 April 2021 as they felt they had reached the end of the road and needed to move on, individually and collectively. The bringing of people to court also lent credence to the group having done as much as it could. This example can provide encouragement for those persisting in their demand for justice for the lost lives, and bereavement and suffering of the victim-survivors of the Grenfell tragedy.

Conclusions

The Grenfell Tower was an avoidable tragedy, had lessons been learnt from earlier fires of a similar nature, like the Lakanal House Fire of 2009. As this did not happen, many mistakes were made in Grenfell.

Thus, residents feel that justice has not been obtained for either those that lost their lives or those who survived on 14 June 2017.

The social workers who went to assist were poorly prepared, and their endeavours to focus on empowering the residents and ensuring that they upheld their human rights and access to services were limited by political decision-makers who failed to grasp the enormity of the impact of the fire on the lives of those who survived. Social workers' human-rights, person-based approach was not what the political authorities in central government wanted to promote, and the key worker system of providing 'wraparound' care was halted in favour of a managerialist approach. This inadequate intervention means that the victim-survivors of Grenfell are still fighting for social justice and their entitlements, including housing and an end to the use of ACM cladding in high rise buildings. It will be interesting to see if one of the lessons that the politicians draw from their involvement in the Grenfell Tower Fire tragedy is that they become better at providing adequate resources to prevent fires from occurring in buildings with combustible cladding and facilitate the work of those practitioners whose responsibility it is to turn lives around after a disaster.

7 Terrorist attacks

Immediate and long-term consequences for social work interventions

Introduction

Terrorist acts have featured in world history for some time. An early recent one in the UK was the bombing of Pan Am Flight 103 on 21 December 1988. This was a regular transatlantic flight going from Frankfurt to Detroit. It had a stopover in London and was on its way to New York City when a bomb went off as it was flying over Lockerbie in Scotland. The airplane crashed, destroying 11 houses on Sherwood Crescent and killing 11 of its residents. All those on board died alongside 11 townspeople, bringing the total to 270 fatalities. Abdelbaset al-Megrahi was found guilty of this mass murder in 2001, but he died of cancer in 2012 and did not finish his prison term. Determined to find all those guilty of this atrocity, the Americans have taken a suspected accomplice of al-Megrahi, Abu Agila Mohammad Mas'ud Kheir Al-Marimi, to face justice in the USA in 2022.

The word terrorism has become part of people's everyday vocabulary since George W. Bush unleashed the 'War on Terror' following the Attack on the Twin Towers of the World Trade Center in Manhattan, New York on 11 September 2001 (9/11). On that date, an airplane was deliberately crashed into each of its two towers, killing 2,996 people. This disaster shifted Americans' perceptions of the destruction that they would face if they did not take the 'external' terrorist threat seriously. Despite the unanimous condemnation of this atrocity throughout the world, the definition of what constitutes 'terrorism' remains elusive. In this chapter, I consider the diverse definitions of terrorism amongst key players attempting to control potential attackers, the international structures that seek to bring concerted action in dealing with the people committing terrorist atrocities. I then focus on examples from within the UK and consider the lessons that can be learnt from such illustrations and what the role of social workers is in dealing with those labelled 'terrorists' entails.

DOI: 10.4324/9781003105824-8

Defining terrorism

Terrorism is a form of violence that is used for political purposes by state actors, criminal gangs, collective groups, and individuals. Most state actors eschew the label 'terrorist' because it is usually employed as a pejorative term indicating that the use of violence is immoral and illegitimate. Also, the state cloaks its use of violence within a grand military agenda aimed at meeting specific geopolitical ends, and at minimising its use of violence by claiming to use it strategically, e.g. Bush's War Against Iraq to get rid of 'weapons of mass destruction', and Putin's War Against Ukraine to cleanse Ukraine of the 'neo-Nazis running the state'. Civilians, i.e. the ordinary residents caught in the crossfire become the 'collateral damage' of war. Those labelled as 'enemies' become stripped of their humanity. Once this occurs, they are not people, and can be and are treated with cruelty and with total disregard of their human rights. It is crucial that those perpetrating these crimes which violate international law and UN Conventions and protocols for proper military behaviour during armed conflicts are charged with 'crimes against humanity' to hold them accountable for their brutality. For example, holding dictators accountable for their ruthless behaviour occurred from 2002 to 2006 in the UN International Criminal Tribunal when the former Yugoslavian leader Slobodan Milošević was tried for crimes committed during the war against Kosovo. Slobodan Milošević died before the trial concluded. No verdict was reached for him, although others acting alongside him were found guilty.

On 9 December 1994, a UN General Assembly Resolution sought to eliminate international terrorism. It stated that terrorism is, 'Criminal acts intended or calculated to provoke a state of terror in the general public, a group of persons or particular persons for political purposes. [These actions] are in any circumstance unjustifiable'. Moreover, this Resolution rejected the justification of such acts on a political, philosophical, ideological, racial, ethnic, religious or any other ground. Nonetheless, the term remains ambiguous, as has been expressed in the statement that, 'One state's 'terrorist' is another state's 'freedom fighter'.

At a meeting in Cairo in 1998, the Council of Arab Ministers of the Interior and the Council of Arab Ministers of Justice defined terrorism in fairly comprehensive terms. It was captured as:

> Any act or threat of violence, whatever its motives or purposes, that occurs in the advancement of an individual or collective criminal agenda and seeking to sow panic among people, causing fear by harming them, or placing their lives, liberty, or security in danger, or seeking to cause damage to the environment or to public or private installations or property or to occupying or seizing them, or seeking to jeopardize national resources.

A few years later in 2004, UN Security Council Resolution 1566 considered terrorism as:

> criminal acts, including against civilians, committed with the intent to cause death or serious bodily injury, or taking of hostages, with the purpose to provoke a state of terror in the general public or in a group of persons or particular persons, intimidate a population or compel a government or an international organization to do or to abstain from doing any [violent] act.

A UN Panel on 17 March 2005 again proclaimed terrorism as: Any act 'intended to cause death or serious bodily harm to civilians or non-combatants with the purpose of intimidating a population or compelling a government or an international organization to do or abstain from doing any act'. This definition can be applied to a government that indiscriminately bombs civilians – in breach of international law, to obtain concessions from another government, as has occurred in Ukraine, Syria, and other countries. State-induced terrorism is much harder to contain and control because it requires unanimity among Security Council members to act. This feat would be impossible to achieve if one of the accused parties were one of its members, as Russia is with regards to Ukraine, for example. Such impotence on the part of the Security Council raises questions about what can be done to control states that violate their responsibility to uphold the UN Charter and protocols, e.g. by suspending such a country from Security Council membership until the matter is resolved and/or a legally binding agreement is reached following their removal from the Security Council.

The European Union uses Article 1 of the Framework Decision on Combating Terrorism (2002) to reflect upon terrorism from a legal framework. It pronounces terrorism as:

> criminal offences set out in a list comprised largely of serious offences against persons and property which: given their nature or context, may seriously damage a country or an international organization [with the aim of] seriously intimidating a population; or unduly compelling a Government or international organization to perform or abstain from performing any act; or seriously destabilizing or destroying the fundamental political, constitutional, economic or social structures of a country or an international organization.

This definition can include virtually anything, including Putin's aggressive acts within its ambit. The UN definitions and European one focus on a terrorist, whether an individual, group or state, inculcating fear and insecurity in other states, organisations, populations, or individuals.

On a country basis, the UK's Terrorism Act 2000, counts 'a serious act of sabotage that disrupts an electronic system' as terrorism. Physical violence is irrelevant in this approach to the issue. The United States uses Title 18 of the Federal Criminal Code to define terrorism within a range of crimes contained within Section 2331 of Chapter 113(B). This encapsulates terrorism as:

> activities that involve violent ... or life-threatening acts ... that are a violation of the criminal laws of the United States or of any State and ... [are] intended to: (i) intimidate or coerce a civilian population; (ii) influence the policy of a government by intimidation or coercion; or (iii) affect the conduct of a government by mass destruction, assassination, or kidnapping; and ... occur ... within the territorial jurisdiction of the United States.

Following the attack on the Twin Towers in 9/11, the coverage of this Criminal Code was enlarged to encompass provisions under the US Patriot Act of 2001. This stated that terrorism is, 'threatening, conspiring or attempting to hijack airplanes, boats, buses or other vehicles; or threatening, conspiring or attempting to commit acts of violence on any 'protected' persons, e.g. government 'officials'.

These definitions suggest that there are three kinds of terrorists: the individual ('lone wolf' including far right supremacists); the group inspired one (e.g. Al-Qaeda, ISIS, Al Shabab, Boko Haram, the Klu Klux Clan); and state-induced terrorism, usually perpetrated as acts of war or armed conflict. Moreover, these definitions draw upon an 'othering' or binary relationship between the 'good guys' (us) over here, and the 'bad guys' – the terrorists, (them) over there. After 9/11, Western discourses drew upon diverse forms of ideological profiling that focused on Islam and those from Islamic countries as characterising the terrorists 'over there'. These characterisations underplayed the role of white supremacists who were inculcating a reign of terror, primarily against black and minority ethnic communities (BMEs) and white people whom they labelled 'traitors' of the race for defending BMEs. Individuals embedded within a white majority population were not portrayed as 'terrorist'. For example, on 16 June 2016, Labour MP for Batley and Spen, Jo Cox, was murdered by white supremacist Thomas Mair for her anti-Brexit views. He was unknown to the police before this killing. Another MP, Sir David Amos, Conservative MP for Southend West, was murdered in his surgery at Leigh-on-Sea on 15 October 2021 by Ali Harbi Ali. Ali had been referred to the PREVENT Programme in his youth, but not formally detained under it.

Countries will have experiences of terrorist attacks arising from either home-grown or international varieties because people will cross borders in pursuit of a cause. Consequently, the UN has created structures and procedures to address terrorist issues and has a global counter-terrorism strategy to hold together national, regional, and international endeavours in countering terrorism. Its strategy was adopted on 8 September 2006 and is subject to review every two years by the UN General Assembly. The review process enables the document to be updated and respond to current priorities concerning counterterrorism, especially those anticipated by member states. The Security Council also has an interest in the counter-terrorism strategy and structures across the UN system.

The United Nations Office of Counter-Terrorism (UNOCT), was formed on 15 June 2017 under UN General Assembly Resolution 71/291. UNOCT aims to formulate, coordinate, and provide leadership on the General Assembly's current counter-terrorism initiatives. These seek to tackle terrorism and violent extremism throughout the United Nations system. UNOCT is led by Under-Secretary General Vladimir Voronkov. It also aims to improve the visibility of the UN's counter-terrorism activities and mobilise and advocate for more resources. UNOCT conducts capacity building endeavours among Member States to strengthen their preventative measures and responses against terrorism within national borders and beyond through various subsidiary bodies. These include the Counter-Terrorism Committee, 1267/1989/2253 ISIL (Da'esh) and Al-Qaida Sanctions Committee, and the 1540 Committee that focuses on the non-proliferation of nuclear, chemical, and biological weapons. The Counter-Terrorism Committee is supported by its own executive directorate (CTED) which implements policy decisions and carries out expert assessments of Member State initiatives. Business in the 1267/1989/2253 ISIL (Da'esh) and Al-Qaida Sanctions Committee is supported by a monitoring team.

The UN's counter-terrorism system consists of 45 entities holding the role of either members or observers. These entities included 41 from the UN itself, INTERPOL, the World Customs Organization, the Inter-Parliamentary Union, the Financial Action Task Force (FATF) and WHO (World Health Organization). The WHO also contributes specifically to the prevention of and responses to radiological and/or nuclear hazards. Including all these members in ONOCT deliberations can make them unwieldy. So, on 23 February 2018, UN Secretary-General António Guterres's sought its reform.

UNOCT also works with members of the United Nations Global Counter-Terrorism Coordination Compact (COMPACT). COMPACT offers a coordination framework that ensures coherence on policies aiming to oppose and prevent terrorism and the spread of violent extremism. COMPACT covers the three pillars on which the work of the United Nations is based. These are: peace and security; sustainable development; and human rights and humanitarian affairs.

Moreover, UNOCT attempts to engage young people in this work, using roundtable formats to do so. Its second roundtable involved civil society organisations (CSOs). It was held virtually on 30 June 2022, with the theme, Youth Engagement, Empowerment and Protection in Counter-Terrorism and PCVE Efforts. Peer-to-peer (P2P) support was utilised to empower young leaders and those in CSOs. The 2022 Civil Society Roundtable Series engaged senior UNOCT officials, UNOCT programme managers and civil society representatives together to assist in designing, implementing, monitoring and evaluating UNOCT's global programmes. Raising awareness about terrorism and the motivation of those promoting such activities among young people is crucial to ensuring that young people become engaged in counter-terrorism measures (Ponsot et al., 2017).

Awareness of the dangers in contemporary warfare

The 'war on terror' signalled a new type of warfare—one that accorded with the features of what Kremlin advisor, Vladislav Surkov, argues is 'non-linear war' (Pomerantsev, 2014). Traditional war, Surkov argues, places war in a particular geographical location, with an identifiable enemy. A traditional war strategy has rarely been evident in the modern warfare practised by Putin since 2014 because ballistic and Cruise missiles are used to pulverise everything in their path. Thus, contemporary warfare is a more fluid phenomenon. The concepts in Surkov's paper can be usefully applied to current developments in social work practice in the UK. Tracing the origins of key anti-terrorist policy developments in the UK (PREVENT and CHANNEL) following the proclamation of 'the war on terror', I argue that such policies have serious implications for social work. Surkov's paper concludes that social workers need to: (a) recognise the tactics at play in the situations of non-linear war; (b) become critically aware of conflated rhetorical turns in political discourses; and (c) actively resist securitised discourses which deny people their human rights; and (d) reject discriminatory notions of so-called 'dangerous' people and communities. In other words, we should actively re-engage with and promote social work values including human rights and social justice even in situations of conflict and terror (Pistone et al., 2019). Moreover, there is an increasing securitisation approach in addressing contemporary social problems. In the UK, this reflects conflated rhetorical logic, notably the linking of the Troubled Families programmes with 'terror'. I now turn to considering specific terrorist acts.

The Manchester Arena bombing in England

The UK is no stranger to terrorist attacks either within the UK mainland or its overseas territories (past and present). This section considers one of the latest terrorist attacks on Manchester, a city that had previously been subject to IRA bombs being detonated in its city centre. The Manchester Arena bombing occurred on 22 May 2017 at the end of the Ariana Grande Concert which had 14,000 young people attending. Thus, the attack was aimed specifically at them. The Manchester Arena had been categorised as a Tier Two risk (terror attack very likely) by the NaCTSO assessment conducted by counter-terrorism police in 2014. The Manchester attack resulted in the largest number of people killed by terrorism following the London bombings of 7 July 2005 (Hind et al., 2021). On that May night in Manchester, 22 people were killed, hundreds wounded and thousands of people's lives, including some of those who came to help, were devastated. Arguments abound about whether the emergency services responded appropriately, and others question why, when Salman Abedi carrying a huge rucksack and hanging about the City Room of the Arena, was not stopped and questioned by a security guard from Showsec, even when a member of the public raised concerns about Abedi being a security risk (Saunders, 2022). Had Showsec staff taken these warnings seriously, they may have asked Abedi to open his rucksack. This may have prevented the slaughter of young people. However, there is no guarantee that had this request been made, Abedi would have not detonated the bomb then and there if he had been able to do so. However, the number of casualties might have been smaller. Salman Abedi was abetted by his younger brother, Hashem Abedi. Both had been radicalised through the propaganda of Islamic State.

The public inquiry into the attack, The Manchester Arena Inquiry, chaired by the Hon, Sir John Saunders, produced a report in several volumes (Saunders, 2022). Volume one considered the security arrangements operating on the night of the Concert. Volume two addressed the concerns about the responses of the emergency services. Volume 3 will raise questions about how the security service and counter-terrorism police could have prevented the attack and how Salman Abedi became radicalised. Had he and his brother been identified as security risks they would have been subjected to the counter-terrorism strategy (CONTEST) and may have been assigned to social workers to work with them. However, this did not happen. And, on 22 May 2017, Abedi's meticulous 'hostile reconnaissance' for assessing the target site for camera blind spots and easy opportunities to avoid the security procedures in place ensured that he waited in the City Room, coming and going as he pleased for some time awaiting the end of the concert before detonating his bomb. Security at the venue was sub-optimal according to the report on the attack, and there were many lessons to be learnt about providing security in complicated buildings with complex arrangements. The security in the Manchester Arena could have been improved if the security ring had been drawn beyond the City Room as this would have meant that Abedi could have been checked before he could enter the area where he could inflict the most damage – when people were leaving the venue and where people, especially parents and children coming to collect concert goers would be waiting (Saunders, 2022).

Group exercise: The Manchester Arena attack

In a small group, consider the following issue. Make notes of your deliberations and responses to present to the plenary group.

The Manchester Arena Attack left many people – parents, children, family members, and emergency workers traumatised. Interventions in such situations are more effective if planned beforehand. Given the relevance of pre-attack planning and exercise drills regarding psychosocial responses to terrorist attacks, convene a group to discuss a response that would ensure effective communications systems, up-to-date information, data sharing, protocols, procedures, and workforce capacity to deal with an atrocity like the Manchester Arena Attack.

You may find it helpful to read the *Manchester Arena Inquiry Report* to get an idea of the complexities to be covered. The article by Hind et al. (2021) will also give you some idea of the issues to be covered. Read these before you begin the group exercise.

Terrorism is a difficult issue to define and prevent. National security forces have securitised many state institutions by drawing public sector workers and practitioners in the health and social care sectors into their remit involving them in straddling the contradictions between care and control. Poynting (2012) cautions that this could engage professionals in state political violence.

The UK's Counter-Terrorism Strategy

Through the Terrorism Act 2000, the UK signalled its recognition of new and emerging threats alongside more traditional ones of which the UK has an extensive history. Responding to these included the use and misuse of new technologies. Consequently, alongside activities to counter terrorist financing and extreme Right-Wing terrorism, it seeks to prevent terrorist abuse of the internet, a concern that has been incorporated into the country's counter-terrorism measures.

The UK's counter-terrorism strategy as part of the National Security Strategy (NSS), was reviewed during the Strategic Defence and

Security Review (STDSR) of 2015. These two documents, the NSS and the STDR, expressed the Government's determination to create a secure and prosperous UK that displayed a global reach and demonstrated substantial influence globally. These aims led to the promulgation of the Counter-Terrorism and Security Act (CT&S Act) 2015. It secured Royal Assent on 12 February 2015 and seeks to prevent people travelling overseas to participate in terrorist activities and come back to the UK. The CT&S Act authorises the removal of a person's passport. The Counter-Terrorism and Sentencing Act 2021 identifies the sentencing options open to the court.

Opposing terrorist groups through a counter-terrorism strategy has been a concern of the British state for decades. After the Second World War, it had to deal with Zionist Terrorism in Palestine – then a British Protectorate. Zionists bombed the King David Hotel on 22 July 1946, killing 91 people and injuring 41 others. The Hotel was operating as the British Headquarters in Palestine then. Other terrorist actions included: the long-standing struggles of Irish Nationalists to re-unify Northern Ireland with Eire; espionage as a product of the Cold War; the terrorism that followed George W Bush's 'War on Terror' following the 9/11 attacks and the War in Iraq, War in Afghanistan and Putin's War Against Ukraine, among others. Many of those accused of 'terrorism' define themselves as liberation fighters, thus highlighting difficulties in reaching an agreed definition of terrorism.

The UK's Counter-Extremism Strategy defines extremism as 'the vocal or active opposition to our fundamental values, including democracy, the rule of law, individual liberty, and respect and tolerance for different faiths and beliefs. We also regard calls for the death of members of our armed forces as extremist'.

This definition was significant in focusing on the ideological dimensions of terrorism and extremism, and defence of the armed forces who are often engaged in wars and other acts of state-endorsed violence.

The bombing of the London Underground on 7 July 2005, under the then government of Tony Blair, and subsequent bombings in this country and abroad have encouraged the development and revision of the UK's counter-terrorist strategy. Initiated in 2003, it was based on lessons learnt during 9/11. Overseas examples covered the bombing of a train in Madrid on 11 March 2004 and later several coordinated attacks that included the Bataclan Concert Hall in Paris on 13 November 2015, and in Belgium, the 22 March 2016 attacks at Brussels airport and Molenbeek underground station (Brion and Guittet, 2018). Responsibility for these attacks was accepted by Al-Qaeda and Islamic State (Da'esh) and fed into the Islamophobic tropes popularised after the 9/11 attacks. However, in the UK, and in Western Europe more generally, there were terrorist actions associated with extreme right-wing ideologues and

individual actors (lone wolves) who were inspired by terrorist organisations and connected with each other on the internet. One of these was
Ali Harbi Ali who killed David Amess, MP on 15 October in 2021. In
the UK, some Far Right extremists attacked elected representatives, e.g.
the murder of Jo Cox, MP by Thomas Mair, neo-Nazi activist and Isla-
mophobe, in 2016. On 25 June 2022, Zaniar Matapour went on a mass
shooting spree in Oslo, aiming to maim and kill people involved in the
Oslo Pride Event organised by the LGBTQ+ community. These developments have led to criticisms of the profiling of people of Middle Eastern
origins, and delayed recognition of the dangers posed for democratic
societies by white supremacists and other Far-right ideologues.

Although the majority of young people who have become radicalised
are young men, the numbers of women and young people under 18 years
of age who have become involved in terrorist activities have risen. Some
have gone to Syria to fight for Da'esh/ISIS. Some of the young women involved became 'jihadi brides' and gave birth to children in the desert. One
of the most quoted of these is Shamima Begum. In 2015 when aged 15,
she left London for Syria. There, she married an ISIS jihadist – a Dutch
convert to Islam, Yago Riedijk, and gave birth to three children, all of
whom died. She was captured when the ISIS caliphate fell and sought to
return to Britain from the Syrian refugee camp, el Hawl. In 2019, Sajid
Javid, then Home Secretary removed her British citizenship despite her
being born in Britain and lacking any other nationality. Javid argued
that she was a Bangladeshi citizen (she was and is not), and Bangladesh
refuses to accept her as such just because her mother was born in that
country. Although she has been fighting to have her citizenship status
reinstated (Knight, 2020), she has failed and still supports ISIS' claims.

The UK's CONTEST counter-terrorist strategy

The CONTEST counter-terrorist strategy (HO, 2015) seeks to reduce terrorist threats in the UK by preventing people from becoming terrorists,
supporting terrorism by being drawn into its ambit, or engaging in terrorist acts. The STDR suggested that CONTEST should be reviewed in
2016. CONTEST contains four key strands (HO, 2011, 2015). These are:

- *Pursue*: This aims to investigate, disrupt, and prevent a terrorist
  attack.
- *Prevent*: This seeks to stop people from either becoming terrorists or
  supporting terrorism.
- *Protect*: This attempts to improve the UK's protective security and
  prevent a terrorist attack.
- *Prepare*: This tries to minimise the impact of an attack and support a
  speedy recovery from it.

PREVENT

PREVENT is the part of CONTEST that is concerned with extremism and the threat posed by both internal and international terrorists. There is a connection between the two, as extremists in the UK can seek inspiration from international terrorists. Thus, PREVENT endeavours to reduce the threats, risks and vulnerabilities posed by domestic extremists from the far-right, far-left, animal rights' activists, and those engaged in terrorist acts related to Northern Ireland. Consequently, all terrorist ideologies fall into the PREVENT frame and this includes examples of unclear, mixed, or unstable ideologies. PREVENT also intervenes to stop people moving from extremist actions to terrorist ones.

All public sector workers, especially those in education (all levels) and in the medical and health professions are legally required to report anyone they suspect either of being radicalised or in danger of becoming radicalised. Those who are reported are offered help to become deradicalised or be supported to ensure they stop becoming prey to radical ideologies or ideologues.

Within the CONTEST framework, PREVENT contains four key objectives. These are to:

- Respond to the ideological challenges of terrorism and the threats posed by terrorist ideology and its causes.
- Refrain individuals from being attracted to terrorism by providing appropriate advice and support as soon as possible.
- Work with various sectors and institutions to address the risks of radicalisation within them.
- Enable those already involved in terrorism to change and be rehabilitated (see www.gov.uk/government/publications/prevent-duty-guidance).

Despite its objectives, PREVENT, is not considered effective (O'Toole et al., 2016). Key reasons for this include: its negative impact on social cohesion (Thomas, 2012); the securitisation of Muslim communities (Kundnani, 2009); its failure to convince professionals and community residents that they are not being spied upon (Birt, 2009); and the linking of diverse policy areas to counter-terrorism (Thomas, 2012).

Moreover, various people who have committed terrorist acts have been on deradicalisation programmes, thus indicating a failure to deradicalise them. For example, Usman Khan, murdered two people on London Bridge before he was shot on 29 November 2019. He had already been convicted of plotting to bomb the London Stock Exchange in 2012. He had also completed the Healthy Identity Intervention Programme while in prison and undertaken the Desistance and Disengagement Programme post-release.

CHANNEL

As part of CONTEST, CHANNEL refers to the national process of identifying and providing early intervention and support for a person who is deemed to have been or is in the process of becoming radicalised. A person who is being supported is being 'channelled' to receive help through a specified process. Piloted in 2007 and rolled out in 2012, CHANNEL occurs within a multi-agency approach that seeks to stop people becoming radicalised. A risk assessment is usually carried out to establish what intervention is required (Knudsen, 2018). CHANNEL draws upon existing collaborations between local authorities, statutory partners that include the police, education, health, social services, children and youth services, offender management services, and local community. This collaboration aims to:

- Identify individuals who are at risk of radicalisation or have become involved in terrorism.
- Assess the nature and extent of the risk that such individuals pose.
- Develop an appropriate support plan for the individuals referred to them.

As a result, CHANNEL seeks to safeguard children and adults by protecting them from engaging in terrorist activities through early intervention, addressing vulnerabilities, and diverting people from causing harm (CHANNEL Duty Guidance, On https://assets.publishing. service.gov.uk /government/uploads/system/uploads/attachment_data/ file/964567/6.6271_HO_HMG_Channel_Duty_Guidance_v14_ Web.pdf).

This multi-agency approach to identifying and supporting individuals at risk of becoming attracted to terrorism has no fixed profile of such a person. Hence, it is not possible to have a threshold whereby a person is considered at risk of becoming a terrorist (Kruglanski et al., 2018; Koehler and Fiebig, 2019). Signs of upholding extremist views are utilised to determine whether a person should be offered support to desist from such ideas. However, specific guidance on the issue of when to refer someone to PREVENT to obtain an assessment and specialist support is lacking. Additionally, the individual concerned may also need a safeguarding response from social workers alongside PREVENT support. However, an individual considered to have a 'terrorism vulnerability' would be seen as requiring CHANNEL support, and if posing a 'terrorism risk', they would be referred to the police for specific consideration. If the risk is deemed high, the person may be removed from the CONTEST programme and be subjected to court proceedings.

CHANNEL Panel

CHANNEL Panels are constituted according to local authority areas. In these, the local authority responsible for the Panel, provides the Chair and Deputy Chair. The police for the relevant local authority area have principal responsibility for CHANNEL in that area. According to the CT&S Act, a local authority is defined as one of the following: a county council in England, a district council unless it is already included in the area's county council, a London Borough Council, the Common Council of the City of London, the Council of the Isles of Scilly, a county council or county borough council in Wales, and a council constituted under section 2 of the Local Government (Scotland) Act, 1994.

The partners of a CHANNEL Panel are specified in Schedule 7 of the CT&S Act. The Panel's members are comprised of representatives from the following groups. They are required to undergo vetting procedures if they do not already have clearance, for example, from the Disclosure and Barring Service (DBS). Panel members can be social workers or come from the following organisations:

- NHS
- schools, further education colleges, and universities
- youth offending services
- children's and adults' services
- local safeguarding arrangements
- local authority safeguarding managers (adult and/or children)
- local authority Early Help Services
- Home Office immigration (immigration, enforcement, UK visas and immigration)
- Border Force
- housing
- prisons
- probation providers.

The CHANNEL Panel has the duty to develop a support plan for cases that it accepts. For those that are rejected, it devises alternative forms of support including health care and social care services. This Panel is charged with maintaining accurate records for each case. These should detail the support plan, agreed actions, decisions made, and outcomes. The CHANNEL Panel is also responsible for carrying out the monitoring and escalation framework. It covers: the review of referral and case data, utilising the approved Home Office Case Management System, performing CHANNEL observations, using peer reviews to provide support and training for Panel members and Chairs. All Panel members are required to cooperate with the police in conducting their roles and duties.

Various inspection regimes are required to include aspects of PRE-VENT within their inspection frameworks. These inspection regimes include the Office for Standards in Education (Ofsted), Care Quality Commission (CQC), and Her Majesty's Inspectorate of Constabulary and Fire and Rescue Services (HMCFRS). These inspections are likely to be instigated when concerns are raised.

Referrals

CHANNEL draws upon local authority-led support in carrying out its duties as stipulated in the CT&S Act. Separate guidance covers Scotland. A case is progressed in the local authority area where the young person resides. If the young person is from another area, the original local authority gives consent for the young person to obtain CHANNEL support. The young person's social worker from the original local authority attends or reports to the CHANNEL meetings. His/her role is to: keep an eye on the care plan; ensure that it is revised and updated; and undertake the social care work covered by that person's care plan. More immediate services such as accessing CONNEXIONS, obtaining school and mental health support are procured from the local authority where the young person resides.

CHANNEL Panel governance arrangements

Governance in the CHANNEL Panels requires the demonstration of clear lines of accountability. Consequently, the Chair for Strategic Governance (CSG) should not be responsible for oversight or delivery of CHANNEL Panel activities. Governance arrangements may fall within the remit of existing statutory multi-agency partnerships, including the Community Safety Partnerships or County Strategy Groups, or other local strategic bodies like the CONTEST Boards. These governance structures must be able to assess compliance with CHANNEL duty requirements, oversee the implementation of development plans, assess referral data, and monitor performance through anonymised case studies. The Chief Executive of the relevant local authority must provide statements of assurance, confirm the suitability of arrangements, and name and designate the officers responsible for undertaking all necessary roles.

The Chair of the Panel Assurance Statement is expected to have sufficient authority to direct multi-agency partnerships in delivering the programme. Additionally, the Chair is required to have previous experience in chairing multi-agency meetings, a sound understanding of CHANNEL, within the context of PREVENT and CONTEST, and be willing to undertake any necessary training. Also, the Chair cannot hold a Home Office-funded position within the CHANNEL or PREVENT programmes.

Moreover, the Chair would: oversee the development of the counter-terrorism local profile (CTLP) for the local authority area; be briefed on CTLP content; and stay abreast of changes to the varying nature of local threats. The CTLP comprises of a report that outlines the threat and vulnerability from terrorism-related activity within a specific area. The relevant details are provided by the local Counter-Terrorism Policing Unit. The Panel also receives the agreed process for escalating a case.

The CHANNEL Case Officer can be either the police counter-terrorism case officer (CTCO) or the Home Office-funded CHANNEL Coordinator that is employed by the local authority. This person undertakes a regular review and amends the vulnerability assessment framework (VAF) as the case progresses so that it reflects accurately all relevant vulnerabilities and risks. The CHANNEL Case Officer refers to the police or PURSUE and consistently applies the VAF to assess vulnerability. The VAF is formulated around three criteria to determine whether the person: engages with extremist groups, causes or ideologies; intends to cause harm; and has the capability to cause harm. The CHANNEL Case Officer's motto is, 'Notice, Check, Share'.

Vulnerability, assessed on the following factors, can indicate problems in finding a stable place in society for a suspected terrorist. These factors are:

- peer or family pressure
- influence from other people or the internet
- bullying
- being a victim or perpetrator of crime
- anti-social behaviour
- family tensions
- hate crime
- lack of self-esteem or identity
- personal or political grievances.

Vulnerability can be exacerbated through other negative influences such as having direct contact with extremists in the community, family and/or wider networks, and materials obtained from the internet and/or social media platforms.

Referral process

Specialist police officers compile a 'gateway assessment' that gathers information by utilising police databases and other resources to assess the level of vulnerability and risk relevant to a referred individual. Once the gateway assessment has been completed, the case is referred for consideration about moving into PREVENT or CHANNEL for consideration under section 36. The decision taken will lead to the person either being managed in a police-led partnership or escalated to PURSUE. The decision must be recorded on the Home Office-approved case management system that records and manages CHANNEL cases. The CTCO should receive and be cited on partner requests for information and responses to them. The minutes of all CHANNEL meetings are also recorded on this system. Information sharing is authorised for lawful purposes under Article 6 of the GDPR (General Data Protection Regulation) and Section 36 of CTA. (CONTEST, on https://assets.publishing.service.gov.uk/government/uploads/system/uploads/attachment_data/file/964567/6.6271_HO_HMG_Channel_Duty_Guidance_v14_Web.pdf).

Multi-Agency Risk Assessment Conference (MARAC)

If a young person is considered at a very high level of risk, including of domestic violence that can threaten or endanger the person's life, they may be referred to the MARAC (Multi-Agency Risk Assessment Conference) for protection within a wider context and involving various agencies including social services, housing, probation, and the police. This person will be assigned an independent domestic violence adviser (IDVA) who will represent them at MARAC meetings. Here, the representatives from multiple agencies will discuss the person's situation and devise and agree an action plan which the IDVA will convey to the person concerned and ensure that it is carried out.

Support for CHANNEL Cases

Those on the CHANNEL caseload are offered theological and ideological support through structured sessions using a Home Office-approved Intervention Provider (IP). This will enable the referred person to understand and challenge their ideological, theological, or fixated thinking. The Home Office would like an IP to be considered for all referrals. Those on the CHANNEL programme examine other important areas of their lives and acquire understanding and skills for behaving differently. These include:

- Life skills in the areas of work or social skills that include how to respond to peer pressure.
- Anger management sessions to deal with anger. These can be either formal or informal.

- Cognitive/behavioural contact, cognitive behavioural therapies and working to improve attitudes and behaviours.
- Constructive pursuits such as supervised or managed constructive leisure activities.
- An education skills person to facilitate the undertaking of activities like education or training.
- Careers contacts to address employment issues and job acquisition.
- Family support contact through activities that support family and personal relationships and engage with formal parenting programmes.
- Health awareness contacts to assess or address both physical and mental health concerns.
- Housing support contacts to address living arrangements, accommodation provision, and neighbourhood issues.
- Drugs and alcohol awareness and substance misuse interventions.
- Mentoring from a suitable adult who acts as a role model and gives personal guidance and/or pastoral care.

Social workers' involvement in the counter-terrorism strategy and programme

Social worker involvement in the CTS&P is ambiguous due to the securitisation of social work which has taken place in a context of uncertainty and fear. Limited training and uncertainty in the work revolve around finding the balance between care and control, especially when working with individuals who struggle with mental health, abuse, social isolation, and identity problems. This has created a vacuum that has been filled by officials and leaders concerned with maintaining their position and power by controlling the uncertainty (Curtis, 2014). Incorporating new tasks through the securitisation of the profession has social workers concerned that PREVENT measures entail the 'soft policing' of vulnerable individuals and groups (Chisholm and Coulter, 2017; McKendrick and Finch, 2016) and stigmatise Muslims (Qurashi, 2018).

Social workers are involved in identifying individuals at risk, assessing the nature and extent of that risk, developing the most appropriate support plan for the individuals concerned, assessing vulnerability, and involving individuals and families as protective factors. They also worry that such work may challenge their anti-oppressive values and find themselves in professional dissonance with others including their peers. The support of social workers involved in this work over time is an issue that has been poorly addressed. Most practitioners end up finding informal peer support, but this may be insufficient if the worker has become traumatised by a particularly difficult case, including one in which the horrors of an atrocity must be faced repeatedly. Thus, employers must divert resources to supervision, regular debriefing, and mental health support facilities for their workforce.

Exercise – Radicalised young people in a youth group

You are a youth worker helping young people in your local youth group become more skilled at finding employment. The group is small and has five or six young people who are regular attenders and a similar number floating in and out of the group. One day, Grace, one of the regular attenders comes to you to report a concern she has about Douglas, a young man in her school, whom she has overheard talking about how he intends to go to Syria, become a jihadist and return to kill people in the local community. Grace is worried about Douglas and is also anxious that she may be doing him an injustice. Maybe she misunderstood what he was saying. The youth worker reassures Grace by saying she was right to raise the issue with him, and not to worry, he will not let on that she has spoken to him. Instead, he will raise the issue with his colleagues running other youth groups in the city to (a) decide how to approach Douglas; (b) ascertain whether this is the only incident of potential radicalisation; and (c) devise an action plan if onward referral is warranted.

Working in a small group, choose a person to chair the discussion and someone else to take notes so that you have a record of what was said and decided, especially if the action is to be referred further. Role-play your meeting with your fellow youth workers and ensure that you cover the following elements:

- What information can you gather about Douglas' behaviour at school, in his community, in his religious institution, and from his GP, and whom would you involve in this task?
- How would you gather information from peers and others that Douglas hangs out with, especially after school and on weekends?
- At what point, and how would you involve Douglas' parents in the discussion, other members of his family, and Douglas himself?
- How would you determine whether Douglas needs to be referred on to the CONTEST programme or even the police?

Young people can be vulnerable to radicalisation if they lack protective factors including a loving, stable family life, achievement in school, satisfying peer relationships, feeling connected to their community, and aspirations for a better life that are anticipated to be fulfilled. These will enable a person to feel supported and deal with any hardship that life brings. Acting on such insights forms the basis of relational social work practice (Folghereiter, 2003).

Social workers involved in disaster work including counter-terrorism tasks can become emotionally drained through such work. Haugstvedt (2022) asks that the profession openly acknowledges the importance of addressing the emotionality of engagement with distressed individuals for these social workers. Both managers and peers should understand that this work impacts personally upon professionals. Help in dealing with these emotions is an essential part of their interaction with peers and managers. Their colleagues should offer supportive measures including peer support, debriefing, and regular supervision, and the individuals concerned should set aside time for self-care.

Social worker involvement in CONTEST

If a child or an adult is in receipt of social care support, as well as support through CHANNEL, the social worker from their local authority should be present at the CHANNEL Panel meetings and be involved in all the decisions that it makes. CHANNEL can run alongside other safeguarding programmes where the relevant thresholds have been met, but it must not replace these and\or be replaced by them.

In cases of radicalisation, social workers would consider both risk indicators and protective factors and seek to strengthen the protective ones and reduce the importance of the risky ones. Some risk indicators might be: a child's willingness to follow others who seem to be leading exciting lives when they are manipulating the child to think the same as they do; over-identification with a particular group or ideology; having a sense of grievance about a social injustice whether it applies to them or not. A protective factor could be the parent's willingness to support their child and engage in changing their behaviour. This could involve their learning to become more aware of the dangers posed by the internet and how they can support their child to avoid them. Additionally, they would explain why their child might face travel restrictions (imposed through the police), involve an IP who would help them understand how inappropriate ideologies might be resisted, and help parents access counselling, pastoral and other support for their child including engaging in leisure activities more suitable for children and young people. The social worker would also be mindful that the ideologues who had entrapped a child earlier might resume their activities to recruit them for their purposes and be on guard for any signs that this might be occurring. The social worker would attend any meetings held to discuss the case, including the exit review to ensure that any potential lessons would be considered, and good practice guidelines identified for future eventualities. Another case for consideration is presented below.

Case study – Radicalising Ash

Ash was a 13-year-old boy who was bored with living in a small town. He was constantly online in his bedroom, looking up anything that struck his imagination. His parents rarely ventured into his room now that he was a teenager and thought he was looking at 'normal teenage things' on his computer. He was normally studious and quiet, and they had never had any problems with him. So, they were shocked when the police came to talk to them about things he had been saying at school, and especially when he started asking how he could get a passport to travel abroad. The school, concerned that he was being radicalised at home, referred him to the PREVENT programme. The school had noticed changes in Ash's behaviour for about 6 months, but initially put it down to becoming an adolescent. Seeking to go overseas without his parents suggested something more serious was occurring. Indeed, unknown to his parents, Ash had discovered a way of accessing terrorist networks in Syria and had been groomed into thinking it would be 'fun' to go and join them.

The parents were surprised that it was the police, and not a social worker, who had come to speak to them, and were totally unprepared for what they were told.

Discussion

In a small group, discuss the following questions:

- Why you think the police and not a social worker came to see Ash's parents in the first instance?
- If you were the parents, what course of action would you want to see Ash undergo to ensure that he became deradicalised?
- Imagine you are the social worker brought into the case, how would you want to engage with and support Ash and how would you want to relate to his parents? What support would you offer them, and how?
- How would you involve the parents in supporting Ash and how would you support them?

Parents need support in dealing with the many new dangers that radicalisation poses for their children. They may be unaware of what their child is doing in the privacy of the bedroom accompanied by a computer screen. Social workers have a role in helping them understand the issues they face and work with them to protect, support and advise their children in living worthwhile, rewarding lives. The social workers supporting these parents may also be in need of support, including supportive supervision (Haugstvedt, 2022).

Conclusions

Terrorism raises issues regarding the deliberate harm of individuals by extremist individuals, groups, or states. Although there is agreement that terrorist acts must be prevented, the definition of what constitutes terrorism is contested. The UN and all nation-states assume prime responsibility in establishing counter-terrorism structures to ensure the safety of their nation and peoples. In the UK, the CONTEST programme with its four elements aimed at preventing radicalisation is one such mechanism. However, achieving deradicalisation at individual, group, or organisational level is not an easy task. Social workers are drawn into these structures and measures, usually seeking to deradicalise individuals or avoid their becoming radicalised in the first place. This entails difficult decisions being made. Some of these may challenge their fundamental values as individual professionals interested in enabling individuals to behave according to accepted norms rather than tackling extremist ideologies. Recognising the emotionality of engaging with troubled individuals is essential to maintaining worker and individual wellbeing, social cohesion and societal safety.

Part II

Learning lessons from disasters occurring in other countries

8 Storm surges and hurricanes

Introduction

Extreme weather events occur in many guises. Contemporary extreme weather events are the outcomes of climate change. These are many, and may assume the form of floods, droughts, heatwaves, wildfires, cold-snaps, storm surges, hurricanes, and coastal erosion. Heavy rains called *monsoons* have featured in many countries for a very long time. But now, people living in monsoon-affected countries are complaining that these do not come as predicted and when they do, they are heavier than usual and can cause more damage than anticipated (Loo et al., 2015). Pakistan has become a recent case in point. Rainfall during a period of global warming is likely to be heavier than previously because warm air holds more water vapour (moisture) that can fall as precipitation. Recent extreme weather events have caused significant loss of life and billions of dollars in damages. Such events can be linked to climate change which is altering weather patterns across the world, thereby causing extreme weather events to increase in frequency and intensity. In this chapter, I focus on extreme weather events such as Hurricane Haiyan in the Philippines, Superstorm Sandy in the USA and the 2022 floods in Pakistan. Hurricanes are called typhoons in the Philippines and cyclones in India. I will examine the differentiated experiences of such events and their implications for the groups that bear the brunt of these. I also consider the roles that social workers have played in the past and can play in future to help prevent and mitigate the risks that these events pose for people in their everyday life practices and routines.

Typhoon Yolanda or Hurricane Haiyan

Background

Extreme weather events are now anthropologically caused, i.e. are the outcomes of human actions. The top ten contemporary polluters

DOI: 10.4324/9781003105824-10

contributing heavily to climate change in 2021 were China, the United States, India, Russia, Germany, the United Kingdom, Japan, France, Canada and Poland, in that order. Extreme weather events affect poor people disproportionately because although they contribute least to climate change, they are more vulnerable to the impact of anthropogenic climate change and suffer the devastating effects of extreme weather events much more. Floods and rising sea levels are particularly evident in low-lying countries like Bangladesh and small island states like Kiribati and Tuvalu. The Climate Change Vulnerability Index identifies 10 nation-states that are most vulnerable to climate change. Ranked among the poorest countries in the world, these are: Bangladesh, Guinea-Bissau, Sierra Leone, Haiti, South Sudan, Nigeria, the Democratic Republic of the Congo, Cambodia, the Philippines and Ethiopia. This line-up highlights the lack of climate justice prevailing in the world and requires something to be done about the inequality it portrays. Extreme weather events cause heavier precipitation, more intense heat, and more damage through storm surges and coastal flooding resulting from sea level rises.

The Philippines is the third most disaster-prone country in the world because it experiences regular occurrences of disasters in the normal course of events. These cause much loss of life and property and environmental damage. Additionally, climate change has undermined previous valuable features of a significant number of islands. These include the bleaching of coral reefs, and a decline in the copious abundance of fish, thereby endangering initiatives aimed at securing environmental justice (Yamada and Galat, 2014).

The Philippines has high levels of poverty. In 2021, nearly one-quarter of the population lived below the national poverty line. High levels of financial poverty have an adverse impact on the disaster resilience of families in the Philippines. Additionally, many families have members working overseas who send remittances to family members living in the Philippines. These workers are largely comprised of women working as care workers or domestic workers, and men working in construction. In 2020, their remittances from all the countries in which they were employed totalled US$29.9 billion, despite the pandemic. Neither the economy nor the families in the Philippines could survive without such remittances. Fishing is an important part of the local economy, especially on its numerous islands, and boats are often purchased with remitted funds. Moreover, those with relatives overseas can ask for help to rebuild homes devastated by natural disasters including earthquakes, volcanic eruptions, and hurricanes. However, many homes are rebuilt in the same way as previously, meaning that they will be unable to withstand future high category storms. Whether they are local or have arrived from overseas as volunteers, humanitarian aid workers distribute aid, especially of medicines and food, to those in need.

Typhoon Yolanda or Hurricane Haiyan

Climate change led to events like the 8 November 2013 Typhoon Yolanda/Hurricane Haiyan. Super Hurricane Haiyan/Typhoon Yolanda, was a Category 5 storm. Its intensity was similar to the 2005 Hurricane Katrina in the USA. Hurricane Haiyan also affected Vietnam, Hong Kong, Taiwan, Palau, and Guam (BBC News, 2013). In Palau, the residents of the state of Kayangel (Ngcheangel) were adversely affected. No one died although people refused to evacuate their homes, even when houses had been destroyed and local infrastructures had been seriously damaged. Vietnam had to evacuate 800,000 people living primarily in the southern and central provinces. It also ordered 85,328 fishing vessels to seek shelter due to the expected ferocity of the storm. The military and the IFRC assisted with relief efforts, especially the provision of food. Hurricane Haiyan also impacted 3 million people living primarily in the provinces of Hainan, Guangdong and Guangxi in China. Its State Flood Control and Drought Relief Headquarters was in charge and ordered boats back to port by 9 November 2013. Hong Kong was also affected. It announced a strong Monsoon Signal on 9 November. Taiwan also experienced losses which included 16 people being washed out to sea. Of these, 8 died, the other 8 survived. Taiwan also suffered infrastructural damage valued at about US$16.9 million.

Hurricane Haiyan or Typhoon Yolanda as it was called in the Philippines, hit the island state on 8 Nov 2013, as a Category 5 superstorm and caused a storm surge of more than 5 metres in height. It had winds of 315 km/hr, caused 6,268 deaths, injured 28,689, had 1,061 missing persons, and cost $10 billion of damages (Belen, 2015). An early warning system was in operation, but the strength of the storm was underestimated. Thus, many people did not evacuate their homes as advised and failed to go to the evacuation centres. Tacloban, an autonomous urbanised city in the province of Leyte in the Eastern Visayas region of the Philippines, was badly affected by Typhoon Yolanda's 315 km/hr winds and huge storm surge. There, 6,201 people were killed and the airport was virtually destroyed. The destruction of most of the built infrastructures in Tacloban depicted an 'acute-on-chronic crises' resulting from rapid unsustainable urbanization, extreme climate change, severe natural disasters, major biodiversity crises, and the 'emergencies of scarcity' (Burkle, 2014). The provinces most affected were Eastern Samar, Western Samar, Leyte, Southern Leyte, Iloilo, Capiz, Aklan, Palawan, Cebu, and Bohol. The last two provinces had also suffered the 7.2 Mw Visayas earthquake on 15 Oct 2013 in which 156 people had died in Bohol alone. They were recovering from that when Typhoon Yolanda struck. President Aquino III declared a state of calamity because over 4 million people from 900,000 families were displaced due to 1.1 million houses having been damaged and 550,000 destroyed. Damage to the communication systems in the Philippines, reduced capacity in getting messages to people and hindered the distribution of aid. Communication difficulties impacted upon access to information about where to seek shelter and how to keep abreast of developments. These problems highlighted the importance of local community responses in letting people know where to seek aid and support, a lesson highlighted elsewhere by Pyles (2007)

Various overseas NGOs, e.g. World Vision, came to help (World Vision, 2013). During the calamity, donor priorities and recipient priorities diverged. The citizens of the Philippines defined the Typhoon as a momentous everyday event which disrupted communities. Donors conceived of it as an exceptional event that affected individuals and responded to their assessments of individual needs. Donors used predetermined categories of need and vulnerability, leading to the delivery of culturally inappropriate aid in many cases (Bandyopadhyay and Vermann, 2013). Moreover, aid was distributed inequitably. Thus, many victim-survivors went without help. Humanitarian aid providers in Hurricane Haiyan were criticised for overlooking the everyday realities and politics of lives in the Philippines. President Aquino and the Mayor of Tacloban disagreed about processes and procedures for humanitarian aid. This complicated and disrupted procedures and delivery efforts for 6 million displaced people. These funds were lodged within the Yolanda Reconstruction Program and remained unused until Dec 2017 when President Duterte used them.

Furthermore, emergency response capacity was in limited supply. Yet, responding appropriately required capacity at all stages of the disaster cycle, including prevention, preparedness, response, and recovery. Engaging communities in mitigation activities that reduce risk, prepare communities, and promote preventative work is crucial. Yet, low-income countries lack the resources necessary for implementing such measures. Pressures on scarce resources can create conflict among potential recipients because greed can become a major motivator of action aimed at acquiring such resources. These pressures can produce environmental refugees when people flee armed conflict.

Other tensions can impact directly on those delivering aid. For example, health care workers face increased personal risk. They may also feel overwhelmed by facing constant, unremitting stress in environments with high levels of complexity, complicated organisational structures of assistance, fraught political and religious influences, and endless health care needs exacerbated by severe poverty and malnutrition and a lack of medical supplies and clinics or hospitals.

Exercise – Overcoming difficulties in delivering aid

In small groups, discuss the following questions. Choose a chair and notetaker who will make notes to feed back to the plenary:

- Can humanitarian aid be sustained indefinitely? Discuss in relation to both 'natural' disasters and conflict-based ones like Palestine, Syria, Iraq or Afghanistan.
- How would you try to convince those who will not evacuate (for whatever reason) to do so? Discuss these questions in your small groups.

Assisting people in complex disasters is complicated and requires sensitivity, cultural knowledge, and preferably communication in the local language, or a skilled interpreter. It also requires the transparent and equitable distribution of aid (Dominelli and Vickers, 2014). Disasters can provide opportunities to end structural inequalities if communities pick these up (Pyles, 2011). Post-disaster change can include transforming systems that might otherwise block future adaptive capacity. Community resilience planning is facilitated by pre-existing planning capacity, strong political leadership, and non-governmental funding resources. Community support is available in the immediate aftermath of such disasters and in the medium- and long-term. Community assistance is the first to reach devastated locales, not least because the victim-survivors are on site and determined to help restore as much of their community structures as possible. Such responses indicate a commitment to solidarity and investment in social resources locally, often led by women (Drolet et al., 2015). Community responses to resilience building activities require collective efficacy which varies according to socio-economic status, levels of community cohesion, resources, informal social control, and social capital expressed as social networks and exchanges. Below, I consider how Superstorm Sandy was used to build capacity in Red Hook following the devastation of this hurricane.

Superstorm Sandy

Hurricane Sandy, or Superstorm Sandy, as it later became known, began as a tropical wave in the Western Caribbean Sea on 22 October 2012. It turned into a Category 3 storm on 25 October 2012 when it reached Cuba. By the time Sandy reached the New Jersey and New York area, a rise in ocean levels created a storm surge that reached 13 feet (4 metres) in height, causing casualties and substantial damages. Fortunately, although many residents refused to evacuate when advised to do so, the operationalisation of evacuation measures initiated by government reduced the number of deaths. Airplane, train, bus and car travel, and electricity supplies were disrupted due to high winds and flooding. At one point; the New York subway was submerged by water. Sewage flowed into the water, impacting negatively upon the environment and water supplies. While Manhattan faced a deluge of water, snow featured in the higher elevations nearby, e.g. Appalachia. The storm was of substantial proportions, and Jim Cisco called it a 'Frankenstorm'. He liked the term because the American celebration of Halloween, had just passed. However, the media called it a 'superstorm' and this term caught on. As a result of Superstorm Sandy, emergency personnel had their leave cancelled. And, Obama, then a Presidential candidate seeking his second term, cancelled a campaign stop on 28 October 2012. Meanwhile, various musical celebrities had raised $23 million for the American Red Cross. The storm covered more terrain as it moved from the Caribbean into Canada. As it coursed through the continent, Superstorm Sandy deprived 8.5 million people of power, destroyed 650,000 houses, caused US$70 billion in damages, and killed 233 people (World Vision, 2012). On 2 November 2012, Storm Sandy was absorbed by an extratropical storm.

Flooding in Red Hook, New York City

Red Hook was built on a tidal marsh and housed low-income New Yorkers. Located in New York City's floodplain, it is extremely vulnerable to coastal flooding such as that wrought by Superstorm Sandy. Red Hook lies on a low, flat peninsula which is the term given to land surrounded by water on three sides. Given rising sea levels, its geographical location makes it extremely vulnerable to extreme weather events like floods. After the flooding which devastated much of Red Hook, investors from outside the area arrived to purchase land and housing at inflated prices to build housing, bars, restaurants, and other recreational amenities catering for middle-class lifestyles which were beyond the means of the Red Hook residents who lived in the neighbourhood prior to the Superstorm-induced flooding. Around 6,000 residents rented from the New York City Housing Authority, which refused to invest in flood protection to safeguard their futures. Self-help was an important element of the recovery process and neighbours helped each other (Cagney et al., 2016). Following this flooding, various residents formed the Red Hook Coalition Fund to channel money to rebuild their community. The Coalition Fund assisted businesses to hold meetings, identify the needs of the community, and organise programmes for young people. Volunteers, including social work students were brought in to assist the devastated community (Pottick and Pottick, 2014).

Case study – Reviving Red Hook, Brooklyn

Superstorm Sandy hit the New York area on 29 October 2013, causing 97 deaths and billions in damages. One area that suffered extensive damages was Red Hook, Brooklyn. It was a low-lying, low-income urban area which was very vulnerable to storm surges. It also had extensive health inequalities featuring asthma and diabetes. Moreover, Red Hook was home to Latino and Black populations, nearly half of whom (45%) lived in poverty. Additionally, Red Hook had large public housing complexes, small businesses, and large multinational companies like IKEA in it (Schmeltz et al., 2013).

Superstorm Sandy impacted badly on everyday life in Red Hook by making existing inequalities in income, health, and infrastructures much worse (Ruskin et al., 2018). The infrastructural damage caused by Superstorm Sandy, denied this population of electricity, drinking water, health services, and garbage collection for weeks. This intensified the susceptibilities of its vulnerable populations. Mitigating these vulnerabilities requires robust vulnerability assessments. A vulnerability assessment considers 'how the adaptive capacity of individuals, households and communities is shaped and constrained by social, political, and economic processes at higher levels' (Smit and Wandel, 2006: 284). The vulnerable populations in these communities had multiple vulnerabilities and multi-faceted needs that required attention. Some of these groups endured greater vulnerabilities and hardship than others. For example, older people without resources and in poor health were unable to advocate proactively for themselves. However, planners could utilise their experiences to collect evidence that would assist the redesign of such communities. Moreover, the search for funds and adaptive measures could be used to enhance older people's lives. Addressing vulnerabilities and creating and creating resilience could also reduce the costs of intervening and responding to a disaster (Carbone and Wright, 2016). Communication issues were also seriously impacted despite the availability of social media for some residents (DSadri et al., 2018).

Volunteers became a crucial resource that built the social capital necessary in helping those in need in Red Hook. For three weeks, around 300 volunteers came every day to coordinate service delivery, provide hot meals, distribute information and resources, and facilitate access to electricity for victim-survivors. Their assistance mitigated the lack of refrigeration and fuel for cooking. Volunteers visited housebound individuals to ensure that they received food, medicine, and ice for medications like insulin which must be kept cool. Those volunteers skilled in digital technologies used online tools to procure donations, food, and other supplies. Without their endeavours, the transmission of diseases would have been higher and upper tract respiratory infections would have risen, and communication with victim-survivors would have been poorer. However, volunteers have a limited role in raising huge infrastructural issues. Consequently, key public health matters such as sanitation, flooding, lighting, and transportation required government authorities to take the initiative to resolve them (Schmeltz et al., 2013).

The activities of local community organisations, residents and volunteers that came to the aid of victim-survivors and worked hard to resume services, highlighted the lack of coordinated planning by the authorities before the event. Additionally, these groups lobbied government for responses, particularly in the public health arena, and identified key areas in preparation for future disasters. The rapid responses of the local community enabled many residents to survive the devastation that the storm wreaked upon their lives, but it also highlighted the importance of government taking the initiative in providing the bigger items like infrastructure developments which are beyond the resources of the local community to manage. Such precautions need to be considered before a disaster occurs to build adaptive capacity and promote resilience (Kelly and Adger, 2000; Smit and Wandel, 2006).

Volunteerrs play a crucial role in assisting communities and their residents receive practical support and survive their conditions in a more human rights-based and supportive manner. They often arrive on the spot quickly. Although some are untrained or have received a crash course in disaster interventions (Pottick and Pottick, 2014), their contributions can be invaluable. Organisations such as the national Red Cross (American in this case) use volunteers in an effective and planned manner.

Schmeltz et al. (2013) raised important questions about the responses of authorities to the difficulties experienced in Red Hook. They even queried the policy of mandatory evacuation because often the transportation that was used to transport those who were expected to leave the affected area(s) was inadequate, especially for those with diverse mobility considerations. They also questioned the extent to which evacuation centres had the facilities necessary for providing social care and health care to those with special medical and other needs. Another issue of concern for humanitarian aid workers was that of ensuring that evacuation centres could continue to provide resources and services to those living in these temporary lodgings for as long as was necessary.

Policy considerations in Red Hook

Safety for women and children in Red Hook

Other general issues revolved around safety and the formulation of appropriate policies for the health and safety of the populace. These safety issues usually covered violence, especially violence against women and children living in Red Hook. Shortages of shelter places for women who wanted to leave their abusers were severe. Many survivors of domestic violence found themselves having to choose between living with an abuser, relocating out of the state, moving to a homeless shelter, or living on the streets. However, some shelters were able to use some money from the 2013 Disaster Relief Appropriation Fund for women seeking to escape violent men. Preparations to mitigate violence from occurring is critical given that research has already demonstrated that violence against women and children can rise dramatically following a disaster (Thurston et al., 2021). Thurston and colleagues (2021) suggest realigning policy and practice to address the safety needs of women and children. Their suggestions include:

- Viewing violence against women and children as both a public health and disaster management issue.
- Initiating gender-sensitive disaster risk reduction policies and ensuring that women play key roles in determining disaster management and social protection programmes, coordinating disaster management, law enforcement and health authority endeavours in preventing such violence, and addressing the subsequent health matters that might arise.
- Conducting high-quality research to ascertain the scale of the violence perpetrated, the mechanisms through which it is conducted, and how it can be eliminated.

Gentrification issues in Red Hook

Moreover, there will be various other issues for policymakers to address. These include the extent to which people will want to relocate or return to their previous communities and how this might be achieved, especially given the pressures on housing availability following a disaster. Another housing danger is the gentrification of an area (Berner, 2018). Disaster gentrification is a real risk faced by poor, devastated communities like Red Hook (Schmeltz et al., 2013). Meanwhile, Schmeltz and colleagues (2013), argue for a bottom-up approach to disaster responses and highlight the importance of listening to the victim-survivors, what they say about what they need, how these needs should be met, and how their communities should be rebuilt. Following such advice would enable people to feel more committed to proposed evacuation plans. For Schmeltz et al., (2013), vulnerability assessment theory and the practice literature endorse a bottom-up approach to enhance adaptation, promote resilience, reduce vulnerabilities, and mitigate the negative impact of climate change-induced extreme weather events. In their framework, engaging directly with people and their adaptive capacities provides the most useful avenues forward in disaster mitigation strategies. This approach would also indicate the levels of local resistance to gentrification of places like Red Hook.

Recovery processes draw upon collaboration, coordination, technical assistance, and resilience building to drive adaptation and mitigation strategies to avoid future disasters. Federal, local, and regional agencies need to collaborate effectively to provide useful capacity building and inclusive reconstruction activities. However, in the case of Superstorm Sandy, the New York City Hazard Mitigation Plan was a top-down affair and lacked community level information on adaptative capacity. This made planning to grow local resilience difficult because it was experienced as remote (Finn et al., 2019). Social workers can assist communities in mobilising to have their voices heard and lobby politicians to develop resilient, sustainable communities.

Health issues in Red Hook

Many victim-survivors used social media to obtain information, pass on information, and engage different stakeholders in thinking about the future. These reported many stories about the hardship people faced after the disaster struck. The lack of medical resources meant that not everyone needing health services could access these when needed following the flooding. This had detrimental implications for health, wellbeing and mental health care. Most of those who did not obtain access to medical facilities were men who had either a low socio-economic status or a pre-existing medical condition. The failure to secure health services when required increased PTSD (post-traumatic stress disorders), anxiety, depression, and mental stress. Struggles to access health care affected other members of the family. The emotional impact of Superstorm Sandy increased levels of depression in the population, and increased demand for psychosocial support by 25 per cent.

Hurricane Sandy exposed many gaps that require extensive research for rigorous future data inputs into policy and practice including flooding, climate change, public health, mental health services and built infrastructures including housing (Heid et al., 2016). Research is necessary to improve preparedness, crisis responses and resilience to cope with future disasters. Ideally, local victim-survivors should be involved in such research, particularly action research which allows space for coproduction (Dominelli, 2012a; Pyles, 2015). Additionally, first responders were exposed to hazardous chemicals and other toxins while providing relief to stricken residents. These instances need tracking for long-term health impact to improve responses and prevention at all stages of the disaster cycle. Social workers can assist in tracking such developments as their work is community-based.

Floods in Pakistan

Pakistan has become increasingly susceptible to climate change and extreme weather events including floods and landslides following heavier than usual monsoon rains, and droughts. Yet, Pakistan is not a major greenhouse gas (GHG) emitting country, contributing 1 per cent of the global emissions annually. Of this, 43 per cent is produced through agricultural activity, and 46 per cent through energy use including transportation. Individual usage at 2 megatons per year is low.

Climate change is one factor leading to such calamitous events. The country's distinct geography, demographic patterns, socioeconomic aspects, and lack of adaptive capacity combine to produce disastrous outcomes (IPCC, 2012). Sea level rises and glacier melt intensify these pressures. During the summer of 2022, these factors combined to produce floods that affected 33 million people, killed 1,717 persons, and submerged one-third of Pakistan under water. Roads and bridges were washed away. Much agricultural produce was destroyed. Among those who died were 639 children. A further 12,867 people were injured, and around 2.1 million people had to be rehoused in temporary camps. Around two million children were unable to attend their schools and 15 per cent of Pakistan's population had to leave their dwellings. The provinces of Sindh and Baluchistan were the most seriously impacted. A multi-sectoral multi-needs assessment identified needs and gaps in resources, with priority given to 10 severely affected districts in Baluchistan. The Baluchistan Provincial Disaster Management Authority requested that humanitarian aid be delivered to those in most need quickly. The Pakistan Red Crescent Society was a key player in delivering aid to victim-survivors. Health was severely affected through the lack of clean drinking water and the persistence of flood waters in many areas. Damages are estimated at $40 billion, but international humanitarian aid has been limited. The biggest country donors of aid have been China with $150 million and the USA with $97 million. Even when adding the more modest sums given by the UK, Canada, the Nordic countries and others, the overall amount remains far from that needed in a country that lost around 10 per cent of its Gross Domestic Product through this disaster alone. Pakistan had had severe flooding in 2010 when 20 million people were affected, particularly in Sindh Province (Kirsch et al., 2012). Around 1,800 died. Then, as now, the government of Pakistan, the World Health Organization (WHO), UNICEF, Médecins Sans Frontières (MSF) were among the key players delivering aid. The floods, occurring in a very poor part of the country, made existing structural inequalities, especially in health, much worse. Although the impact of this disaster was widespread, with an estimated $43 billion in damages, only $1.3 billion was received from international aid donors. Some authors are calling donor reluctance to give generously 'compassion fatigue'. Cocker and Joss (2016: 1) describe it as 'stress resulting from exposure to a traumatized individual'. This definition focuses on individual reactions to prolonged exposure to stress, but in a major disaster, the numbers involved are scaled up considerably, and the sense of unending numbers and powerlessness in responding to overwhelming need can lead to 'compassion fatigue'. I remain to be convinced of this being the crucial consideration, as Ukraine, enduring an invasion from Russia has secured much more in both state and individual donations. With no end to the invasion in sight, such support looks likely to continue for some time. A similar generosity of giving was evident during the 2004 Indian Ocean Tsunami (Askeland, 2007). The 2022 floods in Pakistan occurred while the Russian Invasion of Ukraine was ongoing, but donations were much more modest from the start. Such examples indicate that geopolitical factors are critical if unspoken dimensions of the responses to calls for assistance (Bandyopadhyay and Vermann, 2013).

Exercise – Planning to deliver aid in Pakistan

Working in small groups, consider the following request. Choose someone to chair the discussion and another to take notes of it for presentation to the plenary group.

You are organising a small group of people to assist an aid organisation in Pakistan that is looking for help in securing the following items:

- *Food packs*, each of which should contain enough food to support a family of six people. Ensure that the food contains the local staples, is nutritious and easy to transport.

- *Hygiene packs* that include water purification tablets, soap, shampoo and conditioner, hairbrush, comb, deodorant, toothpaste, toothbrushes, floss, mouthwash, lip balm, skin lotion/moisturiser, antiseptic cream, wet wipes, disinfectant hand gel, face masks, sanitary napkins, tampons, diapers, incontinence pads, toilet rolls, tissues, kitchen rolls, razor and shaving cream, scrubbing brush, nail clippers, bandages, face cloth (make these items age and gender appropriate).
- *Temporary shelters* such as weather resistant tents, each of which is capable of housing a family of six.
- *Setting up a temporary learning centre* to provide a safe space where children victim-survivors of the floods can learn, be fed, and be cared for.

Choose how you might provide this assistance, e.g. raising funds for these materials to be purchased locally; sending volunteers to assist with tasks locally; creating and staffing the Temporary Learning Centre; and so on.

- What ethical issues, linguistic and cultural matters do you also need to consider?
- What logistical issues are relevant, e.g. transportation, communication, record-keeping?
- How would you ensure the health and wellbeing of local people? Of humanitarian aid workers?

Note that if sending people anywhere, you need to ensure that they are security cleared to work with vulnerable groups, especially children, to ensure that safeguarding concerns are addressed.

Financial assistance to local organisations is usually a preferred mode of supporting disaster affected communities overseas because it leaves choice in how to spend the money to meet their needs effectively in the affected localities and their governance structures. However, it is also important to ensure that aid is delivered equitably and transparently. Having report-back instruments in place can be one means of ensuring accountability for how the funds were used and which players were involved in the distribution processes. Pyle (2011, 2015) highlights the dangers encountered in Haiti.

Social work involvement in hurricane disasters

Social workers have a long history of being involved in philanthropic activities aimed at enabling people to deal with personal and collective catastrophes. The three key social work responses pivot around:

• Practical aid in the immediate aftermath of the disaster.
• Psychosocial support for victim-survivors.
• Community reconstruction and development.

Social work students have also been drawn into the ambit of providing humanitarian aid. For example, during Superstorm Sandy, social work students from Rutgers University assisted in the humanitarian responses (Pottick and Pottick, 2014). They received supplementary training in disaster responses and disaster mental health to enable them to enhance their understanding of the situation and become better equipped to respond to the needs of the victim-survivors. However, useful as such training is, it may be insufficient for dealing with the vast range of complex factors that they may have to address in the realities of disaster practice where the unexpected occurs regularly.

Social workers use a strengths-based, person-centred, transdisciplinary holistic approach to respond to victim-survivors of climate change disasters such as floods. This means focusing on:

• Understanding people's needs.
• Understanding the relationships between different systems and their impact on each other.
• Using a strengths-based approach.
• Engaging with a range of stakeholders, e.g. practitioners, policymakers, and entrepreneurs and forming alliances with other stakeholders who may be able to help.
• Securing additional culturally appropriate and necessary resources.
• Mobilising communities to reconstruct their futures.

The assessment of need should calculate whether a community has the capacity to cope and recover from the impact of the disaster and use that information to devise an effective intervention strategy (Collins, 2009). A disaster such as a flood will affect communities differently, depending on their respective susceptibilities and resource availability. Hence, an assessment of vulnerabilities must be locality specific, culturally relevant and take account of the context (Dominelli, 2012a; Vincent et al., 2013). Moreover, social workers favour coproduction, whereby they involve people in identifying and implementing disaster interventions and risk mitigation activities (Zastrow, 2010).

Guidelines for social work intervention

Intervening in disasters is tough, and practitioners whether social workers or humanitarian aid workers need to be prepared adequately for such work. Social workers can be sceptical about some disaster practices, including the language used in disaster risk management circles of referring to a disaster as 'an incident'. They feel this downplays the seriousness of what happens and strips people of their humanity and emotional reactions to disaster situations. In storm surges and hurricanes, social workers can assist in mobilising communities to mitigate risk by arranging for self-help groups to support each other. This can include: covering windows and doors with boards or other protective materials to reduce the likelihood of windows shattering and doors being blown in; piling sandbags at points where water may ingress buildings. They may also assist people in planning their evacuation and preparing their 'grab and go bag'. Other activities can focus on conducting awareness-raising sessions, helping people to support each other and share food and other materials in short supply after the disaster has occurred. They may take a longer-term view and discuss reconstruction initiatives such as bringing additional resources into the community, relocating people and reunifying family members. Finally, those with the relevant expertise may run practical psychosocial first aid sessions and refer people onwards for medical and psychiatric treatments.

Social workers emphasise the stressful nature of disaster intervention work, and how it relies on personal, professional and community resilience, each endeavour feeding the other. Understanding one's own role and skills in carrying it out is critical to retaining a balance between helping others and not feeling overwhelmed by the incessant demands while in the field. One social worker insisted that retaining this balance required ensuring that the 'work did not stick to you'. In other words, drawing professional boundaries enabled one to leave the work in the field, and find some down-time for oneself. This had to be supplemented by staying healthy, self-care and exercise, and regular debriefing locally with peers and within the employing organisation including online sessions. Additionally, intervention models which were easy to implement assisted practitioners to feel in control of daily demands.

Other helpful strategies included thinking of oneself as a community activist there to support the disaster-affected community and thinking theoretically about what one was doing in practice. For most practitioners, this meant sticking to familiar theories, e.g. social development theories, systems theories, crisis intervention theories, and understanding that there might be lessons arising out of the 'nothing works' approach. Another important point was having clarity about the departure date and making this known from the point of arrival to avoid raising unrealistic expectations about the duration of the assistance provided.

Paying attention to the practitioner's own emotional reaction to the situation is also relevant to effective interventions. Emotional reactions include: acknowledging feelings of being overwhelmed and deskilled; worrying about what procedures and processes you are expected to follow and being aware of other services' expectations of your role and behaviour. Social workers also encounter ethical dilemmas when undertaking disaster work. These include feeling guilty about wanting to leave the scene when the work becomes personally distressing; rejecting the imposition of services on victim-survivors by donors insisting that they follow top-down approaches and not bottom-up ones rooted in community engagement and coproduction; and knowing when to end the constant and endless repetition of a victim-survivor's narrative when that person is attempting to deal with the immediacy of their grief. Having countless cups of tea available can facilitate this discussion.

In responding to the victim-survivors' expressed wishes, various themes keep coming up, and require social work support and help in dealing with them. They are: forming helpful relationships with other service-providers and victim-survivors; establishing clear guidelines for the frequency and length of contact; being prepared to diffuse violence and its constant presence; maintaining a sense of balance about the disaster; responding to victim-survivors' wishes to return home; accompanying them to funerals to help deal with their grief and finding local, culturally appropriate rituals to help deal with that; and meeting various local officials associated with service provision. Always be aware that there is no one-size-fits-all response to disasters and be prepared to do things differently.

Responding to local demands in locality specific and culturally relevant ways may challenge social workers who are unfamiliar with a particular setting. They may become distressed if they experience that their ethical dilemmas remain unresolved despite the support offered by peers and line managers (Pyles, 2015, 2016; Boddy and Dominelli, 2017).

Exercise – Peer support

George was a social worker who lived in Florida. He was so busy helping people prepare for Hurricane Season that he was unable to take safety precautions to protect his own home. Then disaster struck. When George returned home after a terrible day helping people get to the evacuation centre to find his house totally devastated. He started calling for his wife and two children, but no one answered. He started looking for any signs of them in the debris while phoning the hospitals and the Helpline. However, he could not get through to anyone. He finally decided to go to the evacuation centre to see if they were there. The journey to it seemed interminable. When he got there, he found his wife and two children. They had been submerged in the floodwater and some debris had caused injury to their limbs. They had received basic medical care, but as they were otherwise fine, they were expected to manage under their own resources. George started to think about where they could go for safety and privacy. He had a sister who lived in Kansas. He rang her up to explain his circumstances. He was told he and his family would be welcome to join them there. So, he set off, hoping he had enough fuel in his tank to get out of the hurricane-stricken area. Fortunately, he did, but it took him 20 hours of driving with his children and wife moaning in the back seat. He finally reached his sister's house. They settled the injured trio into warm beds, gave them some chicken broth and told them to go to sleep. They were so exhausted that they quickly fell asleep. Only then did George realise that he had been soaked through from head to foot and was chattering from feeling cold. His sister suggested he soaked in a hot bath for a while, then had a bowl of chicken broth. He was then also told to go to bed. This he did, and he also fell asleep. He woke up during the night feeling extremely hot. His skin was burning. He took a couple of aspirins to reduce his temperature and went back to bed. The next day when his sister came to call him, he had passed away in his sleep. It turned out that he had injured his leg some days earlier, but he had ignored it to meet the demands that were being placed upon him and it had become seriously infected. He had died of sepsis.

Discussion

Working in small groups, choose someone to chair the session and someone to take notes and report back to the plenary group. Make sure you cover the following points in your discussion:

- How could you convince George and other social workers like him to take seriously their own health?
- How would you support George's wife and two children to cope with both his death and their devastated home? What resources would you draw upon and which services would you refer the family to?
- How would you support George's wife, and their two children to acquire housing (either rebuild their previous one, or move elsewhere)?
- What lessons would you want to pass on to George's employers?

Self-care is an important if often neglected issue among social workers. It is poorly covered in training when it is essential to know how to look after both oneself and others. This constitutes a training deficit that must be rectified. The lack of work-life balance needed to care for oneself can be detrimental to one's health, or even be fatal. Consequently, line managers should include questions about self-care and how well a practitioner is looking after themselves as a normal and regular part of the discussions during supervision (Dominelli, 2012a).

Conclusions

Storm surges and hurricanes can cause horrendous loss of life and damage to property. They are the outcomes of extreme weather events linked to climate change. Implementing preventative action that tackles climate change is a crucial consideration for social work practice, and requires adequate education and training to act effectively in the field. Social workers can support people throughout the disaster cycle from prevention to risk mitigation and reconstruction. This would enable people to consider strategies and action plans for preparing to address flooding catastrophes better in future. Building adaptive capacity and resilience in a sustainable environment are important strategies in keeping people safe and adapting to the dangers they face. Social workers must also look after themselves and their families alongside the residents of a community and the victim-survivors once disaster strikes. Finding a way of balancing all these demands on their time and energies is crucial to social workers' health and wellbeing. The social work curriculum must take seriously the inclusion of training regarding disasters at all levels of training.

9 Earthquakes

Socio-economic and political structures turn a natural hazard into a social disaster

Social workers from across the world went to these locations to provide humanitarian aid. Others raised funds for victim-survivors. Their endeavours highlighted the invisibility of social work interventions in disasters, lack of capacity in social work education and training, and led to the creation of the Rebuilding People's Lives Post-Disasters Network (RIPL) by IASSW (International Association of Schools in Social Work) in 2005. This enabled social workers to consider the preparation and skills set needed by social workers going overseas to assist in disaster situations. These disasters also led to the formation of the Earthquake Disaster Virtual Helpline in 2010, but which came into its own in the Nepal earthquakes of 2015. The case studies presented in this chapter will focus on the different skills and knowledge required to work in earthquake-induced disasters and identify the importance of working with seismologists and other physical scientists to address the need to build earthquake-proof houses and other resilient infrastructures that will protect people better in future.

Introduction

Earthquakes lead to deadly situations. Around 2.5 million people died in earthquakes that occurred between 1900 and 2000. Some earthquakes with the largest number of casualties occurred after that time. More people die in the industrialising countries than the industrialised ones. For example, in 2003, a 6.6 Mw (magnitude on the Richter scale) earthquake in Bam, Iran killed 40,000 people or 30 per cent of its population; in 2010, Haiti's 7.0 Mw earthquake killed over 250,000 people and ruined most of the built infrastructures including government buildings. In contrast, Chile's much more intense 8.8 Mw earthquake in 2010, which was spread over a much wider area in terms of its impact, had 500 deaths. The 2023 earthquake that struck southern and central Turkey and northern and western Syria reached 7.8 Mw. The figures of confirmed casualties one month later reached 50,000. This figure is likely to

DOI: 10.4324/9781003105824-11

rise as the response moves to the recovery phase and people are removed from the rubble, Poverty is an important variable in determining vulnerabilities, especially in infrastructures including housing and health, and exacerbates the casualties and hardship that low-income people encounter in such disasters. It also makes them vulnerable to exploitation not only to traffickers and people smugglers, but also developers wishing to impose their own ideologies and agendas in the reconstruction of devastated communities (Pyles et al., 2015).

Earthquake survival rates are affected by physical and social factors. These include the: magnitude of the earthquake and various features associated with it; topography or terrain in which the earthquake occurs; country's investment in resilience measures, especially in building codes for building including dwellings; built infrastructures; resource availability; preventative measures; resources for promoting community-based resilience; and people's involvement in forward planning to prevent damage and deaths in future disasters. The training of the relevant professionals and local populations in dealing with local hazards is crucial in devising preventative and preparatory measures. These should be devised through coproduction and fully engage populations vulnerable to the earthquake and other hazards so that they will 'own' these and follow through on them.

There are two major geographic locations for large earthquakes:

- The continents within the Alpine Himalayan subduction belt which has many fault-lines that stretch from Portugal to China.
- The 40,250-kilometre (km) 'Ring of Fire' or Circum Pacific Belt, which runs along the basin of the Pacific Ocean and includes countries where major earthquakes can occur. It consists of a horseshoe-shaped line of more than 450 volcanoes. It runs from Alaska, through Western Canada and the USA, down to Chile, around to Australia and New Zealand/Aotearoa and then up to Japan. It features active volcanoes and has frequent earthquakes along its entire 25,000-mile length.

The Huaxian Earthquake of 23 January 1556 is among the world's most catastrophic earthquakes. It occurred near present day Xi'an, in Shaanxi Province, China. In it, more than 800,000 people died (Feng et al., 2020). The slow response of the Ming Dynasty, then holding the reins of power in China, and the large numbers of people living in caves that liquefied under the shaking caused by the earthquake led to these high levels of deaths. Some very recent ones, e.g. those occurring in Nepal during April 2015 and May 2015, suffered much fewer casualties.

In this chapter, I consider major geological and seismological points about earthquakes, and then delve into examples that depict different strengths and weaknesses in responses to them. This is to derive lessons that can be learnt to enhance earthquake resilience. I also discuss the roles of social workers and their interventions in earthquake disasters.

Brief seismological introduction

The rocky ground upon which we tread is part of the Earth's lithosphere which is composed of two parts, the Earth's crust, and the upper mantle. The solid rock of the lithosphere runs from the highest mountain to the ocean floor. Located beneath the mantle is the Earth's dense, very hot core. The lithosphere is broken into large rocky plates that lie above a partially molten layer of rock called the asthenosphere. The rocky plates of the lithosphere are called tectonic plates. These plates are around 100 km (62 miles) thick and consist of two principal types of material: the oceanic crust which is also termed *sima* due to the silicon and magnesium minerals that make it up; and the continental crust which is termed *sial* because it is composed mainly of silicon and aluminium minerals. The composition of the two types of crust differs markedly, with mafic basaltic rocks dominating the oceanic crust, while continental crust consists principally of lower-density felsic granitic rocks.

Tectonic plates are dynamic in that they are constantly moving in diverse directions and speeds. Earthquakes cause violent shaking. Such shaking can: rupture or create crevices in the Earth, trigger landslides; and turn the surface of the Earth into liquid. This latter process is called liquefaction. In it, the motion of an earthquake can cause loosely packed, water-saturated soil to become liquid. As liquefied soil loses its density, it eventually loses its ability to support roads, buried pipes, and other forms of built infrastructures including houses. Earthquakes can also push and pull the ground. In the course of doing so, they tear the surface and push the ground apart and upward to create 'surface ruptures'. A surface rupture may occur slowly or suddenly during an earthquake. A surface rupture usually occurs along pre-existing faults. Additionally, seismic waves travel through hard rock more quickly than they do through softer rock and sediments such as soil and sand. Moreover, as the waves go from harder to softer rocks, they slow down and their strength increases. Consequently, the shaking is more intense at spots where the ground is softer. Nonetheless, houses on hard rock, but close to the surface rupture, are likely to undergo intense shaking and damage.

Plate tectonics has become the unifying theory of geology because it explains how the Earth's surface has moved in the past and currently. The movement of tectonic plates has created the tallest mountain ranges and the deepest oceans. The science of plate tectonics refers to the study of how tectonic plates behave and move to create the Earth's landforms.

For example, Pangea was a single landmass that encompassed all the current day continents. It began to break up during the early Jurassic period. And, as the American and African plates split apart around 175 million years ago, the Atlantic Ocean formed between them.

Volcanic and earthquake activity is more likely to occur at the margins of these tectonic plates. The Earth has seven major tectonic plates. These are known as the African Plate, the Antarctic Plate, the Eurasian Plate, the Indo-Australian Plate, the Pacific Plate, the North American Plate, and the South American Plate. Most tectonic plates are composed of both oceanic and continental crust. The Pacific Plate is composed mainly of oceanic crust. The oceanic crust, which is mainly basaltic, is thinner than the continental crust. The continental crust, which is made of granite, is lighter and floats more easily than the oceanic crust.

There are three types of plate tectonic boundaries, namely the divergent, the convergent, and the transform plate boundaries. When two plates move away from each other, they are called divergent and cause the formation of crust. Earthquakes usually happen at the divergent plate boundaries, e.g. the Rift Valley in Ethiopia, or mid-ocean ridges such as the Mid-Atlantic Ridge. The Mid-Atlantic Ridge is 65,000 kilometres long and forms the largest mountain chain on Earth stretching from the Arctic towards the Antarctic, all under water. When two tectonic plates come together or collide, they form convergent plate boundaries. Mountains are formed when tectonic plates converge. If one of these converging plates moves underneath the other, the process is called subduction. Deep trenches form at these points and can produce earthquakes, as does, the Alpine-Himalayan subduction zone that runs from Portugal to China, for example. If these colliding plates are pushed down, underwater trenches can be formed. Trenches form the deepest part of the ocean, e.g. the Mariana Trench in the Western Pacific, east of the Philippines near the Mariana Islands.

If two tectonic plates slide past each other, they form what are termed transform plate boundaries. An illustration of a transform plate boundary is that occurring at the San Andreas Fault where two tectonic plates meet in western California. The Pacific Plate on the west moves northwestward relative to the North American Plate located to the east. Earthquakes frequently occur along transform plate boundaries.

Taking protective measures

Whether people own or rent their homes, emergency services and disaster management agencies such as the American Federal Emergency Management Agency (FEMA) advise making a risk assessment of any potential geologic threats to your dwelling and taking preparatory and mitigating action before a major event such as an earthquake occurs.

Involving all members of the family in forming your plan is crucial. Such conversations should enable you to form an earthquake safety plan that you can all understand, follow through, and own. The earthquake hazards and risks you face depend on various factors. These include the location of your home, the type of construction used in your home, whether your home is located on or near an active fault, your community's population density, current building codes, and your family's emergency preparedness. The geologic hazards that you might face after an earthquake range from ground shaking and surface rupture to landslides and liquefaction.

If your home was constructed before building codes mandated earthquake proofing houses, it may be vulnerable to serious structural damage. Such a potential hazard requires safety planning, earthquake proofing the structure of your home, securing your personal property, and buying earthquake insurance to increase your resilience or ability to cope in the event of an earthquake. Specific actions you can undertake include:

1 Identifying the potential hazard, e.g. a surface rupture, a landslide, and assess what you can do to minimise the damage it can do to your home and potential injury to the individuals living within it. You may need to find out whether you live in a seismologically active zone.

2 Involving experts including a civil engineer knowledgeable in how to seismically retrofit and strengthen the foundations of your home so that it can become more resistant to shaking. This is particularly important in older homes constructed when building codes did not require earthquake proofing.

3 Identifying the safest places in each room of your home because finding such a spot may save your life. Remember windows and glass can shatter from the shaking.

4 Undertaking practice drills including getting outside (be mindful of falling debris and electrical wires and sparks because fires are a major risk after an earthquake) and if remaining inside, follow the 'drop, cover and hold' advice. A strong dining room table may be useful for this response.

5 Creating or buying an earthquake safety kit. At minimum, this should contain food, water, medicine, bandages, disinfectant, an emergency blanket, a battery-operated radio, and torch/flashlight with spare batteries.

6 Ensure that each person has a 'grab and go bag' that has specific items for each member of the household, e.g. baby formula and diapers for babies, sanitary products for women, and a means of keeping specific medicines cool, e.g. insulin, and ensuring that oxygen supplies can be

used safely. Reduce your risk of damage and injury from a serious earthquake by identifying possible home hazards. These include:

a. Securing tall, heavy furniture that could topple to walls or floors, e.g. bookcases, china cabinets or modular wall units. Strapping water heaters to prevent them rupturing. Preventing stoves and other appliances from moving and thereby break gas pipes or electrical lines.

b. Close all supplies of gas or electricity and water to your home if you have time, and practice how to do this quickly. It could be a specific task assigned to one person.

c. Securing hanging plants in heavy pots to prevent them from falling off their hooks.

d. Removing heavy picture frames or mirrors over a bed that could drop upon you during your sleep.

e. Replacing latches on kitchen cabinets or other cabinets if they will not remain closed during shaking.

f. Moving breakable and heavy objects to low locations or use closed secured cabinets so that they cannot fall, break and cause further damage or injuries.

g. Ensuring that a masonry chimney will not collapse and fall through the roof.

h. Keeping flammable liquids including paints and cleaning fluids in a garage or an outside shed.

It might also help you to understand some of the terminology that is used in the context of an earthquake disaster. Key ones are:

- *Aftershock*. These are earthquakes that occur after the first one and are usually of a lower magnitude (measurement) than the first earthquake.
- *Epicentre*. This refers to the centre of an earthquake. Vibrations are sent from the epicentre in many directions.
- *Fault lines*. These refer to the cracks in the rocks that lie below the Earth's surface.
- *Seismic activity*. This is used as another word for earthquakes, as are tremors, quakes, and shakers.
- *Seismograph*. This is a machine that is used to measure the strength of an earthquake.
- *Tsunami*. A tsunami is a series of waves (not just one) caused by a large and sudden disturbance of the sea. Tsunami waves move outward in all directions from where they began and can traverse oceans. The big waves approaching shallow waters along the coast can grow to a height of up to 100 feet and smash into the shore, causing much damage along it. Tsunamis are mainly caused by undersea earthquakes, but they can also be triggered by landslides, volcanic activity, and meteorites.

Human rights and ethics

Human rights and ethics are essential ingredients in the practice reper-toire during a disaster and are linked to bioethics. Bioethics focus on vul-nerability as a way of moving away from the focus on how to save lives to ascertain how to address structural violence, economic injustice, and global solidarity. Addressing structural inequalities is central to build-ing resilience and reconstructing societies after a disaster. UNESCO's Declaration on Bioethics and Human Rights illustrated the importance of this shift which now provides the dominant ethical framework for humanitarian aid during the disaster phases of prevention, relief, and re-covery and underpins human rights-based work. Consequently, victim-survivors become the bearers of rights. However, these human rights can be violated through neoliberal policies that ignore the negative impact of their tenets on social contexts, trading relations and progressive visions of human development. Neoliberal policies can act as barriers to human flourishing by withdrawing resources, especially through austerity poli-cies. However, promoting human development is best underpinned by enhancing compassion, solidarity, and beneficence in delivering humani-tarian goods and services.

To achieve these ends, human rights are implemented as holistic, interconnected and embedded throughout the disaster cycle: prepared-ness, emergency relief and response, recovery, and reconstruction. Ad-ditionally, these rights cover the right to life (safety); access to all basic needs (food, clothing, shelter, water, medicine, health, and education); longer-term socio-economic needs (land, housing, property, livelihoods); and civil and political protection including having appropriate docu-mentation, being able to exercise the right to movement across borders, freedom of expression, and participating fully in decision-making or governance structures (Costa and Pospieszna, 2015).

Humanitarianism has traditionally focused on individual recipients of help and support. Humanitarian aid workers doing such work may have neglected the relevance of social justice, human dignity, and the so-cial, structural contexts to their interventions, alongside humanely just responses based on collective action. Moreover, individual approaches can lead to deficit-based thinking about the roles that victim-survivors can play in their recovery because these approaches fail to focus on re-inforcing local individual and communal strengths, tackle structural in-equalities and other social issues that deepen human suffering, especially those linked to poverty, malnutrition, and poor governance. Individual-ised models are usually top-down in their approach. In them, the experts tell the victim-survivors what to do, and humanitarian aid workers can be portrayed as 'saviours' in tough situations.

However, this top-down approach was unable to meet the challenges that arose during the 2004 Indian Ocean Tsunami. This failure led to the

2005 Operational Guidelines on Human Rights and Natural Disasters. In these, the UN Inter-Agency Standing Committee (IASC), connected human rights to disasters. This embedded the protection of human rights in managing a disaster throughout the disaster cycle. This encompassed prevention, planning, relief, recovery, and reconstruction. Yet, the 2005 Guidelines have no sanctions through which to compel governments to implement human rights-based services before, during or after a disaster. A study of the 2004 Indian Ocean Tsunami by Dominelli and Vickers (2014) revealed that community-based, bottom-up interventions that linked local and external organisations and engaged residents were preferred over top-down ones.

Vulnerability is a key concept in the provision and delivery of humanitarian aid. Vulnerability revolves around an assessment of an individual or community's exposure to the potential danger, i.e. the risk posed by a specific hazard and the likelihood of becoming susceptible to its impact. Thus, the mitigation of risk and enhancing resilience to a hazard is crucial to limiting the impact of a disaster when it hits. Vulnerability can be attributed to a physical location such as living in an earthquake-prone area, or linked to social attributes including gender, age, ethnicity, disability, and poverty. Additionally, vulnerability is raised if human rights are violated through violence, fraud, corruption, and tradition. Additionally, overcoming vulnerability factors requires social and political institutions to provide collective security for individuals and communities.

Universality is a concept that affirms a common humanity that underpins human rights across the globe. The realisation of this concept challenges the notion of human rights being based on ideas that foster individual autonomy and equality. Instead, universality now promotes notions of social justice, capabilities, human rights, and a global ethics of care that includes the planet (Dominelli, 2012a). At the same time as having these positive possibilities, globalisation has instigated its own vulnerabilities. Neoliberalism also promotes asymmetrical power relations and prioritises the wellbeing of markets over that of human beings (Kirby, 2006: 95). Under its auspices, people experience deprivation, precariousness, inequality, exclusion, privatisation, commercialisation and increasing insecurity. Neoliberalism has enabled 85 of the world's richest individuals to accumulate substantial financial resources. These, Oxfam (2014) has calculated, are equivalent to those held by 3.5 billion of the poorest people. Moreover, the mechanisms of injustice that precede a disaster will continue to operate during it, a reality brought home globally by the COVID-19 pandemic (IASSW, 2020).

Such dynamics and market mechanisms reinforce structural inequalities and have enabled neoliberalism to undermine poor people's coping mechanisms (Pyles, 2011). Enforcing social justice, equality and solidarity enhances an individual's adaptive capacities to address structural concerns collectively and thereby reduce risk, usually at the local level. A human-rights framework endorses social inclusion, equality, and institutional support. Creating new alliances of solidarity will facilitate the 'collective capacity to act' (Robinson, 2011). Developing collective responses to disasters like earthquakes can prevent human rights challenges that result in unequal access to assistance, discrimination in aid provision, unsafe resettlement, inadequate property compensation, and wide-scale displacement of victim-survivors.

Question – Prioritising needs

During a disaster, you may not have enough resources for all those in need. You may have to prioritise specific distribution activities at the micro-, meso- and macro- levels to cope with a scarcity of resources.

How would you proceed to prioritise the needs that you have identified in your needs assessment following an earthquake disaster when resources are insufficient to meet all needs? Consider the following questions in your response. Discuss your answers in small group and prepare to report back on your deliberations:

- What should be the basis for prioritising those who should receive aid?
- What might be the response(s) of individuals who do receive aid?
- Could you think of strategies other than prioritising individual need that might be useful in coping with insufficient resources for distribution to those who are already traumatised by the disaster? Discuss what these might be.

Prioritising aid distribution in the context of resource scarcities pose difficult issues for humanitarian aid workers to address. Some practitioners caught in such dilemmas seek to find additional materials from other sources with varying degrees of success (GHD, 2003; Holtz et al., 2020).

Specific earthquake situations

Earthquakes are considered 'natural' disasters. I tend to think that the earthquake is a 'natural' hazard, but the disaster occurs when the hazard and society interact, and people suffer its impact. A 'natural' earthquake occurs when there is shaking in the Earth's crust where strain has been building up in the rocks, which are large slabs of crust called plates, causing these to move and rupture suddenly. Within the 'natural' hazard domain, this movement or rupture is a fault or the point at which rocks can slide past each other. These plates can move past each other in several ways according to the direction in which they move. These are: a strike-slip fault, normal fault and reverse (thrust) fault. However, if their movement interacts with people, social institutions, or built-infrastructures, this results in devastating effects on people and their environments. Moreover, people's social vulnerabilities usually enable the event to surpass the 'natural' hazard phase. Landslides and dam lakes are major secondary hazards in an earthquake. Also, earthquakes can be caused by human activities such as fracking and nuclear explosions.

The 2010 earthquake near Concepción, Chile

On 27 February 2010, Chile experienced what locals called the Concepción earthquake. It was an earthquake of 8.8 Mw that began in the ocean at the convergent boundary between the Nazca and South American tectonic plates. This caused a tsunami that inundated many coastal towns from Valparaiso in the North to Concepción in the South. The tsunami impacted 9 per cent of the region's population, caused 525 deaths, 25 people were missing, and damages to the infrastructures and the environment were high. One of the towns badly affected was Talcahuano (near Concepción). Family, friends, neighbours, various community groups and local organisations were among the first to provide aid. Chile Grows With You, a social agency, created in 2007 provided victim-survivors with rights-based support. Its explicit rights-oriented mandate included intersectoral mechanisms, relationships, and human behaviour. Initially, it sought to establish common understandings about human development and needs and focused on working with both local and national governments. As a human rights-based entity, Chile Grows With You, based its services on universal access and support for all Chilean children to ensure that it reached children at greatest risk of getting into difficulties, including crime. This supportive, rights-based framework was invaluable in supporting children and families immediately after the earthquake (Arbour et al., 2011). Its earlier experiences enabled Chile Grows With You to quickly organise, define, operationalise, prioritise and sustain collective action to meet earthquake-induced needs and continue supporting children and families following the immediate aftermath of the earthquake.

Moreover, its human rights-based approach facilitated the assessment of people's capacity to claim their rights; review the state's obligations to victim-survivors; and identify and analyse the structural barriers to the implementation of their rights. Furthermore, the agency used the

CRC (Convention on the Rights of the Child) to affirm children's right to health services and early years education. National staff visited the health centres in the disaster-affected areas to assess needs. They found assessing the needs of mothers and children difficult. Thus, they developed protocols to inform people of their rights to services, identify those requiring services, prioritise services for people who were injured and/ or ill, link children to services and train parents and health personnel to work from a human-rights based perspective. A team of earthquake experts put together by IASSW provided training for social work practitioners in Talcahuano. Housing was identified as a key problem that was beyond the capacity of local communities to provide. Local engineers claimed that earthquake-proofing housing would add 10 per cent to the cost of rebuilding a house. This additional cost meant that poor people's houses were less likely to be earthquake-proofed, despite building code requirements because people built their own homes whenever possible.

Lisbon, 1755

Lisbon, a thriving city of 275,000 inhabitants in eighteenth-century Europe, was the centre of a large colonial empire. However, on 1 November 1755, the Lisbon Earthquake virtually destroyed the city, and by the time of the third aftershock, between 30,000 and 100,000 people were dead. Moreover, the earthquake was followed by a tsunami that flooded the downtown centre. This event caused many people to drown. The earthquake was followed by a fire, a major risk after earthquakes, that was not put out for 6 days. Overseas media coverage of this cascading catastrophe through pictures and newspapers left much to be desired. Media depictions of victim-survivors focused on a suffering nation, but their condition of being part of humanity and entitled to be treated with dignity and respect was lost on the media's audiences, i.e. their readers (Sliwinsky, 2009). The Lisbon Earthquake depicts the fragility of ensuring that those different from oneself are judged as being human. It also symbolised the loss of optimism and growth of tele-pathos, as the 'sympathetic identification with another's suffering at a distance' was termed. This was intended to acknowledge the rights of the other, i.e. the victim-survivors, and their closeness to one's own rights. The scenes of horrendous damage and suffering continue to provide a lens through which the media view major disasters.

Nepal, 2015

The Ghorka earthquake was composed of two earthquakes that occurred in Nepal, during April and May 2015. On 25 April 2015, a 7.8 Mw earthquake killed 9000 people, injured many others, and destroyed

600,000 structures including world famous heritage buildings in Kathmandu. Following this, on 12 May 2015, a sizeable aftershock which some classified as a second earthquake of 7.3 Mw killed 100 people, and injured 1000. Nepal, as a poor country, found this disaster difficult to cope with, so required external assistance. Additionally, the national poverty which featured strongly in Nepalese society was endemic and had crucial gendered dimensions which disadvantaged women.

After the earthquakes, a significant number of women became subjects of internal trafficking to address family economic insecurity (Nikku, 2016). In one recorded incident, 70 children were taken away from traffickers who were exploiting their various vulnerabilities by subjecting them to prostitution and domestic exploitation. There are three core dimensions to trafficking. These are: activities linked to recruitment, transportation, and transfer; the means which included threats, deception, and coercive force; and the purpose of trafficking which can engage family and friends in initiating the endeavour. Trafficking is a lucrative business. In 2016, traffickers extorted $150 billion from their victims. For some poor families, the sexual exploitation of young women was a significant way of enabling other family members to survive the damages caused by the earthquakes (Nikku, 2016; Gurung and Clark, 2018).

Rural populations are more vulnerable than urban ones because poor transportation infrastructures mean that aid takes longer to reach cutoff rural areas. Despite their predicament, survivors lack government protection and attention to their need to obtain their share of scarce resources and income. Moreover, the Nepali government weaponised aid by refusing to distribute it in areas that were suspected of having supported the Maoist insurgents earlier. Yet, a peace agreement had been reached in 2006. Similar principles were followed in the Sri Lanka Civil War when the Tamil Tigers were also refused aid. Such institutionalised state coercion indicates that the state can fail to safeguard the rights of victim-survivors following an earthquake or other disaster.

Case study – Preparation work in Nepal before the April 2015 earthquake

The week before the April 2015 earthquake struck Nepal, I was teaching green social work at the Nepal School of Social Work at the invitation of the then headteacher. We went around the school's premises, and I was pointing out risks or hazards that could cause harm or damage should an earthquake strike, and what actions they might take to mitigate these risks. We considered securing bookcase, books, furniture, areas to stay away from if an earthquake did occur, secondary hazards such as fire, falling debris from buildings that grew upwards to provide male children with property and thus weakened their basic structures, where it would be safe to shelter should an earthquake strike, and what should go into a 'grab and go bag' (Dominelli, 2018a). The suggestions were well-received. However, none were implemented before the earthquake struck a week later. Lack of time, and a shortage of resources were the reasons given for not making any progress on mitigating the risks we identified together.

In your small group, consider how you might have prioritised mitigating the risks identified. Consider the following points, and prepare to report-back to the larger group:

- How might you obtain more resources for a poor school, what resources you would seek and where would you get these from?
- How could you develop existing strengths within the staff and student groups, and the nearby community?
- What could you do to influence policymakers and ensure that all public buildings including schools and universities were made earthquake-proof (Make sure that you are acting with local organisations and ensuring that what you do is locality-specific and culturally relevant)?
- What allies might the Nepal School of Social Work develop to ensure that it had a range of individuals and groups that could support its requirements and provide aid during a disaster?

Note: The Nepal School of Social Work was closed after the earthquake and its different parts were integrated into other universities and institutions.

Advance preparation is crucial to mitigating the damage that a disaster might cause when a hazard interacts with society. Preparing a family action plan and organising a 'grab and go bag' is essential to survival (Dominelli, 2019a). Earthquake-proofing buildings is an important strategy in reducing risks (Nygon et al., 2007; UNISDR 2009, 2015).

Sichuan, 2008

The 7.9 M Wenchaun earthquake occurred in the mountainous terrain of Sichuan, China on 12 May 2008 along the then unknown Longmenshan fault. This earthquake claimed nearly 90,000 lives and caused $146.5

billion in reconstruction costs and affected 15 million people. Children formed a significant proportion of those who were killed because they were in school. The epicentre was near Yingxiu where 30 per cent of the population died. Yingxiu School, destroyed during the 2008 Wenchuan Earthquake, rose from the rubble, and was rebuilt along with the rest of the town. Hence, it is currently a thriving place that has retained much of its previous charm. However, given its geographic location among mountains and rivers in Sichuan Province, it remains subject to landslides and flooding as well as earthquakes.

The town of Beichuan was one of the most severely damaged towns in the 2008 Earthquake. Consequently, the original town has been left as a memorial and a museum nearby is where people can visit and find out about the earthquake. Additionally, the old town has been replaced with a new one called New Beichuan which is located about 45 kilometres away. It has been purpose-built with earthquake-proofed buildings and wide boulevards. This relocation of people is consistent with China's policy of moving rural populations into purpose-built dwellings to mitigate the risk of being caught in an earthquake disaster.

Social workers intervene in earthquake scenarios using coproduction to engage residents in rebuilding their communities. Coproduction involves processes that include validating both local or indigenous knowledges and scientific expertise, listening to the wishes of residents and facilitating the incorporation of their ideas into any solutions that are created so that these are locality specific and culturally appropriate and considered theirs (Sun, 2005). This process is indicated in Figure 9.1.

Many volunteers from Hong Kong, other parts of China, and overseas descended into Sichuan to help the victim-survivors devastated by the earthquake. Many of these volunteers were helpful. However, numerous untrained ones hampered relief operations and used resources that were required by the victim-survivors whose needs were far greater.

Many people went into the Wenchuan area to offer psychosocial counselling and support. These included social workers from overseas countries, many who did not speak Chinese, let alone the local language used in the area. These volunteers offered psychosocial support when it was not wanted. Initially, the victim-survivors rejected their help. There was a saying, 'Run from dogs, psychotherapists and fire', which was popularised during this period to capture this reaction. The victim-survivors were more interested in finding missing family members, getting practical assistance in the form of food, medicine, and shelters near their original communities, than in receiving psychosocial aid, or facilitating a need to mourn their losses (Zhang et al., 2012). The services addressing emotional and mental health needs were wanted much later, several years, later for some victim-survivors.

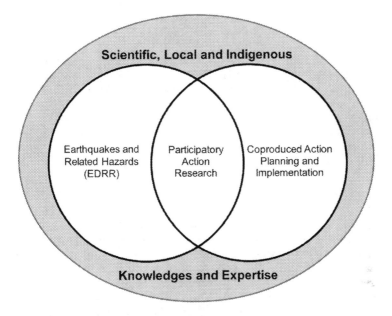

Figure 9.1 The coproduction processes in earthquake interventions.

However, there were initiatives which followed strengths-based, locality specific and culturally sensitive approaches to the needs of the affected populations. Some of these involved Hong Kong Polytechnic University (PolyU). Its main approach was to send social work academics (many of whom were trained in social services delivery) to support people affected by the earthquake, develop social work programmes, and offer training courses that covered a range of topics including psychosocial social work. These endeavours were community-based, centred around creating Social Work Stations where people could go to seek assistance (Sim and Dominelli, 2017; Ku and Dominelli, 2018). These initiatives built on existing strengths among the populations involved. Using locality specific, culturally relevant interventions, such projects empowered communities to increase their self-reliance, become self-sufficient as far as possible, and seek the support that they wanted, when they required it.

The Sichuan Model of expanded mental health

An example of these was provided by Tim Sim from PolyU who developed the Sichuan Model of psychosocial social work, which promotes community-based interventions drawing on cultural traditions including dancing, eating, and celebrating their achievements together (Sim and Dominelli, 2017). The Sichuan Model for mental health and wellbeing is based on the following principles:

[S] Step-by-step
[I] Involvement
[C] Contextually respectful
[H] Help people achieve self-help and mutual help
[U] United effort
[A] Add causing
[N] No trouble, no chaos and no harm

The Sichuan Model encouraged local practitioners to learn how to work with their communities during the recovery and reconstruction periods, and engage through the Social Work Station which acted as a one-stop shop for services and support. In these encounters, practitioners and residents built on local, traditional strengths and cultures, promoted collective processes and accountability, and encouraged residents to interact with the local leadership to promote a top-down and bottom-up model of intervention.

Hok Bun Ku, also from PolyU, developed community development projects that provided women with income generation projects based around women's traditional skills such as growing vegetables, cooking, and embroidery, as in Cai Po. Eventually, these community projects facilitated interdisciplinary work as advocated by the green social work paradigm. Thus, for example, architects were drawn into a scheme aimed at exploiting the skills of constructing more beautiful community infrastructures and buildings using traditional knowledge and know-how (Dominelli and Ku, 2017; Ku and Dominelli, 2018). Working with communities in Sichuan, as in other disaster areas underlines the importance of interdisciplinarity across physical and social sciences, arts and humanities, and of locality-based, culturally relevant solutions that involve local residents.

There have been initiatives to control the flow of volunteers into devastated areas. But these have tended to be small-scale and under-resourced. Others sought to use professional associations to channel assistance into disaster-stricken communities. For example, the International Association of Schools of Social Work (IASSW) and the International Federation of Social Workers (IFSW) use their networks, especially their regional ones, to support skilled social workers to offer voluntary assistance. Under the auspices of IASSW, Dominelli (2012a) developed RIPL (Rebuilding People's Lives After Disasters) to assist victim-survivors of the 2004 Indian Ocean Tsunami and the Earthquake Virtual Helpline after the Christchurch and Haiti earthquakes to advise overseas volunteers not to go into affected areas and exhaust local resources to meet their own needs, but leave them for the relief efforts, and offer empowering training and support through the internet (Dominelli, 2012c). However, this ethical dilemma about resourcing being diverted to meet the needs of volunteers is not acknowledged by all volunteers. Some argue that by being present on the ground, they can achieve more than they could by relying on remote technologies.

Conclusions

Earthquakes can happen in many countries, and it is essential that houses are earthquake-proofed and that mitigating actions are taken to prevent deaths and minimise the damage these hazards cause. People cannot rely on formal mechanisms alone to assist them. They must help themselves, including preparing an emergency kit of water, food, medicines, clothing, radio, batteries, and other relevant supplies that cater for the specific needs of individuals. Social workers can help people advocate for earthquake-proof housing and to prepare for emergencies and mitigate the risks they face. Social workers can also engage in reconstruction endeavours when they should coproduce the solutions with local people and other stakeholders, e.g. in China, the model they would use would be top-down, and bottom-up.

The Wenchuan earthquake experience, as the Nepali ones highlighted the importance of collaboration with local people, officials and local organisations to coproduce solutions and new knowledges. Disaster interventions are both serious and local social occasions for fun. Or, to quote Tim Sim, 'life is a dance'.

10 Volcanic eruptions

A local natural hazard with sometimes unanticipated global impact

Introduction

Volcanic eruptions are rarely considered in social work in most European countries, including Italy which has three active ones. Until recently, even social workers in Iceland which has 32 volcanoes in this condition paid limited attention to the topic. Social workers in Europe became aware of volcanic eruptions when Eyjafjallajökull erupted in Iceland in 2010, brought the airline industry to a halt, and delayed people's travel plans for a week. Not flying planes was a precautionary measure aimed at preventing damage to jet engines as ash and silica getting into them might cause them to fail and thereby endanger life. Social workers in other countries had been involved in supporting victim-survivors of volcanic eruptions in e.g. Mexico, Japan, the Philippines, for decades. As most of their work was available in languages other than English, social workers in the UK were rarely aware of their activities.

The NERC (Natural Environment Research Council) and ESRC (Economic and Social Research Council) collaborated through a cutting-edge project called STREEVA (Strengthening Resilience to Volcanic Hazards) to address the lack of knowledge about volcanoes in the social sciences. This focussed on finding new ways of assessing the economic damage that volcanic eruptions could cause. A project funded by the Wellcome Trust and DfID (Department of International Development in the UK), Health Interventions During Volcanic Eruptions (HIVE), considered the health impacts of ashfall following volcanic eruptions and included social work. It undertook research in Mexico, Japan, and Indonesia. The HIVE research project helped to devise guidelines around wearing masks which became very useful in developing the social work guidelines for mask wear under COVID-19. Volcanic eruptions are, like earthquakes, difficult to predict, so preparations usually take the form of stockpiling masks. These must be made of the correct filtration material and fitted properly to prevent small particulate matter (PM) of 2.5 PM from entering the nose and mouth. In this chapter, I consider volcanic

DOI: 10.4324/9781003105824-12

eruptions and their impact upon societies that have found ways of accommodating to life in the shadow of a volcano and use case examples to explore such situations. I also consider social work interventions in the case of the volcano in Montserrat.

Volcanic formation and eruptions

Volcanoes form when magma reaches the Earth's surface, causing eruptions of lava and ash and can kill people, damage human health, and destroy parts of the environment. They can also provide minerals to improve soil fertility. Volcanoes can be active, dormant, or extinct, depending on the state of the magma in the chamber at the bottom of the volcano. An active volcano will have a history of recent eruptions and will have a strong likelihood of erupting again, e.g. Mauna Loa in Hawaii or Sakurajima in Japan which are currently spewing out ash. Dormant volcanoes have a very long period of inactivity but could erupt at some point in the future, e.g. Mount Kilimanjaro in Tanzania on the African continent. Extinct volcanoes have an extensive period of inactivity – usually over 10,000 years and are not likely to erupt in the future. Ben Nevis in Scotland is an example of an extinct volcano. Volcanoes that erupt only once are called monogenetic while those that erupt multiple times are termed polygenetic. The British Geological Survey (BGS) claims that the magma that rises to the Earth's surface as lava forms different types of volcanoes. The type depends on:

- The magma's viscosity, i.e. its 'stickiness'.
- The amount of gas contained within it.
- The mineral composition of the magma.
- The way in which magma reaches the surface.

There are four main categories of volcanoes used to describe volcanic landform types:

- *Cinder cone volcano* which is the simplest and smallest type of volcano and usually has a symmetrical cone rising up to 1200 ft.
- *Composite or stratovolcanoes* are tall volcanoes that have steep sides and a cone shape that is formed by layers of ash and lava flows. They are symmetrical volcanoes that typically rise to 8000 ft although some reach 10,000 ft and are illustrated by some of the most famous mountains in the world, e.g. Mount Fuji in Japan. Their eruptions are more likely to involve pyroclastic flows rather than the slower lava flows because these give off hot gases, ash, lava, and pumice alongside stiff, slow-moving lava when they erupt. They may also be

accompanied by deadly mudflows which are termed 'lahars' as has occurred on Mount Fuji.

- *Shield volcanoes* which have a broad structure, are often 20 times wider than their height. Such volcanoes can be massive. It can look like a warrior's shield. This is typically formed by the eruption of highly fluid lava that is less viscous than that of a composite or stratovolcano and so travels farther and becomes thinner the further it travels. Shield volcanoes, formed by fluid, basaltic lava flows, are among the largest active volcanoes and can rise above 9 kilometres above the sea floor as occurs around the island of Hawaii. There, the shield volcanoes Mauna Kea and Mauna Loa are among the largest in the world.
- *Lava dome volcano* is a small volcano which has a circular dome shape and rises up to 330 ft and usually results from the slow extrusion of viscous lava from a volcano which occurs following the collapse of the summit of the composite volcano which then forms a depression wherein magma begins to ooze out. The lava that forms this mound is very viscous and cannot flow easily and so it accumulates near the vent. A lava dome volcano can be found in the crater created on Mount St Helens which began erupting on 18 May 1980.

Some authors mention other types of volcanoes besides those listed above:

- *Maar* which is a volcanic crater that has the crater lying below the level of the surrounding ground and is encircled by a low pyroclastic cone. It is created when groundwater or permafrost hit hot lava or magma and causes an explosion. Maars often have a lake in the crater.
- *Tuff ring* which is a small volcanic pyroclastic cone that rises above the ground and surrounds a shallow crater (maar) that is formed by explosions caused when hot magma reaches cold groundwater. The ensuing explosion shoots fragments of bedrock, tephra, and ash from the crater.
- *Caldera* which is formed by the depression left by an eruption that causes a wide area of the ground surface to collapse. The Yellowstone Caldera is technically a 'supervolcano'. A 'supervolcano' involves an eruption of magnitude 8 on the Volcano Explosivity Index. This indicates an eruption of more than 1,000 cubic kilometres of magma. The last eruption of the Yellowstone Caldera occurred over 640,000 years ago. It has been estimated to have been 2,500 times larger than the eruption of Mt. St. Helens in Washington State which occurred on 18 May 1980 in the USA. Also, the Yellowstone Caldera eruption collapsed the supervolcano upon itself. This formed an enormous sunken crater or caldera that has an area of approximately

1,500 square miles. The magmatic heat of that eruption remains to power Yellowstone National Park's geysers, hot springs, fumaroles, and mud pots.

Other authors refer to fissure volcanoes and monogenetic volcanic fields. These are not included in the above categorisation because the individual vents and volcanoes in monogenetic fields each erupt only once. However, the fields themselves are polygenetic as they may experience multiple eruptions. Fissure volcanoes are essentially neither constructional nor excavational because they do not build edifices, experience subsidence, or have explosive eruptions that form craters.

The BGS argues that there are only two significant types of volcanoes, the stratovolcano and the shield volcano. However, the BGS accepts that there are many different volcanic features that can be formed when magma erupts to include cinder cones and/or lava domes. Moreover, the BGS adds that the different processes that shape volcanoes can account for variations in these two basic types of volcanoes.

There are two volcanic landform types: *constructional* and *excavational*. Constructional volcanoes are created by eruptions that build high volcanic edifices, e.g. cinder cones, composite volcanoes, and shield volcanoes. Excavational volcanoes have negative relief (below the general land surface). These are formed through either violent blasts or from collapses over a magma chamber. Maars, tuff rings, and calderas are excavational.

Lava flows are emitted by erupting volcanoes. There are various types of lava flows: mafic, andesite and dacite. Which one it is depends on its silica and mineral content. One type is called mafic because it is dark in colour and is composed of iron and magnesium. It produces basalt. Lavas of andesitic or intermediate composition form a block lava flow. These have tops made of loose rubble with fragments that are more regular, having a polygon shape with reasonably smooth sides. If there is more silica in these flows, then the lava is more fragmented than a block flow. Dacite lavas are viscous and tend to form thick blocky lava flows or steep-sided piles of lava which can form lava domes. Dacitic magmas have explosive eruptions in which ash and pumice are ejected abundantly. A basaltic lava flow has the lowest silica content of these three types. Thus, it has low viscosity or resistance to flow. This means that it can move quickly and easily away from a vent to a distance of up to 20 kilometres. Andesite lava flows are viscous and thick. They arise from stratovolcanoes by forming small-volume flows that advance short distances down the sides of a volcano. A dacitic flow occurs when a young oceanic crust slides under a thick felsic continental plate during the subduction process. This alters the oceanic crust hydrothermally so that it gains quartz and sodium in its composition.

Active volcanoes emit a mixture of gases, vapours, aerosols, tephra, and particulate matter including ash which contains a variety of potentially toxic elements (Covey et al., 2021). These can vary substantially depending on the eruption (Hillman et al., 2012, Hillman et al., 2013; Doocy et al., 2013) and could adversely impact human wellbeing and health. Volcanic ash is known to exacerbate acute respiratory conditions including asthma and bronchitis (Baxter et al., 1983). However, there is limited knowledge about the impact of volcanic emissions on human health (Horwell and Baxter, 2006), even though 9 percent of the world's population lives within 100 kilometres of an historically active volcano (Auker et al., 2013).

Measuring volcanic eruptions

Volcanic eruptions can produce a pyroclastic flow which is a fluidised mixture of hot rock fragments and gases, and entrapped air that moves at high speed in thick, grey-to-black, turbulent clouds that stick close to the ground while flowing along with enormous destructive power. These eruptions are measured by the Volcanic Explosivity Index (VEI). It is a scale that describes the size of explosive volcanic eruptions based on magnitude and intensity. The numerical scale ranges from 0 to 8 and it is a logarithmic scale. It can be considered similar to the Richter scale used to measure the magnitude or size of an earthquake.

There are six types of volcanic eruptions:

- *Icelandic.* An Icelandic eruption has molten basaltic lava that flows from long, parallel fissures and can form lava plateaus.
- *Hawaiian.* A Hawaiian volcanic eruption occurs when lava flows from a volcanic vent in a relatively gentle, low-level eruption with basaltic magmas. These are of low viscosity, have a low content of gases, and a high temperature at the vent. Very small amounts of volcanic ash are produced. This type of eruption occurs most often at hotspot volcanoes, e.g. Kīlauea on Hawai'i's Big Island as Hawai'i Island is known.
- *Strombolian.* A Strombolian eruption has relatively mild blasts, often with a Volcanic Explosivity Index of between 1 and 2 which release incandescent cinders, lapilli, and lava bombs, to a height of up to several hundred metres. In these eruptions, gas within the volcano forms bubbles called 'slugs'. When these grow large enough, they rise through the magma column, and once they reach its top, the lower air pressure causes the slugs to burst and throw magma into the air.
- *Vulcanian.* A vulcanian eruption has a dense cloud of ash-laden gas exploding from a volcanic crater and rising high above the peak of a stratovolcanic volcano. They usually commence with

phreatomagmatic eruptions which can be extremely noisy due to the rising magma heating water in the ground.

- *Peléan.* A Peléan eruption occurs when viscous magma, usually of the rhyolitic or andesitic type, explodes to generate pyroclastic flows or dense mixtures of hot volcanic fragments and gas. It has some similarities with Vulcanian eruptions. A Peléan eruption features a glowing avalanche of hot volcanic ash, or pyroclastic flow, and forms lava domes and pumice cones.

- *Plinian.* A Plinian eruption is an extremely explosive eruption that involves the exsolution of magmatic volatiles in the volcano's channel. This causes a disruption to and an explosive ejection of pyroclastic material in an eruption column that can continue for hours or days above the volcano. The ash columns it creates can extend many miles into the stratosphere and spread out in an umbrella shape, as occurred when Mount Vesuvius erupted in Italy in 79 AD. The strongest of these eruptions is called 'Ultra Plinian'. Such extremely explosive eruptions have a VEI of 8. One of these occurred at Lake Toba, Sumatra, Indonesia about 74,000 years ago. This spewed out 2800 times more material than Mount St. Helens in 1980. These large eruptions produce widespread deposits of fallout ash. Eruption columns may also collapse due to their density to form thick pyroclastic flows.

Volcanic eruption case example: Montserrat

The Small Island Developing States (SIDS) of the Caribbean are among the world's most vulnerable regions due to the worsening impacts of climate change and extreme weather events. SIDS are also at frequent risk of volcanic events, such as the 1995 eruption of the Soufrière Hills Volcano in Montserrat after a period of being dormant. Montserrat is disaster-prone place which has earthquakes, hurricanes, and volcanic hazards endemic to it. Finding new ways to respond to ongoing and future disasters including those involving volcanoes and to improve communities' resilience is urgently needed to protect the vulnerable countries of the Caribbean. I consider the volcanic eruption in Montserrat at length below.

Montserrat, a British Protectorate, is one of the UK's overseas territories comprised of a small Caribbean Island 11 miles long and 7 miles wide. The island of Montserrat lies southwest of Antigua in the Caribbean and north of Venezuela. Montserrat is a largely undeveloped island called the 'Emerald Isle' due to its lush vegetation. It had a population of 11,000 before the volcanic eruption of 1995, and around 5,000 people now living there. In 1995, Montserrat had a few towns and one main city, the capital called Plymouth. The capital was covered by the volcanic debris and is currently uninhabitable. Montserrat is located on the boundary between the Caribbean and North American tectonic plates. This is a destructive plate boundary, and the Soufrière Hills volcano is composite one.

Montserrat lies on a destructive plate margin meaning that the volcano lies at the boundary between an oceanic and a continental plate. It is one in a chain of islands known as the Lesser Antilles that form an arc to the west of the convergent part of the plate boundary that separates the Caribbean plate from the North American one. These two plates will converge due to descending branches of active convection cell currents in the asthenosphere. As these two plates merge the oceanic plate is forced down or sub-ducted under the continental plate because it is denser (3 g/cm^3) than the continental crust. As it is forced down, pressure increases, and this triggers earthquakes at a range of depths along the Benioff Zone, or the place where the friction generated by the colliding tectonic plates, creates intermediate and deep earthquakes. At the same time, heat produced by friction melts the descending crust to form molten magma. This magma is then forced upwards and has created the Chances Peak on the Soufrière Hills. Thus, the Soufrière Hills have formed at the convergent plate boundary where the Atlantic Plate is subducting under the Caribbean plate. A convergent plate boundary is where deformation occurs when two (or more) tectonic plates in the lithosphere collide as they move toward each other.

The movement of plate tectonics like these is the product of the rise and fall of convection cell material in the asthenosphere. The convection cells in the asthenosphere move upward until they reach the bottom of the lithosphere. Here, they move laterally. This lateral motion forces the lithosphere to split and for one part of the tectonic plates to move away from another nearby. Thus, convection currents develop within the asthenosphere and push magma upwards through volcanic vents and spreading centres to form new crust. The movement of these convection currents add stress to the lithosphere lying above them, and as the surface crust cracks, an earthquake can occur.

In the Chances Peak, after lying dormant for 300 years, the volcano began to act. The first earthquake appeared in 1992. Then, on 18 July 1995, the volcano commenced to release warning signs of an eruption before erupting. These warnings were mainly small earthquakes and eruptions of dust and ash. Once Chances Peak had awoken, it continued with significant activity for five years, with the most intense eruption occurring during 1997. Prior to the 1997 disaster, the inhabitants of Montserrat enjoyed a relatively high standard of living. The ensuing volcanic eruptions and lahars (mudflows) destroyed large areas of Montserrat including the capital, Plymouth which was obliterated under layers of ash and mud 20 metres high. Many homes and buildings were destroyed, including the only hospital, airport, seaport, and many roads. Much of damage occurred in the south of the island which became uninhabitable and was evacuated. People were evacuated to the north of the island or went overseas. An exclusion zone, set up in the regions affected, prevented people from living in the southern part of the island.

An immediate effect of the 1995 eruption was that two thirds of the island became covered in ash making it impossible to get aid to people in need as many roads became impassable. The sole airport was closed, making getting aid into the country, even from overseas, extremely difficult. The ash also polluted the air. This increased breathing difficulties, cardiovascular diseases, and respiratory illness. About 50 per cent of the population were evacuated to the north of the island into temporary shelters. However, these habitations were over-crowded, the sanitation was poor, and the food provided was inadequate. Moreover, further damage occurred through the destruction of vegetation by acid rain, a feature which took many years to decrease. Besides the decline in agriculture, acid rain polluted lakes and rivers and thus made animal life almost impossible. Additionally, the departure of more than half of Montserrat's population made the island's recovery even more problematic.

During this period of activity, the violence of the eruptions varied. In 1996, the volcanic eruptions became increasingly violent, and the levels of damage rose. Earthquakes continued to occur in three epicentre zones. One was beneath the Soufrière Hills volcano, another lay in the ridge running to the north-east, and another was located beneath St George's Hill, about 5 kilometres (3.1 miles) to the north-west. As large eruptions continued into 1997, the dome collapsed and the large pyroclastic flows that resulted affected much of Monserrat. The eruption on 25 June 1997 created a pyroclastic flow that travelled down Mosquito Ghaut. This powerful pyroclastic surge could not be restrained by the ghaut and flowed out of it. Consequently, 19 people who had been officially evacuated to the Streatham village area were killed. A number of other people experienced severe burns. Many of these people had remained behind to look after their crops.

Many of those displaced in 1995 were evacuated to the north of the island, some went to neighbouring islands, and others escaped to the UK. Although the UK offered £2,500 for relocation purposes, this was condemned as insufficient because four times that amount was calculated as necessary. The British government also donated £41 million to help the island recover and replace destroyed industries. Another £24,000 was given to individual families to help them recover financially and begin their lives anew. Also, thousands of new homes were to be built for the residents remaining on the island. Despite this assistance, riots broke out among the islanders that stayed behind because the UK was accused of not helping them enough.

Volcanic activity has continued since 1997, albeit at reduced levels. For instance, another volcanic event lasted from 12 to 14 July 2003. This caused parts of the volcanic dome to collapse and formed huge pyroclastic flows (fast-moving clouds of hot ash and rock) that spread into the ocean for 2 kilometres. The forest fires and tsunamis caused by the pyroclastic flows, destroyed more farmland, schools, hospitals and endangered more people. The devastation caused by the pyroclastic flows occurring in Montserrat led to the evacuation of around two-thirds of the island's small population of 11,000. Food, clothing, and shelter were initially virtually impossible to obtain, and this lengthy period of continuous volcanic activity made rebuilding the society difficult. This challenged social workers attempting to deliver aid and rebuild communities.

Relief and recovery efforts, including the reconstruction of the built infrastructure, occurred at a snail's pace. For example, the new airport was not opened until 2005. Residents were moved to temporary shelters on more than one occasion before permanent housing was built in the north of the island. In the meantime, inhabitants had been given the option of relocating to other Caribbean islands or the UK. In 1998, the British government granted the people of Montserrat full residency rights in the United Kingdom, allowing them to migrate if they chose. Those that came were granted British citizenship in 2002. Yet, people have returned to the island recently. Returnees from the UK, and others have migrated from nearby islands due to the low cost of living prevailing in Montserrat. As a result, despite existing deprivations, especially in the form of housing shortages, 5000 people are now living on the island.

Many people who had left the island earlier, have returned, having interpreted a pause in the volcano's activities as a sign of it being safe to do so. However, none of this history provides a basis for predicting what will happen in future. Thus, people returning run the risk of there being more violent eruptions in the near future. A volcanic observatory has been built to monitor the volcano, and this may provide early warnings that could ensure that the island's residents can be evacuated safely should another volcanic event arise. The last large eruption occurred in January 2009. Consequently, life on the island has begun to assume a degree of normalcy. New roads and a new airport have been built, and various health and social services facilities in the north of the island have been expanded. Moreover, the presence of the volcano has spurred a growth in tourism.

Social work interventions in volcanic disasters

Social work interventions are an important part of the relief and recovery stage of the disasters. As Montserrat lacked sufficient numbers of locally trained social workers, many practitioners from other parts of the Caribbean came to help. They were crucial in undertaking needs assessments, determining resource availability, and supporting people, using crisis intervention methods and strengths-based approaches. These responses were essential in enabling people to overcome the negative impact of this calamity. Initially, these practitioners focused primarily on practical emergency responses including meeting practical needs such as water, food, clothing, shelter, and medicines. The social workers conducted needs and resource assessments which enabled them to respond to practical concerns. They also used these assessments to identify and respond to child protection issues, loss, grief and bereavement, and provide counselling as required.

Additionally, social workers found that long-term losses included feelings of insecurity, lack of safety, feelings of unbelonging, insecure incomes, separation from family and neighbours, poor or no housing, and not identifying with the places to which they had been relocated. Loss of culture and uncertainty about what it means to be a Montserratian persist among both those who stayed and those who migrated (King and Carmichael, 2007). Insecurity can also exacerbate feelings of isolation and poor mental health which social workers work with to facilitate access to services and wellbeing.

Although longer-term issues such as the provision of housing and employment opportunities were evident, social workers had no such resources available to meet such needs, and some victim-survivors chose to relocate to the UK. By conducting realistic reappraisals of the living situations and environments of the victim-survivors, social workers used their skills to draw upon existing individual and group strengths and promote their problem-solving skills. Also, by identifying protective factors, social workers were able to develop and enhance self-efficacy and self-esteem. This enabled these practitioners to work on overcoming the debilitating effects of grief upon victim-survivors, build on existing strengths and help them to heal.

Additionally, there were specific features of intervening in the specifics of Montserrat's culture that had to be incorporated into their practice. This included drawing upon their religious inclinations and the importance of spirituality in their daily lives. One of these insights was the implications of many residents living in a matriarchal society and their being able to rely on their own individual resources and inner strengths as well as other reliable sources of support such as family, friends, neighbours, and peer groups. Social capital and networking opportunities, e.g. with church groups, were also sources of support. These offered material resources, friendships, and a shared feeling of 'being in it together' with others. With such support, most people adapted quickly to their new environment. However, a few developed post-traumatic stress disorders (PTSDs) and needed specific mental health interventions which were not always available locally. Also, recognition of cultural specificities, a strength-based approach and a solution-focused strategy that considered the situation holistically meant that social workers were able to showcase peoples' resilience in adverse circumstances. Most residents wanted to return to 'normal', i.e. their previous conditions, and social workers found this an effective strategy in helping residents to adapt to the situation and plan for a new future. To achieve these goals, practitioners also drew upon their knowledge of systems theories at the micro-, meso- and macro- levels, and the transdisciplinarity of their work to link the local knowledges of the inhabitants to those of the 'social' and 'natural' scientists. Doing disaster work requires social workers to be trained in how to work in transdisciplinary teams and deal with a range of diverse disasters, of which volcanic eruptions are one. But disasters can also be complex, and volcanic eruptions are only one part of the disaster journey of the victim-survivors. Additionally, social workers have highlighted the impact of their work on their own psyche, and how they have needed supervision and support to carry out their duties and avoid poor mental health themselves.

Social workers have had to acquire an understanding of the hazards associated with volcanic eruptions because they are traditionally unfamiliar with these. A key one of these is that ashfall can affect health, especially asthma and eye irritation (Horwell et al., 2018; Covey et al., 2021). Moreover, social workers had to respond to residents' long-term purposes and goals. Here, institutional support to address long-term recovery and structural problems were crucial in devising income generation schemes, constructing schools and health services, creating community-based resources and infrastructures, and enabling people to return to the island, albeit to its northern parts. Collective activities and community-initiated income generation schemes which social workers supported enabled local residents to work together to reach their development goals. Those residents who relocated to the UK did better in terms of education, housing, and jobs, because more opportunities were available for them to obtain these resources than was the case for those who remained on the island.

Social workers also became involved in consciousness-raising activities to help residents learn what to do in the event of being caught in a future volcanic eruption. Their advice included:

- Staying indoors until the ash settles unless the roof is in danger of collapsing.
- Remaining indoors and closing or covering windows, doors, and other openings wherein ash and gas may enter.
- Evacuating areas as recommended by the authorities.
- Staying clear of lava, mud flows, flying rocks and debris.
- Changing into long-sleeved shirts and long pants before leaving your dwelling, using goggles or eyeglasses, not contact lenses once outside.

- Wearing an emergency mask outdoors or covering your face with a damp cloth to avoid inhaling dangerous particles in the ash. If the emission contains toxic gases, use a gas mask.
- Staying away from areas downwind from the volcano to avoid volcanic ash.

Exercise – Addressing the impact of masculinity on victim-survivors

NGOs tend to focus on empowering women when they intervene post-disasters. Very few NGOs orient their work to helping men re-establish their livelihoods and come to terms with their loss and the impact of this on their masculinity, especially its injunctions to be the provider for and the protector of the family (Dominelli, 2020).

Imagine you have arrived in an area devastated by a volcanic eruption that has destroyed the fishing village near the beach a few kilometres away from the volcano. All the houses, cars, buildings were all destroyed, leaving the villagers bereft. No one knew what to do to rebuild or where they would obtain the resources to do so. Meanwhile, relations between villagers and different members of a ruling family were deteriorating due to lack of action in restoring 'normalcy'. Some women complained about increased levels of both domestic and sexual violence against them, mainly by men that they either knew or were related to.

Groupwork discussion

Your small NGO has some funds to establish projects, mainly to empower women and ensure they have income generation schemes. You begin to set one up when a delegation of villagers comes to your temporary office. They want you to establish an income generation scheme for about 100 men ranging in ages from 25 to 70. You have funds for 3 projects to support 30 women in all age groups.

Working in a small group, discuss how you would respond to this request and how you would resolve both ethical and resource conundrums. Ensure that you choose someone to take notes of the discussion and someone to report back to the plenary group. Ensure that your discussion covers the following areas:

- The state of relationships between men and women.
- Securing additional resources for the community.
- Responding to individual and collective trauma related to their losses.
- Involvement in governance structures.

Resource scarcity can create tensions between different groups both requiring resources and support. Consulting with local people and organisations and involving them in dealing with scarcity issues including equitable distribution of available resources, seeking resources from elsewhere and donor intentions may be a useful way in which to address some of the conundrums posed and the principles to be used in resolving them (Kleinman, 1999; Cagney et al., 2016).

Conclusions

The volcano in Monserrat is of an andesitic type and the current pattern of activity includes periods of dome growth, punctuated by brief episodes of dome collapse which has resulted in pyroclastic flows, ash venting, and explosive eruptions. Earthquakes continued to occur in three epicentre zones underneath the Soufrière Hills volcano. These include those occurring in the ridge running to the north-east, beneath St George's Hill, and about 5 kilometres (3.1 miles) to the north-west.

The eruption that began on 18 July 1995 was the first sign of activity in Monserrat since the nineteenth century. When pyroclastic flows and mudflows began occurring regularly, the capital, Plymouth, was evacuated, and a few weeks later a pyroclastic flow covered the city in several metres of debris. Pyroclastic flows on the Soufrière Hills were caused by andesite lava which was so thick it was unable to flow and thus built up into a huge lava dome. When parts of the lava dome became unstable this collapsed forming hot, fast-moving avalanches of lava blocks, gas, and dust. On 25 June 1997 a pyroclastic surge that travelled down Mosquito Ghaut spilled out of it, killing 19 people who had been evacuated to Streatham Village area; other residents suffered severe burns. The island's airport, directly in the path of the main pyroclastic flow, was destroyed, along with Montserrat's tourism industry. The damaged transportation and communication systems adversely impacted the economy and delivery of aid.

The Montserrat Volcano Observatory (MVO), set up to monitor the volcano, was to predict any future eruptions. Scientists have encouraged a slower pace of development in the island as they anticipate another eruption occurring in the twenty-first century. This may have the potential to end human habitation on the entire island, and thus waste any investment in re-establishing its economy and built infrastructures. A risk map was formulated to identify locations where it was safe to live. This demonstrated that the entire southern half of the island is uninhabitable and would be at serious risk if new eruptions were to occur. The monitoring of the volcano by the MVO is intended to facilitate for early warnings leading to timely evacuations and supportive interventions.

The destruction in Montserrat was wide-ranging because the eruption destroyed its two key industries: tourism and farming. The ash that covered the fields killed the crops and meant a year of failed harvests. This cut-off income for many families relying on agriculture. Tourism also crashed for years, and this undermined the incomes of a further swathe of people. The main visitors to arrive were aboard cruise ships coming to look at the famous volcano. These liners commenced the regeneration of tourism.

With regard to social workers, the situation was dire, but social workers, many who came from overseas, rose to the challenge. Nonetheless, the shortage of social workers meant that not everyone who needed help could be fully supported. This shortage created an obstacle for those requiring assistance in reaching decisions about the new directions their lives had to travel. Moreover, the lack of social work training on disaster interventions and sustainable development resulted in social workers having to learn on the spot. The absence of training could delay their speedy and effective engagement with and support for victim-survivors. A range of social work support was needed to respond to men's needs, given their loss of roles as economic providers, family protectors, lack of access to land and employment opportunities. These realities destabilised men's capacity to cope and encouraged unacceptable behaviour that adversely affected women and children, especially those related to them as domestic violence increased. Finally, inadequate post-disaster planning policies at national level meant that the resources necessary for social workers to do their work were unavailable and thereby disrupted both recovery interventions and reconstruction endeavours.

11 Financial disasters

Introduction

Financial crises are no strangers to humanity. There are the domestic financial crises that are familiar to many households as they struggle to make ends meet so that expenditures and incomes are roughly in alignment to avoid sinking into debt. The opposite is saving money so that incomes are higher than the money that is spent. Then there are institutional failures, namely those involving banks and other financial institutions in which the liquidity and assets necessary to support their banking activities are absent. Institutional failures lead to collective crises which can endanger the global financial system as occurred during recessions such as those that took place in the 1930s and the financial crisis of 2007–8. The latter one featured the instability of financial markets based on trade that was not underpinned by assets capable of sustaining those exchanges.

The Wall Street Crash of 1929 precipitated the Great Depression of 1929–1939. This is considered the worst financial disaster of the twentieth century (Friedman and Schwartz, 1963). During it, 15 million Americans were unemployed and most American banks failed. This economic downturn did not end until President Franklin Delano Roosevelt initiated the New Deal to promote economic investment and employment under the auspices of a state-driven public sector to power an economic revival that spread into the private sector. The advent of the Second World War enabled the economy to take off on a war footing.

A financial crisis can be defined as a condition in which the value of assets suddenly drops, undermines trust in financial institutions, and can cause a refusal to invest in government bonds or a stampede to withdraw money from the banks. A 'run on the banks' is a crisis response to financial breakdown, as people decide the money in their pockets is safer than leaving their funds in an institution that is going bankrupt as occurred to Northern Rock in the UK in 2007. In this chapter, I consider the financial crisis of 2007–2008, its implications for the world economy

DOI: 10.4324/9781003105824-13

and national economies like the UK within it. The impact of collapsing financial institutions on supply chains, people, public welfare, and social services institutions, combined with tax increases to bail out the banks and austerity initiatives that cut deep into peoples' lives to control public expenditures. These were the key policies Western politicians favoured to solve the crisis. These policies affected those on low incomes most and led to greater reliance on philanthropic and charitable impulses (Engelbrecht, 2011). These encouraged the growing use of food banks including in countries like the UK where the welfare state was to have eliminated the need for them (Beveridge, 1942).

I will also consider the exacerbated growth of structural inequalities that has resulted in poor, unemployed, and low-income working people being 'left behind' (UN, 2016) while the number of billionaires rose substantially (Oxfam, 2016). Ironically, at the time of writing, in the second half of 2022, another financial crisis fuelled by Putin's War Against Ukraine loomed. This crisis has caused a deterioration in the capacity of the financial systems in Western economies to prevent a cost-of-living crisis. This has included considerable growth in inflation rates, high interest charges, exorbitant rises in energy prices for consumers and food shortages globally. I update this with the externally driven economic crisis that led to a cost-of-living crisis in 2022 that has devastated the lives of marginalised and poor people. However, high levels of inflation, mortgage interest hikes, and rises in energy and food costs have also touched the lives of middle-class people, especially professionals that have begun to demand an end to stagnating salaries and worsening working conditions.

I then consider what social workers can do to cushion the impact of financial calamities. I conclude that financial crises disrupt the lives of the poorest people most, but they also carry horrendous implications for the environment as addressing climate change gets relegated to a tomorrow that may never come. Thus, the 2022 financial crisis has subjected the commitment to 'net zero' emissions by 2050 to fall by the wayside, leaving the courageous people of the SIDS (small island developing states) battling to keep their heads above the crashing ocean waves.

The financial crisis of 2007–2008

Internationalisation of social problems

Globalisation has increased economic and commercialised cultural integration both within and across countries, making people and events interdependent. This movement has led to the internationalisation of social problems, especially poverty, migration, climate change, humanitarian aid, people trafficking, criminal gangs pushing criminal activities like the arms trade, drug trade, and armed conflict. International social problems reveal the interdependencies and interactions between the local and the global spheres, with travel going in both directions, although either the local or the global can dominate in specific circumstances.

Social workers are usually called upon to deal with international social problems at the local level. Responses may be extensive, and wide-reaching. Kokaliari (2016) describes the impact of the financial crisis in Greece. She argues that stress, depression, and mental ill health accompanied the impact of austerity policies on daily life and placed greater demands on service provision when their funding was declining. Ioakimidis et al. (2014) make similar points for Greece, Spain and Portugal, but argue that social workers in southern Europe, leading precarious existences themselves, became determined to establish radical forms of practice to resist the imposition of the new managerialism and monetarist practices on the profession.

Social workers are familiar with global social problems such as international adoptions as a legal response to finding children substitute families and feel comfortable addressing these. Although familiar, these issues may produce unpredictable challenges accompanying them. For example, Americans returned adopted Russian children when they did not conform to their stereotypes of the perfect adopted child. Addressing the complexities of a financial crisis challenged social workers in different respects because the nation-state which often employed them was responsible for the austerity policies creating mayhem in many lives among poor and disenfranchised populations. Social workers may experience ethical dilemmas about how to respond to unexpected crises, especially if hampered by serious resource shortages. Additionally, social workers often lack the language, cultural skills and knowledge of external factors affecting the local people that they are helping. Relying on interpreters can create additional difficulties around interpretation of vernacular phrases and cultural diversity within the local populace. Linguistic gaps are relevant in disaster scenarios because these may impair practitioners' capacities to respond appropriately. Financial crises also have a jargon that excludes those not used to that terminology. Learning about a local area requires external social workers to form good local partnerships with people and organisations located in the area (Dominelli and Vickers, 2014). Linking the local and the global can complicate the finding of solutions to problems. This requires practitioners to become aware of the competing pressures to be resolved when trying to bring people together in agreed activities.

Solutions that are rooted solely in the locality usually fail to tackle the source of those problems that are affected by the global context. This is exemplified by the increases in energy prices during 2022. Geopolitical forces are driving this outcome and require a solution at the international level. Yet, social workers can collect data that evidences the hardship and suffering endured by those 'left behind' (UN, 2016). Social workers can address internationalised issues more effectively when the local and global are better linked, as is apparent in internationalised social problems like international adoptions. Despite the complications of family-based dynamics in responding to internationalised social problems like international adoptions, social workers are well-placed to address these given their understanding of organisations, legislation, and action traditions. There is a legal and procedural framework and a practice framework to guide their actions in this. But equivalent comforting practice wisdoms are absent in addressing financial crisis at the structural level, and so practice focuses on the micro-level of maximising access to benefits, food banks and charitable donations.

Practitioners feel less confident in responding to more recent internationalised social problems such as climate change and financial crises. They have not been trained to intervene in such arenas and are reluctant to accept that it is their duty to do so. The 2007 financial crisis challenged social workers to respond to a global problem that was experienced harshly at the local level, especially by those 'left behind' globally (UN, 2016). Moreover, it presented a type of disaster for which social workers had received no training. Thus, they lacked clarity about how to comment upon Lehman Brothers and the Royal Bank of Scotland, each being 'a bank too big to fail'. Yet, they had to deal with the aftermath of their bankruptcy, especially the social calamities following on the heal of austerity policies and cuts in public services as people began to experience hardship and lacked the material resources whereby to transcend their financial predicament.

A globalised economy

The 2007 banking crisis began as a subprime mortgage crisis in the US, which drew upon the unregulated use of derivatives. A derivative is a financial instrument or contract that obtains its value from an underlying asset. It aims to mitigate risk for one party by passing it on to another willing to assume it. There are four key types of derivatives: futures, options, forwards, and swaps. There were early warning signs indicating a possible breakdown in these arrangements, but these were ignored.

The 2008 financial crisis began in August 2008 and climaxed in November 2008 as a series of banks were nationalised across North

America and Europe. This banking crises was the largest one to take place since the recession of 1929–1933. This chapter considers the build-up to the crisis, the role of low interest rates in stimulating an asset price bubble. This asset price bubble was stoked by financial innovation and increases in lending through new financial products that had not been tested. Ultimately, this bubble burst, and initiated disastrous consequences for those residents who had borrowed money, mainly to purchase houses. This largescale failure subsequently led to significant improvements in the regulatory structures of the financial sector.

When meltdown occurred, the U.S. Treasury and Federal Reserve Bank had to mobilise their resources to prevent an economic collapse that would deleteriously impact the entire world. This response illustrates how a failure in the private sector demands public sector action to protect private sector interests.

The entry of China into the global market was another contributory factor to the financial crisis. It sought to accumulate current account surpluses and foreign exchange reserves, while maintaining artificially low exchange rates and a positive saving investment balance in that country. However, global interest rates fell (Barrell and Davis, 2008). Low interest rates demanded innovations to produce higher rates of return. This encouraged market opacity and higher risk through higher credit risks embedded in structured products and sub-prime loans. Banks failed to monitor loans, hold sufficient liquid assets, or cover liabilities adequately. Household borrowing rose rapidly, as did house prices because the commodification of housing for the purposes of accumulating capital grew apace. Market instability combined with falling house prices, reduced lending opportunities, and this led to various banks or other lending institutions including building societies failing. These were: Northern Rock in 2007 in the UK; and in 2008, Bear Stearns, IndyMac, Fanny Mae and Freddy Mac. Barrell and Davis (2008: 10) argue that these failures led to a process of deleveraging as financial institutions attempted to reduce exposure to high-risk sectors, sell assets or reduce asset growth, limit dependency on unstable wholesale funding, and rebuild capital adequacy. However, the situation became worse in September when Lehman Brothers went bankrupt. Other banks followed suit as trust in the market disappeared, and people could not see how, without state intervention, this financial nightmare would end. In the UK as major banks including HBS, RSB, Lloyds and others failed. The British government rescued these by basically nationalising (temporarily) the banking sector for it to remain solvent (Mor, 2018). These actions also ensured the stability of the economy and the supply chains serving it and thereby enabling daily life to continue.

Exercise – Raising taxes to save the economy

Thomas was a local politician who was worried about the people he represented on his local council because he could see the tragedies unfolding in so many of the families living within his political jurisdiction. As he walked the empty streets one night, he saw that very few lights were on, even though it was only 20:00. He saw some young people huddled in doorways trying to keep warm. He went over to talk to them. He recognised a couple of them and began to speak to them, asking them a few questions. They told him they were bored, all the youth clubs were shut, their homes were cold, and their parents were depressed, so they went out after having a frugal meal. They told him their parents were 'skint' (lacked money) as they were struggling to pay the increases in council taxes, income taxes, energy, food, and the rent. They also told him that often their parents drank hot water with nothing it, pretending their dinner was a lovely broth.

Thomas left them feeling very perturbed. He ran into Beverley as he was walking down the High Street. She was a youth worker, and he spoke to her about what the young people had said. She said their story was replicated across the town. She was doing the 'soup' rounds and had raised the funds to buy the food to make the soup and was using her own car to distribute it to those places where she knew hungry, young people gathered. She promised Thomas that she would give the group he saw a few extra bowls to take to their parents. However, she complained that this was like sticking a plaster over a gaping wound. She urged him to take the issue up with his fellow councillors and then escalate the issue to the higher levels of government. She said it was totally unacceptable that people who had very little were baling out banks through reduced services and taxation. He simply had to start speaking out. She assured him that were he to do so, there would be many others who would join his anti-poverty campaign.

Discussion

Working in small groups, choose a chair and notetaker to report to the plenary session. In your discussion, cover the following areas:

- Raising the issue of poverty and suffering at all levels of government.
- Leisure provisions for young people.

- Supporting families to meet their energy, food, and shelter bills.
- Holding multinational firms accountable and convincing them to invest in local communities.
- Ensuring that both local and national levels of government passed policies that focused on ensuring that better off residents paid high enough taxes to keep local services running and finding resources to feed every child in the community a nutritious, balanced meal three times a day.
- Attracting allies to join Thomas in his anti-poverty campaign.
- Making taxation policies at local and national levels more progressive.

The 2007–2008 financial crisis highlighted three problems to be addressed. These were: bad lending causing losses that produced liquidity problems, encouraging the growth of complex instruments that gave rise to confusion, and over-reliance on wholesale markets. A measure that was introduced to control the situation was to require financial institutions to increase the capital that they held against debt. However, the situation needs careful and regular monitoring to ensure compliance. Moreover, reliance on wholesale funds should be mitigated by the government raising the capital requirements for banks with high wholesale funding ratios. This financial crisis was also the product of the move away from structural regulation to focusing on the efficiency of the financial system (Ross, 2022). Nonetheless, while bad lending has been tackled by the government, further regulation of the complex instruments was/is necessary.

Neoliberalism

Globalisation, the latest incarnation of which is neoliberalism, prioritises techno-security not social justice or human rights in managing international social problems (Pyles, 2011). Techno-security involves maintaining control over people and the Earth's resources for the purposes of capital accumulation and is prioritised over eradicating injustices. This dynamic of capitalism contradicts social workers' commitment to social justice and places them in ethical dilemmas when responding to the contradictions between care and control when meeting identified needs. The nation-state becomes drawn into the security framework to control and manage its own nationals through austerity policies and exclude non-nationals from making claims on its welfare provisions. Managing discontent and keeping the demands of labour in check are part of this task. Thus, techno-security is used to destroy resistance, opposition and manage disaffected people. The surveillance society epitomises techno-security. The new world order is part of a networked system that allows elites and capital to cross borders with ease, while preventing unskilled workers or ordinary people from doing likewise through nation-state policies, particularly those aimed at controlling the movement of people across borders to curtail demands on their welfare services. These trends featured in the ethno-nationalist discussions about Brexit and the US presidential election in 2016. Both 'othered' migrants, difference and complained about (super)diversity both between and within groups (Vertovec, 2007). The European Union (EU) exemplified what could be achieved by pooling risks through a single market and the free movement of people within its borders. The situation here, was that any EU citizen who crossed borders retained their civil and welfare rights, and in some case, political rights. It offered a more positive vision of the future than those driven by ethno-nationalism. Through the Schengen Agreement, the EU also implemented this vision and showed how readily it could be implemented through the pooling of risk and some elements of national sovereignty. This Agreement enabled people to move freely within its borders and claim welfare rights, entitlements and resident status when needed or wanted by an EU citizen. Brexit has meant that the UK no longer has access to EU membership rights for its citizens.

Although rejection and fragmentation feature strongly in the capitalist system, neoliberal globalisation has also highlighted integration and interdependencies between countries. Neoliberal globalisation is also a key driver of the internationalisation of social problems ranging from poverty in a global economic system to climate change drawing on fossil fuel usage. Migration, whether to avoid the consequences of climate change, negotiate choices about whether to increase one's economic opportunities, or flee to escape violence, is controversial. Countries can claim that they are overwhelmed by the numbers of external migrants that are migrating to their borders, as occurred in Europe during 2015 and 2016. Adverse publicity ensued when many migrants died in the Mediterranean Sea when trying to escape. Thus, the Mediterranean shifted from being a free Mare Nostrum to a controlled entity under the auspices of Frontex. This shift in control affected Lampedusa, in Sicily, Italy and it sought to prevent migrants who had crossed from North Africa by boat from arriving in Europe (Aas and Gundhus, 2015). This scenario is being revisited under a new far-right government currently in power in Italy, under the auspices of its first woman Prime Minister, Georgia Meloni. The British government spoke in similar terms about the thousands of migrants who risked their lives to cross 'The Channel' from France in rubber dinghies.

Their numbers exceeded predictions by significant amounts in 2022. A common thread that links the seven years between these two dates is that employing securitisation and its attendant technologies in policing borders highlights the contradictions between care and control which humanitarian aid workers are poorly equipped to address. Such tensions can also cause deterioration in the mental health of emergency practitioners including health professionals, social care workers and social workers who cannot escape the incessant contradictions inherent in their work on a daily basis (Cagnazzo et al., 2021).

Social interdependencies

Globalisation has also highlighted the social interdependencies or connections between different phenomena, infrastructural systems, societies, and individuals. These interdependencies illustrate the connections between these different phenomena, and the physical environment (Dominelli, 2012a). In disasters, interdependencies are important in relation to physical and social infrastructure system because interdependencies have implications for disaster responses, recovery, reconstruction, and resilience planning efforts (Holtz et al., 2020; Narayanan et al., 2020; Van Eck, 2021). These concerns apply whether the disaster is a '(hu)man-made' one like a financial crisis or a 'natural' hazard-based one like an earthquake. There are tools to assess interdependencies and increase stakeholder and decision-makers' uptake of the infrastructural interdependencies that are needed to plan post-disaster activities. Recognising that a failure in one part of an interdependent system can lead to suffering, fatalities, and other damages in another of its parts is important.

Enhancing resilience requires a shared framework that connects different disciplines in the social sciences, natural sciences, and economics to bring together different units of analysis including individuals, families, households, organisations, and diverse infrastructural structures and physical systems (Dominelli, 2012a). Barriers to resilience can include complex power dynamics playing out within systems, human diversity, and system differences. These can affect the scope and scale of a disaster. Moreover, the flip side of resilience, vulnerability in an interdependent system needs coordinated actions, shared information, and effective communications between different parties if they are to intervene successfully. Gordon Brown, PM in the UK during the 2007–2008 financial crisis, attempted to get global leaders to tackle the financial crisis through a united strategy. However, his plans were truncated when a new PM replaced him in 2010. In disasters, interdependencies are important in relation to both the physical sphere and social infrastructural system interdependencies and their implications for disaster responses, recovery, and resilience planning efforts (Santos et al., 2014).

Failure in any part of an interdependent system can lead to suffering, fatalities, and other damages, especially when the different relationships between them are poorly understood. Building adaptive capacities to enhance resilience can help mitigate the risks of calamities occurring in an interdependent system. However, this requires an understanding of the different elements that comprise that system and the links between them. Furthermore, enhancing resilience requires a shared framework that connects different disciplines in the social sciences, natural sciences, and economics with different units of analysis including individuals, families, households, organisations, politicians, and socio-economic systems. What acts as an opportunity can also become a hindrance. Barriers can include complex power dynamics playing out within systems, catering for human diversity, accounting for system differences, and appreciating how attributes can affect the scope and scale of a disaster. Vulnerabilities in interdependent systems need coordinated actions, shared information, and effective communications between participating stakeholders including emergency workers to address the resultant problems successfully (Holtz et al., 2020; Santos et al., 2014).

Health interdependencies

COVID-19 has exposed how globalisation, anthropogenic climate change and the accelerated evolution of antimicrobial resistance (AMR) are redefining vulnerability and group susceptibility to various threats to health emanating from the animal kingdom (WWF, 2020). Anti-microbial resistant bacteria can result in infectious diseases that have been overcome returning via mutations and travel to and from infected areas. Addressing these problems requires global solutions, including subjecting the overuse of antibiotics within livestock herds to scrutiny. The transgression of the human–animal barrier in the pursuit of agricultural and industrial development have accounted for the transmission of coronaviruses causing illnesses such as SARS, MERS and COVID-19 to humans. Once a new virus reaches human society, it spreads quickly because there is no pre-existing immunity. A virus' rapid spread to many countries produces a pandemic (degree of spread not infectiousness). COVID-19 has now spread to 216 countries and territories through human-to-human transmission enhanced by travel to different locations (internally and externally). As COVID-19 has spread globally to become a pandemic, both rich countries and low-income ones now share similar vulnerabilities, especially in the limited range of effective medical options available because the virus is constantly mutating to produce different variants, some of which can evade existing protection provided by current vaccines. For example, Omicron's Variants BA.4 and BA.5 are not deterred by existing vaccinations. The best that these vaccines have achieved against Omicron's variants is to lessen the seriousness of their infection, reduce overall deaths and cut demands for hospital-based care (WHO, 2022). However, the availability of vaccines cannot overcome economic nationalism or private greed if vaccines cannot be afforded by the poorest countries or individuals and not made freely available to them.

Anthropogenic climate change can result in more fatalities and increase migration due to extreme weather events, e.g. to escape heat waves such as those which occurred in 2003 and 2022. Such movements also require global responses to support migrants because existing international legislation does not cover them, and to curtail the spread of diseases from one area to another. The spread of a virus can be thwarted by looking for similarities to be avoided in specific contexts, and by making patented vaccines and medicine available to all cheaply. But most importantly, the most effective preventative measure for zoonotic diseases is tackling the climate crisis now, by eliminating fossil fuel consumption and eliminating the transgression of human economic profit-making activities into pristine tropical and temperate terrains. COP27 ended in November 2022, without specific agreed actions to keep temperature rises to 1.5°C by 2030 as agreed under the Paris Accord (Carrington, 2022). Moreover, there are no specific penalties for non-compliance with its tenets. This includes not compensating for loss and damages caused by climate change to the poorest people who have contributed least to the problem but suffer its worst consequences.

Global reactions to COVID-19 are minimal as most nation-states have focused on solving their own problems, thus losing opportunities to learn from one another's approaches, and/or to combine their endeavours in solidarity to defeat the virus. Prainsack and Buyx (2011: 49–50) define solidarity as more than person-to-person empathy, seeing it as an 'enacted commitment to carry "costs" (financial, social, emotional, or otherwise) to assist others with whom a person or persons recognise similarity in a relevant respect'.

Solidarity cannot be replaced by charity. Charity-based solidarity produces asymmetrical relationships that do not create effective forms of solidarity. A shift from charity to solidarity seeks to establish equitable relationships between those doing the helping and those being helped. Additionally, solidarity is rooted in the notion of social justice and entitlement. There is a recognition that in in helping another, one is also helping oneself as others become willing to offer help when needed.

Local communities can engage in acts of local solidarity concerned with managing and redistributing resources and protecting individual rights to mitigate hardship and affect social policies, i.e. collective action. Deacon and Cohen (2011) argued that middle-class people should form alliances with poor people to change social policy and the politics of envy. Such actions would facilitate engagement in the politics of solidarity at both local and global levels (West-Oram and Buyx, 2017).

Moreover, solidarity relies on acknowledging human dignity, accepting social responsibility for others, and respecting cultural, ethnic, and religious diversities, providing social recognition, and enjoying mutual security in return. Global solidarity needs a belief in a shared future and hope for achieving it. Additionally, it requires a willingness to share resources – physical as well as financial.

Exercise – Financial crises lead to stressful life circumstances

Edith was a cleaner earning a low wage which was used to supplement the earnings of her husband Jos who worked as a porter on the railways. They had two young children, and although money was scarce, they tended to enjoy themselves with family and friends and were happy raising their family until the cost-of-living crisis arrived. Edith lost her job as a cleaner and could not find another one. At the same time, the cost-of-living exploded as food prices and energy prices rose dramatically. As money became tighter and tighter, they had to choose between essentials and desirable items. They started using food banks to supplement basic meals. Without this, Jos and Edith took turns not eating, and telling the children that they weren't hungry as they sipped cups of weak tea. Edith's mental health began to suffer as she could see no end to this situation. Jos was worried, but he could not convince her to see her GP. One morning, he was walking to work, when he saw the CAB offices and decided to pay them a visit on his way back to see what help they could offer.

Discussion

Working in small groups, choose a chair and a notetaker who can report back on your discussion in the plenary group. Consider the following issues during your discussion:

- If you were Jos, what would you ask for when you talk to a CAB worker?
- If you were the CAB worker, what advice would you offer Jos regarding the cost-of-living crisis, and his wife's poor mental health and lack of employment?
- What do you think the roles of different stakeholders are in addressing the cost-of-living crisis? Pay particular attention to the role of supermarkets, food producers, energy suppliers, policymakers, politicians, and others you think relevant.

Financial crises carry heavy implications for marginalised, low income groups across the world. They lack the resources that can temper the impact of loss of jobs, income, transportation, health care and other services, whereas wealthy people can draw on their reserves. Hence, risk is prominent in their lives and has to be assessed (Cook, 2017). Yet, their resilience and hopes propel them into tackling adversity, often by drawing upon their community social capital and networks to survive, and where possible, 'build back better' (Vincent et al., 2013; Dominelli and Vickers, 2014; McTeer Toney, 2019).

Economic interdependencies, COVID-19 and global solidarities initiated by the United Nations

COVID-19 exacerbated the financial crisis because in curtailing economic activities during lockdown, the economy contracted substantially, and in some countries, employers were subsidised to retain people's jobs when they returned to work after the pandemic. In Britain, this subsidy came through the furlough scheme. The economy declined because productivity declined, and global supply chains were adversely impacted. The leisure industry, particularly hospitality, retail and dining out were negatively affected as people were largely confined to their homes. Additionally, COVID-19 highlighted and exacerbated existing inequalities. The economy was a key site for these. Black and minority ethnic groups, professionals working in public facing sectors, especially the NHS and transportation were seriously affected. Black and minority ethnic groups were adversely and disproportionately affected by the virus with more of them dying compared to the white majority population. This development was evident in diverse countries (IASSW, 2020). Recovering from these negative consequences remains problematic for many sectors of the economy and the people who work within them. The lack of global solidarities in protecting the global economy exposed the absence of unifying leadership among the world's rulers, and their failure to understand he interdependencies between the different parts of the global economy. Ethno-nationalism is now beginning to question the desirability of an integrated globalised world (Nordtveit, 2010)– a thought becoming popularised post-COVID-19.

Exercising global solidarities could create pathways for ensuring economic equality and mutual progress which could be demonstrated by responding to calls for vaccine solidarity and sharing during the health pandemic. But even here, market exigencies dominated global agendas and ethno-nationalistic responses triumphed. The tool known as the Access to COVID-19 Tools Accelerator (ACT) was an attempt to increase global cooperation to speed up the development and production of vaccines, and equitable access to COVID-19 tests, treatments, and vaccines. This goal has not been realised and the money necessary to underpin such action has not yet been allocated to ensure its achievement. COVAX refers to making vaccines available to low-income countries and is co-led by Gavi (the Vaccine Alliance), the Coalition for Epidemic Preparedness Innovations (CEPI) and WHO (World Health Organization). UNICEF is involved in delivering the vaccine. COVAX aims to accelerate the development and manufacture of COVID-19 vaccines and guarantee fair and equitable access to these for every country in the world. COVAX relies on rich country generosity in donating funds and vaccines. However, 'vaccine nationalism' is currently prioritising national vaccination programmes and pharmaceutical companies (Big Pharma) are not keen to waive their patent rights to make vaccines cheaply and easily available so that these can be manufactured in low-income countries in the Global South. COVID-19 knows no borders. Yet, the self-interest argument fails to bridge the economic gaps between the Global North and the Global South and is blocking the realisation of solidarity (Cohen, 2019). More specifically, COVAX aims to:

- Provide enough vaccine doses to cover 20 per cent of a country's population, and these would be targeted on key workers and the most vulnerable people first.
- Provide access to a range of vaccines.
- Ensure vaccines are made available as quickly as possible.
- End the acute phase of the pandemic by the end of 2021 through the distribution of 2 billion doses, a goal that had not been reached by the end of 2022.
- Contribute to rebuilding the global economy at both national and international levels because COVID-19 has decimated these during lockdowns which have shut down industries, productive capacities, and supply chains. These faltering economies are suffering from the impact of Russia's invasion of Ukraine. A key impact of this has been exemplified by the high costs of fossil fuels and food. The combination of low economic growth, high inflation rates and higher interest charges on borrowed money has produced a global cost-of-living crisis.

The 2022 cost-of-living crisis: the outcome of poor economic performance and political instability

As a result of the lockdowns, economic activity declined, and supply chains faltered. By the end of 2022, some economies were struggling more than others. For example, the UK has seen economic activity fall to some of the lowest levels in living memory. China, in following a 'zero tolerance' policy on COVID-19 has seen its economic performance decline and its supply chains internally and externally have become disrupted. COVID-19 induced economic instability has been exacerbated by Putin's Aggression Against Ukraine. It has deepened economic uncertainty across the world, and initiated a crisis in fossil fuels usage, food shortages, and a rowing back from commitments to achieving 'net zero' greenhouse gas emissions (GHG) in the short-to-medium term. Meanwhile, as demand for commodity products is outstripping supplies, prices are rising and fuelling inflation. To curb inflation, central banks generally are increasing interest rates. This complex combination of factors dragging down economic performance has produced a cost-of-living crises that is felt by everyone, but particularly those who are poor, marginalised and disenfranchised across the world, and those who have mortgages to pay. Demands that nation-states intervene to safeguard living standards, support mortgage payments, and reduce energy costs have been rising.

People are having to make tough choices, often expressed starkly as 'heat or eat'. For some, it is even worse than this. For example, school children are going to school malnourished and/or hungry. Some are having to do without new school uniforms, congregating in one room when at home to be in a heated room, cutting down on cooking and using cheaper alternatives to cooking, e.g. microwaving food and hot beverages to reduce unit costs per item of cooked food. Others are going into even larger debts. Those susceptible to borrowing from 'loan sharks' who charge outrageous interest rates can get nasty, violent shocks if a borrower defaults on a payment. Thrive, a programme in northeast England demonstrated how rapidly a small loan would become a huge burden and virtually impossible to pay off, especially if owed to 'loan-sharks'. These financial pressures in domestic life increased depression and other forms of mental ill health among those unable to cope with disasters of various types, especially when their options in finding solutions were severely socially constrained (Ruskin et al., 2018).

While ordinary people are struggling to pay for daily basics, fossil fuel companies and technological giants are reaping enormous profits (McCall, 2022). Such developments can become a threat to the social order, especially if the winter becomes extremely cold, and people cannot afford to heat their homes, employers cannot keep buildings as warm as necessary, especially in sedentary occupations (the legal minimum is 60°F for a factory where people are usually moving about), and community groups struggle (in the context of declining donations and grants) to provide meals, food banks and warm places for those with low incomes to spend time among others.

Exercise – Overcoming a family's financial crisis

Meriam (all names are fictitious) was alone in her office late one afternoon when a tearful woman came in crying as she held two toddlers by the hand. 'Here,' the woman shouted, 'you take them into care. I am an unfit mother and can no longer look after them.' Meriam looked at the mother and the two children. Although Donna was extremely stressed, there were no obvious signs of the children being neglected, and Meriam wondered what had precipitated this outburst. She welcomed the woman into her office and asked her to sit down while she went and made her a cup of tea and got some milk for the two toddlers. Having calmed the woman and the two children down, Meriam asked the woman, Donna, what had happened. Donna explained how for the last three months, she had struggled to pay her bills juggling one against the other, ensuring the children had enough to eat while she went hungry, and getting into debt. Unfortunately, because she had only her benefits, she could not pay her debts when they became due and had no one locally to help her. The lender, who had lent money to many members of her community, charged 25 per cent interest on outstanding loans, and people got into more and more debt. The lender had sent a thick-set man to collect the money owed earlier that day. He forced his way into the flat to find that except for two cot beds and a pram, there was nothing that could be taken as part payment. He had given Donna 24 hours to find the money. Otherwise, he would take her and the two children and sell them to recover the debt. This threat frightened Donna, and she could think of nothing she could do except ask for her children to be taken into care while she went to find a job to pay off the debt.

Working in small groups, think about what Meriam could do or say to help Donna. Make sure you choose a notetaker and someone to report-back to the plenary group. Make sure your discussion covers the following issues:

- What Meriam would have to do to safeguard the children from exploitation.
- What Meriam could do to keep Donna and the children together.
- What Meriam could do to ensure that Donna was receiving all the benefits she was entitled to.

- What Meriam could do to stop the 'loan sharks' from threatening more and more residents seeking to make ends meet and survive.
- What could Meriam do to mobilise the community to initiate actions that would provide the residents with a degree of financial security?
- What could Meriam do to increase employment opportunities for lone parent women?

Disadvantaged communities are income poor, but rich in social capital and a willingness to work together to solve common problems during times of crisis. Many community groups are established to create social networks that will work to meet identified needs, e.g., starting a community garden providing food for local residents, or selling it in a cooperative venture that sells food at cost (Woolcock, 2001; Edwards et al., 2006; Mathbor, 2007).

Conclusions

Financial disasters cause much hardship and despair. Geopolitics and institutional failures can create unsustainable financial conditions that require nation-state interventions to contain fiscal instability and potential economic meltdown. Cutting public expenditures, curtailing wage increases, raising interest rates and increasing individual taxes are well-worn strategies utilised by nation-states in supporting the economic system. Such policies result in the poorest people paying the heaviest price in bailing the system out. However, such a strategy does not solve the hardship faced by families struggling to make ends meet. For this, self-help becomes a collective strategy that can resolve some sticking points like food insecurity. Numerous people facing financial pressures succumb to mental ill health. Yet, austerity has cut back on those services so that they are rarely available when needed by substantial numbers of people, young and old. The straitened circumstances of numerous people raise questions about the suitability of a socio-economic system that fails so many, and what responsibility the privileged few have to resolve the issues which can be traced back to activities from which they benefitted.

12 Conclusions

Introduction

Contemporary disasters are occurring more frequently and with increasing intensity, regardless of whether they are (hu)man-made or 'natural' (IFRC, 2020). The summer of 2022 was notable for its excessive heat from the West Coast of North America through to China, and many European, Asian and Middle Eastern countries in-between. These dreadful droughts caused terrible wildfires which have exacerbated situations which were already fragile due to the climate crisis, a phenomenon which required significant political will to engage in mitigating risk and preventative actions. Added to the usual commercial and domestic causes of climate change emanating from the production and consumption of fossil fuels in all areas of life, are those arising from the military ordinances consumed during the horrendous Russian War Against Ukraine. These have added significantly to this tally, and include the unquantified large-scale release of many greenhouse gases which military ordinances have discharged into the air, soil and waters; the destruction of built infrastructures ranging from homes and public buildings to commercial enterprises; and the additional resources necessary to rebuild all the areas and infrastructures that have been destroyed. Moreover, Putin's War Against Ukraine has disrupted the global economy which continues to reel from the damage caused by the COVID-19 lockdowns, and exacerbated energy insecurities, food insecurities and income insecurities. These have combined to trigger a global cost-of-living crisis. This chapter considers these multiple challenges which will need to be considered in any humanitarian intervention, whether it is to protect people from the cost-of-living crisis brought about by Putin's War, humanity's inaction on climate change, and the price being paid by people, plants, animals, and planet Earth. It also offers suggestions on the next steps that social workers can take to promote the realisation of a more just, equitable and sustainable world.

DOI: 10.4324/9781003105824-14

Globalisation

Globalisation is a contested concept comprised of an economic system and more. It provides a grand narrative that is global in scope and totalising in many respects (Held and MsGrew, 2007). It is a macro-level system that interacts with the meso- and the micro- levels through neoliberal ideologies pursued by political leaders in various countries, especially the UK and USA, and by business entrepreneurs running global enterprises, e.g. Apple, Amazon, Meta (Facebook). Non-Western entrepreneurs have also joined the rush to ever greater profits, e.g. Mittal and TATA from India, Ali Baba from China. Globalisation promotes the exploitation of nature and labour through industrialisation and consumption-based production. This increases the fragility of the environment and maximises greenhouse gas emissions into the air, water and soils. Moreover, globalisation embeds capitalist social relations in every aspect of daily life to impact on every individual's daily routines and all social institutions to ensure that no aspect of a person's lived reality escapes its effects. Globalisation also presents a hierarchical view of the world with a deregulated private sphere and a regulated public sector. It uses digital technologies to surveil human behaviour and elicit compliance with the promise of speedy gratification through excessive consumption. Moreover, business has increased its role in discussions at the UNFCCC COP meetings.

Globalisation has the following characteristics:

- Economic integration by embedding neoliberalism in mainstream economics, especially through the promulgation of austerity as a key policy for curbing public expenditures in the welfare, education, and health care arenas, and in funding green energy measures.
- Communicative integration by encouraging cheap travel, and the use of the internet to conduct many domestic activities, e.g. meetings, paying bills, surveillance via smart phones and video cameras.
- Virtual relationship maintenance with mobile phones, and increasingly teaching through digital media and other internet-based platforms.
- Development and consolidation of virtual communities of interest and maintenance of social capital through the enhancement of interconnectivity between people, places and devices.
- Neoliberal integration to promote capitalist relations and permeate all aspects of everyday life routines in the social and cultural spheres.
- Prioritising neoliberal political and economic practices which give the market ascendancy.
- Encouraging post-modern critiques of neoliberalism for its individualistic ethos and greed biased toward profit making at the expense of poorly paid workers and exploiting the Earth's resources.
- Promoting a reduced role for the state, especially in its role as provider of services for poor people, while retaining the state's role as

a facilitator of the conditions of capital accumulation and financial integration into multinational corporate interests.

- Enhancing the regulation of everyday life through technological tools.
- Valuing diversity while simultaneously discouraging mass migrations from both armed trouble spots and climactic disasters.
- Facilitating freedom of movement for capital, goods and services, and very rich people.
- Enforcing greater restrictions on movement of low-income people and migrants, especially following the 2016 electoral victory of Trump in the USA and the UK's Brexit Referendum.
- Lauding market discipline to encourage competition and make profits, regulating human behaviour, and commodifying social relations in the interests of the market.
- Having 'economics as ideology' replace political discussion and decision-making to subject all human activities to technocratic criteria by restricting and controlling budgets, e.g. those assigned to meeting the targets of 'net zero' emissions to continue fossil fuel consumption.
- Turning social problems into practical ones that can be solved technologically.
- Engaging nation-states in facilitating marketisation, identity creation and becoming global players through the rise of ethno-nationalism.
- Enabling people, goods, services, flora, fauna, and the diseases accompanying them to cross borders easily as commodities.

Globalisation claims to cascade wealth downwards to benefit all through what is termed the 'trickle down' effect. However, globalisation produces winners and losers. The winners are a few rich people holding trillions. In 2006, 946 individuals held $US3.5 trillion and owned and controlled the world's largest corporations and dictated terms and location to nation-states. This unaccountable elite grew to 1645 by 2013 and reached 2755 by 2021. This reality gave rise to the term 'Economy for the 1 per cent' (Oxfam, 2016). The losers are the majority of poor people, 2.8 billion of whom live on less than $US2-00 a day and the 1 billion who live in absolute poverty on $US1 a day, and the planet. Environmental degradation proceeds unabated as profits accumulate (Ungar, 2002; WWF, 2020), making planet Earth a key loser. The losers are created as an integral part of a modernisation, industrialisation, and globalisation. These are interlinked, rely heavily on fossil fuels, and contribute to climate change and environmental degradation.

Globalisation has also polarised the distribution of income and wealth. Under its ambit, the top 20 per cent of the world's population has accumulated 86 per cent of the wealth in the last 30 years while the lowest 20 per cent controls only 1.3 per cent. Precariousness is on the rise as low pay and 'zero hours contracts' increase job insecurity for poor, working-class people, many of whom hold more than one job, find the amount of reliable income at their disposal decreasing while bills rise inexorably. For them, a direct relationship between the cost of living and earning a decent wage seems illusive. These are the people, called 'those left behind'. Raising them out of poverty and eliminating inequalities are key to fulfilling the 2030 Agenda (UN, 2016), SDGs, and ensuring social justice including environmental justice globally. Realising these goals is integral to green social work (GSW) practice.

Globalisation, currently in its neoliberal variant, forms a significant backdrop to current disasters. Globalisation is a two-headed Janus. On the one hand, it has brought benefits to service users, e.g. better aids and adaptations for disabled people. And, it has made travel and communication easier. On the other hand, it has exacerbated and normalised existing structural inequalities, especially income inequalities (UN, 2016) and degraded the world's precious environment.

Social workers are supporting calls for the elimination of poverty and the worst excesses of precariousness by arguing for a social protection floor (SPF) globally to help the poorest people acquire some income security below which no one will fall. The SPF, initiated by the International Labour Organization (ILO), has been adopted by some countries, but its coverage must become universal. Social workers have been involved in conceptualising and overseeing the implementation of the SPF, especially through their global organisations, IASSW, ICSW and IFSW.

Neoliberalism has also facilitated the growth of significant numbers of poor people in the UK, one of the richest countries globally. New Labour sought to eradicate child poverty originally by 2015, a date extended to 2020. Yet, one in four children continues to live in a poor household (Action for Children, 2022). Poverty also damages opportunities for poor children, for example, in education. Additionally, obesity and malnutrition are linked to poverty. And the introduction of user fees in health means that many children, women, and men living on low incomes are doing without needed medicines, health services or dental treatments. Equally harsh in cutting benefits further has been the imposition of the 'bedroom tax' on those living in social housing on 1 April 2013. Disabled people successfully challenged its discriminatory dimensions (Weaver, 2019). Such initiatives were essentially a benefit cut which had the effect of increasing the numbers of people living in poverty.

Neoliberalism is a key ideology in spreading capitalist social relations as globalising practices from a right-wing, monetarist perspective drawing upon the ideas of Milton Friedman, an economics professor at the University of Chicago. Their neo-liberal monetarist ideology focuses on:

- Individual self-sufficiency and commodified social relations.
- Unregulated businesses and liberalised trade.

- Regulating the private sphere of individual lives.
- Regulating labour by ushering in fewer union and curtailing workers' rights compared to the expansion of managerial prerogative.
- Internationalising the state to enhance local competitiveness.
- Turning the welfare state into a site for capital accumulation by privatising public services and turning service users into consumers.
- Exploiting natural and (hu)man-induced crises for profit opportunities (Klein, 2007).

Neoliberalism, a failed ideology, undermined the quality of life of poor people in the Global South with Structural Adjustment Programmes (SAPs) that also destroyed nascent welfare states (Adedeji, 1999). The credit crunch and austerity destroyed people's lives in the Global North (Birch and Mykhnenko, (2010; Maynard, 2017).

Energy imperialism

Globalisation has also been integrated into imperialist ventures, even when it was called the international financial system (Wallerstein, 1974). Moreover, imperialist social relations have always favoured the colonisers and excluded local populations except for a few chosen elites needed to run the colonial system. Today, decolonisation has become the buzzword (Pyles, 2016). However, there are concerns that that globalisation is acquiring a new lease of life in the form of energy imperialism (Musso and Crouzet, 2020). This new form of imperialism no longer needs local elites to run its activities as the internet has globalised decision-making and empowered managers based in global headquarters (HQs) in one country to run their show anywhere else. The collapse of time and space engendered through the new information technologies gives global financial capital, territorial freedom. Thus, a company is not tied to having workers or HQs based in a specific place. Moreover, energy imperialism acts with constant dynamism and fluidity, to take account of new factors and quickly adapt to rapidly changing situations. Under energy imperialism, manufacturing capital can move as it wishes to reduce production costs and maintain profits. Putin has demonstrated the agility of this strategy through his assault on Ukraine. Fossil fuel sales through GazProm, the Russian state-owned petroleum company, have financed and sustained Russia's ability to continue its state-induced terrorisation of the Ukrainian population. Globalised networks including Rosneftegaz of which Russia is the majority stakeholder allow it to prevail. Rosneftegaz is the holding company for Rosneft which exploits, develops, and sells Russia's oil reserves. Other stakeholders owning these assets are implicated in its activities. Among the other countries involved are Japan, China, France and Spain.

Under the new social order of energy imperialism, development as the expansion of local markets for manufactured products is not required. Excluded people must continue to be managed, but capital is indifferent to where unrequired workers live because digital technologies enable capitalist to surveil them anywhere in the world. Moreover, working from home through remote means has initiated the modern variant of the 'cottage industry'. Workers now pay for their heating, lighting, equipment and space while doing their work from home. The internal management of poor people who have acquired criminal records involves warehousing them in prisons in increasing numbers, e.g. black people in the USA (Beauman, 2011). Moreover, multi-national security companies make substantial profits from warehousing them, and imposing external controls at the borders keep them out of a country. The demonisation of migrants and barring them from entry in specific ways has become a norm of immigration control. In the UK, this is illustrated by Priti Patel's scheme to deport migrants caught crossing the Channel in dinghies to Rwanda. The policy is being challenged in court. Despite this, by 20 December 2022, over 45,000 people had crossed the Channel via this route (BBC News, 2022), and a new Home Secretary was enforcing the UK's 'hostile environment' towards migrants (Hayes, 2022).

The nation-state supports neoliberalism

Under neoliberalism, the nation state assumes global, not domestic priorities, i.e. it keeps the nation open for business. In this scenario, poor people lose out through austerity programmes favoured by many Western politicians. The nation-state also becomes part of the security apparatus that excludes poor people by moving domestic priorities away from caring for people to caring about markets that become entrenched as the source of social power and economic resources, especially jobs. The state's growing surveillance and control role has been termed the 'securitisation of the state'. These policies impact largely on poor people, particularly those living on benefits. Following the tenets of neoliberalism and privatisation, the state has become the commissioning state, the enabling state, and the activation state. These policies allow capital to flex its muscles, while ordinary people are treated as expendable, unwanted labour. Homelessness, unemployment, and poverty can be attributed to state policies favouring capital. Therefore, the nation-state has become implicated in creating state-induced crises in poor people's lives. The nation-state becomes part of a new social hierarchy where self-perpetuating elites are drawn into a new energy-based imperialism that skews social development away from local people and services. Consequently, nation-state subservience to capital is responsible for the shift away from citizenship entitlements to self-help and charity as part of the activation state (van Berkel et al., 2011).

Civil society organisations (CSOs) assume the role of plugging the service gaps left by the nation-state. In other words, CSOs pick up the pieces in a mixed economy of welfare that minimises the state's role as a provider of services. Hence, CSOs and NGOs have become crucial providers of humanitarian aid in disaster situations. Additionally, CSOs/NGOs have become part of the ruling elites' social mission to spread democracy (Lundberg, 2021). In conflict situations, they have become embedded within the military for their protection and run the risk of being considered as siding with the enemy group (Hoogvelt, 2007).

Modernity

Industrialisation owes a lot to the philosophic tendency of believing in 'men's' capacity to use technology and industrialisation to promote progress, seemingly without end. Globally, development has been tied to modernity and industrialisation. The early theorists believed that there were universal models and stages of development followed by each country, roughly in the same order. Andre Gunder Frank (1966) questioned this worldview in the 1960s and developed the theory of the development of underdevelopment whereby countries in the Global South, then called the Third World (the West was the First World; the communist countries of the Union of Soviet Socialist Republics and China were the Second World) became underdeveloped to fuel growth in Western metropolises by following models of development imposed by the colonial powers. These geopolitics are shifting, as China, Russia, and the USA are engaged in a struggle for each to show that their model of development is superior to that of the others. This has resulted in the use of soft power such as culture, cinema, film, and literature to draw people into a specific sphere of influence. The Chinese have also developed industrial and agricultural approaches by purchasing large swathes of land and mineral resources throughout the world and helping industrialising countries to develop their infrastructures through loans. Funds were sometimes provided through the BRICS (Brazil, Russia, India, China and South Africa) Development Bank created to curtail the financial power of the International Monetary Fund (IMF) and World Bank (WB) in the Global South. China also formed its Belt and Road Initiative to engage economically with countries ranging from China to the Alps.

Other theorists posited the 'limits to growth', while some continued with the belief that societies would always progress. The view of unlimited progress and the constant exploitation of the Earth's bounty was replaced by the notion of sustainability. Living sustainably was an approach that indigenous peoples argue that they have always followed by acting as and being custodians of the Earth and its resources, so that these would be available for other generations in perpetuity. Environmental movements have sought to promote sustainable development. However, theirs was a narrower view of the concept. Sustainability was defined as in the Brundtland Report of 1986, i.e. as having the capacity to meet today's needs without jeopardising the capacity of future generations to meet theirs. This approach, now supported by the Sustainable Development Goals (SDGs) and 2030 Agenda (UN, 2016), lacks a duty to care for planet Earth and all within it for enduring sustainability.

Development

Development is the process whereby a community or society moves from one phase of social growth to another. Community, as the space in which development occurs, provides possibilities to escape neoliberalism (Homfeldt and Reutlinger, 2008). Development can be human, social, cultural, political, and economic. Development can be incremental, evolutionary, or revolutionary. Sometimes, development can be driven by technology. For example, the Green Revolution in India changed the structure of Indian agriculture by shifting it from subsistence farming to modern agribusiness. This enabled the country to feed its people and produce a surplus for development. The Industrial Revolution in England industrialised agriculture to produce surplus value to engage in export-led development. The French Revolution was one of ideas that changed how people thought about being governed and promoted equality, democracy, and government led by the people.

The right to development

The UN General Assembly adopted the Declaration on the Right to Development (DRD) in 1986. Article 1 of the DRD highlights the link between rights and development. It states:

The right to development is an inalienable human right by virtue of which every human person and all peoples are entitled to participate in, contribute to, and enjoy economic, social, cultural, and political development, in which all human rights and fundamental freedoms can be fully realized.

The DRD asks nation-states to 'take steps to eliminate obstacles to development resulting from failure to observe civil and political rights, as well as economic, social and cultural rights'. The industrialising Global South, frustrated by not reaching the high levels of Western development, maintained its right to development, a right enshrined in international protocols in 1986. The UN's General Assembly Resolution 41/128 covering the Declaration on the Right to Development was agreed on 4 December of that year. This right is now recognised as a human right.

However, there are no sanctions to ensure that nation-states uphold such rights. Environmental rights were not part of the DRD, but if it were to be written now, it would probably include these. Communities are keen to develop sustainable approaches to development, and for those living in the Global South, pro-environmental, sustainable development is key. Sustainability, especially that encompassing the duty to care for Earth forever is also an important concept in addressing the ravages wreaked by climate change (Dominelli 2012a).

An environmentally stressed planet

The 1972 Stockholm Conference on the Human Environment, and the 1980 World Conservation Strategy of the International Union for the Conservation of Nature, separated development from the environment. Their demands gave rise to the Brundtland Commission on Sustainable Development. It coined the term sustainable development to unify the conservation of nature and caring for the environment with intergenerational equity, gender equity and poverty alleviation. The 1992 Earth Summit in Rio de Janeiro, Brazil and 2002 UN Conference on Environment and Development in Johannesburg, SA, sought to promote sustainability. Additionally, limited progress meant that the Rio+20 Earth Summit in 2012 also called for sustainability. These goals were affirmed through the Post-2015 Sustainable Development Goals (SDGs) which replaced the Millennium Development Goals (MDGs) of 2000. The SDGs were agreed in the 2012 UN Conference on Sustainable Development which occurred in Rio de Janeiro, Brazil. Another important mechanism for dealing with disasters was the Sendai Framework for Disaster Risk Reduction 2015–2030. It was signed in Sendai, Japan in 2015. The industrialised West became increasingly concerned about the costs of industrialisation to the environment after 1992.

Environmental stress and mental health

The environment is becoming increasingly stressed by the demands placed upon it by people and their models of industrial production and consumption and urbanisation. In their Report, *The Limits to Growth*, Meadows and colleagues (1972), highlighted the significance of living within the Earth's means. They used computer simulations to demonstrate the stress that endless consumerist demands from rising population numbers would impose upon a planet with finite resources. Meadows et al. (1972) had their critics who deplored their assumptions and insisted that their doomsday scenario would not come to pass. Now, decades after publication, their predictions are close to the reality being faced by a world that has failed to respond to their plea to live sustainably. Current responses to the climate crisis indicate that business as usual, or doing nothing is the foreseeable, if unacceptable response, to building sustainable futures as people compete for food, water, shelter, and space among themselves, and other living beings in the 'natural' world.

Environment stress also has serious consequences for the mental health and wellbeing of people. Not only do people experience eco-grief (Cunsolo and Ellis, 2018) when they cannot access nature easily and enjoy it as they used to, but there is also the additional stress induced by life in degraded environments. Environmental stress has become an important factor in shaping the lives of poor people who reside in the most appalling conditions caused by disasters, whether 'natural' or industrial, e.g. the dumping of toxic wastes in poor neighbourhoods where black and other minority ethnic groups live (Bullard, 1990). Such devastated environments are intensifying the environmental stress and the concomitant extreme climatic havoc endured by poor people. Environmental degradation unceasingly subjects them to various disasters including increased floods, mudslides, and various other disasters including toxic chemical discharges as occurred in 1984 in Bhopal, India, homelessness, and living in urban slums (Bullard, 1990; Warner et al., 2010). Environmental stress contributes to and exacerbates structural inequalities, emotional distress, and mental ill health. Environmental stress, a source of vulnerability runs alongside attributes such as gender, 'race', class, caste, disability, and age. These factors act as major sources of structural inequalities that are aggravated by natural disasters as demonstrated by Hurricane Katrina, the 2004 Indian Ocean Tsunami, earthquakes in Pakistan, Haiti, Chile, and Nepal. Humanitarian workers including social workers intervening in disaster situations have the responsibility of considering environmental stress as a factor impacting upon service provision, people's mental health, and the Earth's physical wellbeing.

Environmental racism

Poor people are more likely to live in environmentally degraded neighbourhoods and endure environmental stress. This matter was initially raised by Roger Bullard (1990) in 1980. He coined the word 'environmental racism' to describe this. UN-Habitat estimated that 863 million people lived in slums in 2013 compared to 760 million in 2000. Their numbers now exceed 1 billion with most of those dwelling in them living in the Global South. Assisting them requires governments to reduce poverty, promote sustainable development and preserve the Earth's environmental health. To achieve these goals, Meadows et al. (1972) called for the following actions:

- Reduction in pollutants.
- Reduced consumption of natural resources.

- More efficient use of natural resources including energy sources.
- Control of population growth.
- Equitable distribution of materials, energy, and resources.

Women, children, and older people bear a disproportionate burden in income inequality, social exclusion, and the stress of living in degraded environments. Health inequalities are experienced differentially, e.g. malaria kills 1 child every 30 seconds. Children suffer from malnutrition even in growing economies like India and China. UNICEF claims 15 million children are caught in armed conflicts which have deleterious impacts on their environment and health. Children experience the greatest impact of heatwaves in an increasingly warming world (Connon and Dominelli, 2021).

Being a woman is a risk factor in disasters, featuring not only in fatality rates, but also in poverty rates and the burdens poverty imposes on them. The feminisation of poverty is evident throughout the world. Women form 70 per cent of world's poor, i.e. 1.6 billion of them (Chant, 2006). Women are asset poor and own little land despite doing most of the agricultural work for their households. Women perform the bulk of domestic caring work and bridge the gap between low wages or none and family needs, by their own labour. Carework or motherwork, done mainly by women (Swift, 1997), is not considered real work! Poverty is toughest for lone mothers with children. Women are disproportionately represented amongst the lowest paid. They may hold several jobs simultaneously, but cannot pay their basic bills (Ehrenreich, 2001). Although it has been a longstanding issue (Stromquist, 1990), 600 million women globally are illiterate (UIA, 2021).

Improvements to women's and children's health and education were prioritised under targets set by the Millennium Development Goals (MDGs). However, these were not met by 2015 and they were replaced by the Sustainable Development Goals (SDGs) in that year. These are due to run to 2030, but progress has been slow, and affected by COVID-19. Moreover, lack of health resources endangers the lives of children and women including during pregnancy. Over 300,000 women die yearly giving birth. Moreover, infectious diseases such as TB, HIV/AIDS are huge killers. New ones have been added to these, including Ebola, Zika and COVID-19 (WHO, 2022).

Poor men, especially those in the Global South, have their opportunities adversely affected and shaped by poverty. Boys form the majority of 'child soldiers' drafted into armed conflicts (UNICEF, 2018). Nonetheless, adult men are the key decision-makers and prime bearers of arms that keep these conflicts going. Men must be held accountable for encouraging the violent resolution of conflict and ending these practices. In the West, excluded black and white working-class men are disproportionately involved in (violent) crime, often in response to exclusion and become over-represented in prison statistics (Grierson, 2019).

Resistance and acquiescence to globalisation

Resistance to globalisation is partially a response to its unitary grind of demanding homogeneity both individually and collectively. This resistance can take the form of mutual learning exchanges, independence movements, and indigenisation. On other occasions, people are resisting neoliberal predations and organising collectively against globalisation, e.g. the anti-globalisation movement, 'We are the 99 per cent' movement, Occupy Wall Street movement. Consumer movements like Earth First oppose capitalist growth and encourage consumer boycotts of practices promoted by agribusiness and chemical companies. More tensions are occurring against GMO (genetically modified) food in the UK since Boris Johnson relaxed the regulations governing it in September 2021. While such opposition has raised public consciousness about the issues, success to date has been limited.

Others acquiesce with neoliberalism's self-help injunctions, especially if they are trying to deliver dwindling services to a larger group of people requiring them. Moreover, the state takes self-help for granted. This policy became a mantra under David Cameron's Coalition Government as the 'Big Society' and was adopted in social care practice as 'contingency planning'. A service provider in the BIOPICCC project on older people and climate change (Dominelli, 2013) commented on this thus:

> When a person is being assessed we'll be asking about whether it is a family member or whoever, about what support they are willing and able to actually provide to that person … [I]t is part of the contingencies.
> (BIOPICCC, professional interviewee)

The integration of policies, theory and practice are crucial to understanding the relationship between people and nature as mediated by government and multinational firms.

Green social work practice under globalisation

Globalisation has had a profound impact upon social work practice. Alongside altering its understanding of people's relationship with nature, it has affected social and labour relations in significant ways. These include:

- Changing the relationship between individuals and the state, with negative implications for entitlement to public services free at the point of need.
- Changing the relationship between people and the natural environment by prioritising economic exigencies over environmental ones.

- Changing the nature of professional labour to give managers greater powers over workers.
- Changing the nature of worker-service user relationships and seeing them as commodified within the commissioning process whereby packages of care are brought to the attention of service users, who can use individual budgets to choose whom to employ to deliver them.
- Internationalising social problems such as those involving international adoptions, human trafficking, the sexual exploitation of children, the drug trade, poverty, and the climate crisis.
- Diversifying populations entitled to demand services in the context of manufactured scarcity within rich countries like the UK where 'economics as ideology' (Dominelli and Hoogvelt, 1996) is utilised to deny needs-based entitlement to services.
- Acknowledging the rights of those involved in coercive or forced migratory movements to receive services, even if denied politically, e.g. refusing asylum seekers the right to work until their refugee status is established.

Green social work takes these points on board in promoting transformations in policy and practice and the duty to care for planet Earth and preserve its beauty for posterity ad infinitum.

Community social work

Social work traditionally has been about individuals, groups, and communities (Younghusband, 1978). Communities are the spaces where people live and enact their daily routines. Social workers and community/social development workers work within them. Social development focuses on communities, its workers advocate for and empower people within them, its methods and values are shared with social work. The International Consortium on Social Development (ICSD) has tended to see itself distinct from social work. It broke away from IASSW several decades ago, under a different name IUCISD – the International University Consortium for Social Development. ICSD is linked to a journal called *Social Development*. The International Association of Community Development (IACD) is also linked to, but separate from, social work. IACD publishes the *Community Development Journal*. Social development follows the traditions of the Settlement Movement, not the Charity Organisation Societies (COS) that pertains to a casework or individually based approach to social work.

Dominelli (2012a; 2019b) argues that community social work is a good approach for social workers and humanitarian workers to adopt when they intervene in disasters. Community social work provides a holistic service to people. Based within the boundaries of a specific community, the social work office provides a one-stop shop where service users will be dealt with directly or be referred to someone else who undertakes direct work with them. Community social work gets social workers out of the office and onto the streets. To work effectively, social workers must: know what resources (material, skills, knowledge and personnel) the community has, and which are missing; understand the community; know who lives there; work with residents to ascertain their needs; and assess how these might best be met. Below is a brief description of questions for compiling a community profile. A community profile can be developed either individually or collectively. It also requires constant updating to be relevant and kept current.

Defining communities

Community is a contested term. Politicians define it as neighbourliness and people having helpful relationships with one another. This provides a nostalgic, essentialised and idealistic view of communities that ignores conflicts and tensions in them. Communities are formed according to:

- interests
- geographic location (spatial)
- identities
- virtual (imagined, on the internet or existing virtually as an entity (Dominelli, 2019b).

Moreover, people can belong to multiple communities and treat the boundaries between them as fluid. This would enable individuals to alter their sense of community according to their audience, intent of the interaction, and negotiate its meaning with those they interact. Virtual communities, usually based on interests, have been popularised through the internet. However, communities often have tensions dividing them, and these cannot be ignored. Even in the distribution of aid, it is important that only those entitled, according to specified criteria, receive aid, and that humanitarian aid workers retain their political impartiality, and do not take sides.

Compiling a community profile

A community profile provides knowledge for use in engaging communities in coproduction activities. Dominelli (2019b) suggests asking the following questions to promote sustainable communities:

- Where is the community physically located?
- What general description would you give it (include the 'feel' of an area, general appearance, and physical and social environments)?

- What are the strengths of the community and its people(s)?
- What categories of people live there and how many belong in each category?
- Who are the major players (agencies, people, businesses) there?
- What formal and informal networks are in the area and who has joined them?
- What industries, enterprises, factories, offices, workplaces are located there and where?
- What shopping facilities exist in the community and where are these located?
- What recreational/leisure facilities exist and where are these located?
- How is land used (include residential land, recreational land, industrial land, brown-field sites, green belt land, agricultural land)?
- What major roads and natural barriers (including rivers, hills) divide the area?
- What economic and other resources (financial, skills, knowledge) are available and who holds them?
- What governance structures exist - include both formal and informal opinion formers?
- What research is needed to collect the necessary information, and who can help with this?

Some of this information can be obtained through websites and publicly available documents, e.g. annual reports that businesses submit to Companies House. Others are collected by talking to people and hanging around places where different groups of people congregate, and others will involve formal interviews, focus groups, or survey questionnaires. Gathering information by conversing informally with residents has several advantages. It gives the residents the opportunity to 'size up' or assess the individual community worker/social worker and determine whether they want to become associated with any of the activities proposed by that person. These encounters are typical of community social work. They are also transdisciplinary, holistic and allow for the formation of trust that provides the oil that lubricates community-based relationships and facilitates the creation of a base for building formal, coproduced dialogue. Such dialogue would reassure residents by valuing their lived-experiences and knowledge predicated upon those. Such valuing of what they know also promotes a willingness to engage with those who have knowledge based on scientific expertise and explore how to improve their own solutions by listening to those proposed by the experts. Figure 12.1 depicts this holist approach.

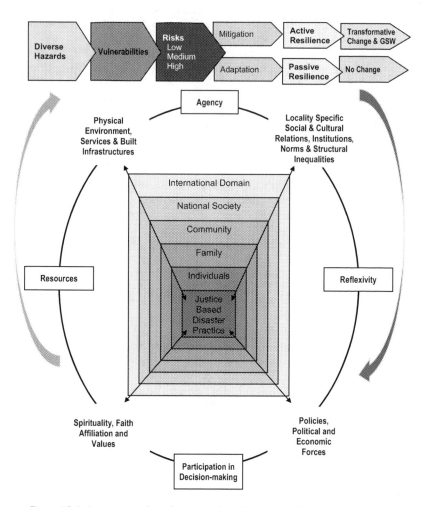

Figure 12.1 A green social work systems-based model for disasters.

Source: adapted from Dominelli (2002)

Exercise – Developing community-based relationships for coproduction

Bart (fictitious names throughout) was a community social worker who had recently joined the Greenacres Social Work Station. He knew no one in the Greenacres Community and was very shy in venturing into unknown quarters. Angie, an experienced community social worker who has worked in this community since the Greenacres Social Work Station was opened, greets him. Angie wishes to integrate Bart into the Team and the community as quickly as possible as there are many outstanding issues to be addressed. One of these is fly-tipping in various community spaces including Greenacres' extensive parkland. Angie thinks that getting Bart to work on this issue could give him a quick win by clearing up the 'rubbish', but it would also enable him to develop friendships with others, seek help from people he did not know, and begin to practice green social work.

Discussion

Working in small groups, choose a chair and a notetaker for the discussion to present its essence to the plenary group. Your task is to answer the following question:

How can Angie facilitate Bart's engagement with the community and his acceptance by his colleagues in the office? When considering this question, think about: Bart's shyness, his lack of knowledge of the area, how he can become acquainted with the community's key stakeholders and opinion leaders (formal and informal), how he would obtain the resources he needs to remove the rubbish, whom he might engage in helping him achieve the various necessary tasks, and how he might break the ice with residents and convince them of his genuine interest in them.

Integrating new members into a team is a substantial part of effective teamwork. Bart is fortunate to have Angie pick this up as an issue and seek to integrate him into the team in a real way that will help build his cache of social capital. She seems to have grasped this intuitively and sought to resolve it as a practical intervention. She utilises her skills as a social community worker going into a person's home for the first time, in a demonstration of transferable skills that she also anticipates Bart as capable of undertaking (Cook, 2017).

Community empowerment

Empowering communities requires practitioners to work from a holistic perspective throughout the disaster cycle from prevention and mitigation of risk to rebuilding a community following a disaster. This becomes extremely important in identifying the relationships that exist and those that need to be developed further to mitigate risk, reduce vulnerabilities, and build resilience. These relationships are encapsulated in the transdisciplinary, holistic green social work model shown in Figure 12.1.

Working holistically requires that humanitarian aid workers understand the community that they are working with – its residents, diverse actors, culture, language, resources, strengths, and weaknesses, and develop a community profile to assist with this. Using empowering values in this work is critical because these treat community residents as agents with the capacity to decide what they want to do and having the potential to acquire the skills and knowledge needed to make their own plans. Practitioners also ensure that the community decides the speed at which it will work by facilitating bottom-up approaches to what they do together. Acknowledging the importance of local culture, rituals, and ways of behaving is crucial in supporting the people who have suffered enormous losses in the disaster. Tensions lying beneath the surface in a community should not be underestimated as these may surface during a disaster and require skills in non-violent conflict resolution and community engagement. These skills are summarised below:

- Entering the community sensitively and establishing trust and credibility.
- Building trust by achieving small successes on issues of interest to residents.
- Identifying problems and creating action plans with residents.
- Identifying community strengths and weaknesses, its internal tensions, and external conflicts, and the individuals and groups involved in them.
- Seeking non-violent approaches to encouraging dialogue and resolving community conflicts.
- Co-producing plans of action to solve the problems/issues.
- Evaluating activities constantly.
- Forming alliances to identify resources and achieve your community goals.
- Looking after the social worker! Look after yourself, develop your support networks involving peers, supervisors, and others, locally and elsewhere.

Empowering people

There are various forms of empowerment. Understanding these can facilitate appropriate responses to specific communities. Dominelli (2012c) characterises those impacting upon people as:

- Legalistic (citizens' charters).
- Tokenistic (superficial).
- Bureaucratic (procedurally driven).
- Consumerist (choice, i.e. focused on the marketplace).
- Commodified (reified market-driven relationships).
- Agent-driven (self-empowerment).
- Collaborative (group empowerment).

All these forms of empowerment are used in practice; and several can co-exist simultaneously. Driven by John Major when PM, they appropriated relationship-based terminology utilised by community workers to prioritise the market. Appropriating this terminology has privileged those who fail to empower residents by not engaging them in defining the provision of first-class services, responding instead to their complaints after poor services have been delivered to them.

Self-preparation and self-empowerment

Preparing to go into the field requires careful thinking, and involves discussions with family, friends, and employers, especially if you anticipate being absent for a period. Minimal preparation before departure on a deployment covers the following:

- Preparing oneself mentally, emotionally, and physically.
- Preparing family and friends for a lengthy absence.
- Identifying the location of the deployment and the nature of the problem/disaster.
- Becoming informed about what is already happening in the disaster-affected area.
- Understanding the local contexts, politics, culture(s) and language(s).
- Learning a few basic phrases in the local language and considering linguistic issues and how to mitigate these beforehand.
- Taking care of insurance cover, home safety and paying bills before leaving.
- Copying all important documents and leaving these in a safe place in the event of the originals being stolen or lost. Tell a trusted person where they might be found. You should also take copies with you, especially of your passport and other important documents.

Building resilience

Undertaking community social work in a community in crisis requires skills in negotiating with unknown others and responding to needs as the victim-survivors define them. Humanitarian aid workers may have to explain sensitively why aid distribution may be dictated by donors, and not needs. Other considerations in building adaptive capacities and resilience include the following:

• Enhancing the educational skills and capacities of people in the community, especially of children and those who are disadvantaged.
• Following the insights of indigenisation or locality specific and culturally appropriate action.
• Developing solidarity with both internal and external actors.
• Acting within a reciprocated framework.
• Encouraging mutuality and support of each other, including building social networks to enhance the community's social capital.
• Inspiring people and maintaining hope.
• Creating allies, both internally within the community and externally with others elsewhere for tactical and strategic purposes.

Social capital

Social capital is a crucial driver of resilience, self-help, and mutuality. It occurs in three main forms: bonding, bridging, and linking social capital (Putnam, 2000; Woolcock, 2001). Support networks are forms of social capital that are vital in addressing internationalised social problems like those that occur during calamities, e.g. preventing the trafficking of children who have lost their parents in a disaster. Developing social networks also enables local communities to extend their reach beyond their community and undertake action that would be impossible locally. For example, in a world dominated by multinational corporations that are unaccountable to anyone, fear of losing one's jobs prevents people from organising or speaking out against local injustices. Having allies overseas who can assume the risks associated with discovering this information on a community's behalf is a useful way of bringing about much wanted change. This occurred in the case of identifying the overseas owners of a mine in Latin America so that grievances concerning its deleterious impact on health could be assessed and challenged. Additionally, reciprocated forms of support become important in maintaining egalitarian social relations between diverse community actors. Community workers and social workers are well-placed to develop and maintain such alliances. These alliances are usually transient, so do not be surprised if they are short-lived. Targeted efforts and hard work are necessary to create, consolidate and develop further social capital networks.

Inclusion and exclusion

Promoting social inclusion and eliminating social exclusion is key to sustainable social development and humanitarian aid distribution. At the simplest level, inclusion is about the right to belong to a society, participate in its decision-making processes, develop one's individual talents to the full and receive collective protection from society. The individual has a responsibility to contribute to that community to the best of their abilities. Social exclusion is the condition of not being accepted as belonging to a society, being rejected and prevented from participating in it, and constantly encountering obstacles to developing one's full potential. The processes of exclusion and/or inclusion become institutionalised through specific policies and practices and become incorporated into development processes (Commins, 2004).

Manufactured scarcity in social work and social development

Political discourses are muted when 'economics as ideology' replaces discussion about choices and power. Working within management stipulated budgets is taken as given, not to be questioned although it configures scarcity. Scarcity becomes manufactured scarcity when resources become rationed for reasons determined by ruling elites. Moreover, in a neoliberal society, relationships are tied to budgets that commodify human relationships through consumerism and the market. This commodification can substitute social work's relational values with techno-bureaucratic ones. This includes contemporary 'contracted-out' agreements and contractual arrangements that cater for service provision and delivery. Besides undermining relational social work, techno-bureaucratic social work increases the likelihood of litigation. However, litigation is rarely conducive to the health and wellbeing of the service user who must object after the fact rather than focus on agreed tasks, coproduction and/or prevention from the beginning. The scarcity of resources increases uncertainty and undermines the sense of entitlement to services and social solidarity. Addressing scarcities requires strategies for obtaining and conserving resources. In a disaster, risk minimisation and harm reduction become key strategies for dealing with uncertainty.

Neoliberal ideologies favour the privatisation of public goods, including asset stripping communities, welfare sectors, and the criminal justice system. The new managerialism and public sector management which focus on performance management, targets, and managerial control of labour processes, have been transferred from business practices into social work. This has led to the bureaucratisation of professional practice and control of both service users and professionals who have lost much of their professional autonomy in decision-making as tick-boxes replace evidence-based judgements about what needs to be done. This has been called the 'modernisation of services' which includes personalisation, individual budgets, and choice. As these are conducted in the context of markets, austerity, and public expenditure cuts, they become somewhat esoteric terms because budgets determine what can be achieved within such frameworks. In a disaster situation, the choices given to victim-survivors are even more restricted as resources are in short supply and the aid available for distribution inadequate for the numbers requiring them. For example, in Afghanistan and Syria, the UN called for billions in aid, but obtained only a fraction of what was needed. Additionally, in the context of decolonisation, and after the 'Black Lives Matter' movement accusations of neo-imperialism and Orientalism (Said, 1978) resonate strongly. Humanitarian aid workers are becoming more conscious of the donors having Western origins and are concerned about delivering culturally appropriate services (Dominelli, 2012a) and determining who is included and excluded. Recent criticisms have included the dignified and generous response to displaced people and refugees fleeing the Russian attack on Ukraine, a situation which was not equalled when Syrians and Afghanis were requiring similar levels of support and comfort. Mass migration to improve the quality of life, escape armed conflict, find adventure, and reunite with family members are likely to increase and challenge future humanitarian responses. This task is also complicated by the internationalisation of welfare states wherein private companies can cross borders with impunity to buy and sell welfare services, e.g. homes for children and older people; custodial settings; using management expertise to replace social workers as occurred during the Grenfell disaster, for example.

Inclusion and exclusion processes also divide service users into those who deserve assistance and those who do not. This binary is a crucial part of the technologies of control used by social workers and has a long history. Professionals use this binary to allocate scarce resources amongst competing demands, i.e. to ration them among deserving and undeserving service users. Rationing resources leaves some claimants destitute. This strategy excludes some from accessing services, cuts corners to meet bureaucratic targets rather than respond to need, and can distribute inappropriate services, as exemplified by rationing social care and health care services to the neediest of the needy (Dominelli, 2013). In rationing resources in conditions of climate change for older people, some providers claimed to:

> provide services to those deemed to be 'critical or substantial' ... It depends on how a person has been assessed in terms of eligibility for services. It might be that if a person is moderate or low that our

carers or private carers might actually not be providing a package of care to them.

(BIOPICCC, professional interviewee)

Moreover, the exclusion of individuals from engaging fully in decision-making about the services they receive can be experienced as oppressive and allow legitimate needs to remain unmet.

Attacks on their professional probity and ability to assess people while being denied resources to provide the services identified by their needs assessment has disillusioned and undermined social workers' morale. As one commented on their situation while echoing the experiences of others:

I feel that managerialism and market forces within a supposedly mixed economy of welfare are destroying social work practice. Increasingly the organisation is driven towards creating an expensive, callous bureaucracy which prides itself on delivering resource-led policies as prime measures of effectiveness and efficiency. Not content with deskilling a professional workforce, the organisation appears to have effectively distanced itself from accountability/responsibility towards social workers.'

(Dominelli, 2004: 29)

Another practitioner, lamenting the encroachment of business practices into the profession said: 'If we become purchasers, we need to change our title and will no longer be social workers, but social welfare brokers' (Dominelli, 2004: 161).

Bureau-technocratic injunctions can reduce relational work within disaster interventions. Social work has acquired porous borders around its professional boundaries and is bequeathing many areas of its expertise to community health nurses, approved mental health practitioners, humanitarian aid workers and others. Some appropriation of professional social work expertise by others has been facilitated by legislative and policy changes that have made it impossible for social workers to defend professional territory that had been theirs earlier. For instance, in the UK, Approved Social Workers became Approved Mental Health Practitioners in 2007, and mental health social work was no longer restricted to those trained in social work as in the 'Approved Social Worker' role. This becomes important in disaster situations where anyone can potentially assume this sensitive work with individuals and families. In the UK, social work is a protected title. However, humanitarian aid workers, personal advisors and many other professionals are currently undertaking tasks once done by social workers without being called social workers. Simultaneously, social work has become more accepted in new roles, e.g. in psychosocial disaster interventions. These important shifts require the profession to realign its education and practice portfolios more in keeping with tackling twenty-first-century challenges, of which addressing disasters and delivering humanitarian aid will be central to the social work curriculum.

Conclusion

Social workers are facing new challenges arising from an economically globalised world, a thriving virtual reality based on internet-based communications systems, cheap travel, internationalisation of social problems, and service-user demands for inclusivity, a valuing of diversity, and involvement in decisions affecting them. These demands are also evident in all stages of the disaster cycle: prevention (avoidance), relief, recovery and reconstruction work. This reality suggests a holistic, co-productive approach to practice to encompass the macro-, meso-, and micro-levels of practice and recognise the interdependencies between its different parts. It also means that social workers require specific training in disaster interventions.

References

Aas, K., and Gundhus, H. (2015) Policing Humanitarian Borderlands: FRON-TEX, Human Rights and the Precariousness of Life. *British Journal of Criminology*, 55(1): 1–18. On https://academic.oup.com/bjc/article/55/1/1/465595

Abbott, D., and Wilson, G. (2015) *The Lived Experience of Climate Change.* London: Springer Nature

Action for Children (2022) Where is Child Poverty Increasing in the UK? Blog on 12 July. On www.actionforchildren.org.uk/blog/where-is-child-poverty-increasing-in-the-uk/

Adedeji, A. (1999) Structural Adjustment Policies in Africa. International Social Science, 51(162): 521–528. On https://onlinelibrary.wiley.com/doi/epdf/10.1111/1468-2451.00223

Agrawal, A., Nepstad, D., and Chhatre A. (2011) Reducing Emissions from Deforestation and Forest degradation. *Annual Review of Environment and Resources*, 36: 373–396.

Albertson K, Aylen J, Cavan G and McMorrow J (2010) Climate Change and the Future Occurrence of Moorland Wildfires in the Peak District of the UK. *Climate Research*, 45: 105–118.

Alexander, D. (1993) *Natural Disasters.* London: Routledge.

Alexander, D. (2002) *Principles of Emergency Planning and Management.* Rheinbeck, NY: Terra Publishing.

Anderson, C., and Brion, S. (2014) Perspectives on Power in Organizations. *Annual Review of Organizational Psychology and Organizational Behaviour*, 1: 67–97.

Askeland, G. A. (2007) Globalisation and a Flood of Travellers: Flooded Travellers and Social Justice. In L. Dominelli (ed.), *Revitalising Communities in a Globalising World*, pp. 171–181. Aldershot: Ashgate.

Arbour, K., Arrieta, F., Moraga, C., and Cordero Vega, M. (2011) Lessons from the Chilean Earthquake: How a Human Rights Framework Facilitates Disaster Response. *Health and Human Rights*, 13(1): 62–73. On www.jstor.org/stable/pdf/healhumarigh.13.1.62.pdf?refreqid=excelsior%3A184f8f350de151aca557e91e3341d75a

Archer, D., and Fowler, H. (2018) Characterising Flash Flood Response to Intense Rainfall and Impacts Using Historical Information and Gauged Data in Britain. *Journal of Flood Risk Management*, 11: S121–S133. On https://onlinelibrary.wiley.com/doi/epdf/10.1111/jfr3.12187

Auker, M.R., Sparks, R.S.J., Siebert, L., Crossweller, H., and Ewert, J. (2013) A Statistical Analysis of the Global Historical Volcanic Fatalities Record. *Journal of Applied Volcanology*, 2(2): 1–24. On https://doi.org/10.1186/2191-5040-2-2

Bandyopadhyay, S., and Vermann, K. (2013) Donor Motives for Foreign Aid. *Federal Reserve Bank of St. Louis Review*, July/August, 95(4): 327–336. On https://files.stlouisfed.org/files/htdocs/publications/review/13/07/bandyopadhyay.pdf

Bankoff, G. (2001) Rendering the World Unsafe: Vulnerability as Western Discourse. *Disasters*, 25I1): 19–35.

Barrell, R., and Davis, E. (2008) The Evolution of the Financial Crisis of 2007–8. *National Institute Economic Review*, 206(1): 5–14. https://doi.org/10.1177/0027950108099838

Barrett, S. (2014) Climate Economics: A Strained Relationship. *Nature*, 508: 179–180. On https://doi.org/10.1038/508179a

Bartoli, A., Stratulis, M., and Pierre, R. (eds) (2022) *Out of the Shadows: The Role of Social Work in Disasters*. St Albans: Critical Publishing.

Bauman, Z. (2011) *Collateral Damage: Social Inequalities in a Global Age*. Cambridge: Polity Press.

Baxter, P., Moller, I., Spencer, T., Spence, R., and Tapsell, S. (2003) *Flooding and Climate Change*. On http://repo.floodalliance.net/jspui/bitstream/44111/1634/1/cap4-6.pdf

Bayrak, M.M., Tu, T.N., and Marafa, L.M. (2014) Creating Social Safeguards for REDD+: Lessons Learned from Benefit Sharing Mechanisms in Vietnam. *Land*, 3: 1037–1058.

BBC News (2002) *The Lynmouth Floods*. On www.bbc.co.uk/devon/news_features/2002/lynmouth_flood.shtml

BBC News (2013) *Facts on Hurricane Haiyan*. On www.bbc.co.uk/bitesize/guides/z9whg82/revision/4

BBC News (2022) How is the UK Stopping Channel Crossings and What Are the Legal Routes to the UK? *BBC News*, 20 December. On www.bbc.co.uk/news/explainers-53734793

Beck, S., and Forsyth, T. (2015) Co-production and Democratizing Global Environmental Expertise The IPCC and Adaptation to Climate Change. In S. Hilgartner, C. Miller and R. Hagendijk (eds), *Science and Democracy, Making Knowledge and Making Power in the Biosciences and Beyond*, pp. 113–123. London: Routledge.

Belen, R. (2015) *Mapping of the Typhoon Haiyan Affected Areas in the Philippines Using Geospatial Data and Very High Resolution Satellite Images*, Paper Presented at Conference in Jeju, S. Korea, 6–9 Oct. New York: UN, ECOSOC publication. On https://unstats.un.org/unsd/geoinfo/rcc/docs/rccap20/15_paper-Mapping%20of%20the%20Typhoon%20Haiyan%20Affected%20Areas%20in%20the%20%20Philippines.pdf

Berner, A.S. (2018) Red Hook: the hip New York Enclave Caught between Gentrification and Climate Change. *The Guardian*, 25 September. On www.theguardian.com/environment/2018/sep/25/red-hook-climate-change-floodplain-hurricane-sandy-gentrification

Besthorn, F. (2012) Deep Ecology's Contributions to Social Work: A Ten-Year Retrospective. *International Journal of Social Welfare*, 21(3). https://doi.org/10.1111/j.1468-2397.2011.00850.x

Beveridge, W. (1942) *The Beveridge Report*. London: HMSO.

Birch, K., and Mykhnenko, V. (eds) (2010) *The Rise and Fall of Neo-Liberalism: The Collapse of An Economic Order?* London: Zed Books.

Birt, Y. (2009) Promoting Virulent Envy? *Royal United Services Institute Journal*, 154(4): 52–58.

Boddy, J., and Dominelli, L. (2017) Social Media and Social Work: The Challenges of a New Ethical Space. *Australian Journal of Social Work*, 70(2): 172–184. https://doi.org/10.1080/0312407X.2016.1224907.

Bøhlerengen, and Wiium, N. (2022) Environmental Attitudes, Behaviors, and Responsibility Perceptions Among Norwegian Youth: Associations With Positive Youth Development Indicators. *Frontiers in Psychology*, 13: 1–22. Article 844324. On https://doi.org/10.3389/fpsyg.2022.844324

Borras, S.M., Franco, J. C., Isakson, S. R., Levidow, L., and Vervest, P. (2016) The Rise of Flex Crops and Commodities: Implications for Research. *Journal of Peasant Studies*, 43(1): 93–115.

Bracken, L. (2017) Interdisciplinarity and Geography. *International Encyclopedia of Geography: People and Earth, Environment and Technology*, https://doi.org/10.1002/9781118786352.wbieg0450

Brion, F., and E.-P. Guittet (2018) *Prevention of Radicalisation in Molenbeek. An Overview* (p. 13) [Research Paper]. Université Catholique de Louvain (UCLouvain). On http://affectliberties.com/wp-content/uploads/2018/12/AFFECT-RP-6-2018-BRION-GUITTET-Prevention-of-radicalisation-in-Molenbeek-VF.pdf

British Red Cross (2022) *Flooding in Pakistan: The Latest News.* 6 December. On www.redcross.org.uk/stories/disasters-and-emergencies/world/climate-change-and-pakistan-flooding-affecting-millions

Bronfenbrenner, U. (1979) *The Ecology of Human Development: Experiments by Nature and Design*. Cambridge, MA: Harvard University Press.

Brown, M., Agyapong, V., Greenshaw, A., Cribben, I., Brett-McLean, P., Drolet, J., McDonald-Harker, C., Omeie, J., Mankowsi, M., Noble, S., Kitching, D., and Silverstone, P. (2019) After the Fort McMurray Wildfire There Are Significant Increases in Mental Health Symptoms in Grade 7–12 Students Compared to Controls. *BMC Psychiatry*, 19(18): 1–11. On https://doi.org/10.1186/s12888-018-2007-1

Brundtland, G.H. (1987) *Our Common Future: Report of the World Commission on the Environment and Development*. New York: Oxford University Press.

Bullard, R (1990) *Dumping in Dixie: Race, Class, and Environmental Quality*. New York. Westview Press. 1st Edn in 1980.

Burkle, F. (2014) Conversations in Disaster Medicine and Public Health: The Profession. *Disaster Medicine and Public Health Preparedness*, 8(1): 5–11. On www.cambridge.org/core/journals/disaster-medicine-and-public-health-preparedness/article/conversations-in-disaster-medicine-and-public-health-the-profession/712F6E7F1D8774807FD96D7B929D86FE

Cabinet Office. (2013) *The Role of Local Resilience Forums: A Reference Document*. London: The Civil Contingencies Secretariat.

Cagnazzo, C., Filippi, R., Zucchetti, G., Cenna, R., Taverniti, C., Guarrera, A., Stabile, S., Federici, I., Monti, M., Pirondi, S., Testoni, S., and Fagioli, F. (2021) Clinical Research and Burnout Syndrome in Italy: Only a Physicians' Affair?, *BMC Nature, Trials*, 22, 205. On https://doi.org/10.1186/s13063-021-05158-z

Cagney, K., Sterrett, D., Benz, J., and Tompson, T. (2016) Social Resources and Community Resilience in the Wake of Superstorm Sandy. *PLoS ONE*, 11(8): e0160824. On www.ncbi.nlm.nih.gov/pmc/articles/PMC5006987/pdf/pone.0160824.pdf

Cannon, T. (1994) Vulnerability Analysis and the Explanation of 'Natural' Disasters. In Varley, A (ed.) *Disasters, Development and Environment*. Chichester: John Wiley and Sons.

Carbone, E., and Wright, M. (2016) Hurricane Sandy Recovery Science: A Model for Disaster Research. *Disaster Medicine and Public Health Preparedness*, 10(3): 304–305. https://doi.org/10.1017/dmp.2015.140.

Carey, R. (2006) Everything Must Go: The Privatisation of State Social Work. *British Journal of Social Work*, 38(5): 918–935. https://doi.org/10.1093/bjsw/bcl373

Carrington, D. (2022) Climate Crisis: UN Finds 'No Credible Pathway to 1.5C in Place. *The Guardian*, 27 October. On www.theguardian.com/environment/2022/oct/27/climate-crisis-un-pathway-1-5-c#:~:text=There%20is%20E2%80%9Cno%20credible%20pathway, %E2%80%9Crapid%20transformation%20of%20societies%E2%80%9D.

Carson, R. (1962) *The Silent Spring*. Boston, MA: Houghton Mifflin Press.

Carulli, G., and Slejko, D. (2005) The 1976 Fruili (NE Italy) Earthquake. *Giornali di Geologia Applicata*, pp. 147–156.

Chambers, R. (1989) Vulnerability, Coping and Policy. *IDS Bulletin*, 20(2): 1–7.

Chant, S. (2006) The 'Feminisation of Poverty' and the 'Feminisation' of Anti-Poverty Programmes: Room for Revision? *The Journal of Development Studies*, 44(2): 165–197.

Chartes, N., Bero, L and Norris, (2019) A Review of Methods Used for Hazard Identification and Risk Assessment of Environmental Hazards. *Environment International*, 123: 231–239. On https://reader.elsevier.com/reader/sd/pii/S0160412018322979?token=87565E4BC163FA86C738F8C09889AC2DE49117718CE0DC63D078CB744AC6127C6738211E298FC661D22A3C25A653C401&originRegion=eu-west-1&originCreation=20230319155417

Chisholm, T., and Coulter, A. (2017) *Safeguarding and Radicalisation: A Report*. London: DoE. On https://assets.publishing.service.gov.uk/government/uploads/system/uploads/attachment_data/file/635262/Safeguarding_and_Radicalisation.pdf

Cianconi, P., Betrò, S., and Janini, L. (2020) The Impact of Climate Change on Mental Health: A Systematic Descriptive Review. *Frontiers in Psychiatry*, 11: Article 74, pp. 1–15. On www.frontiersin.org/articles/10.3389/fpsyt.2020.00074/full

Cocker, F. and Joss, N. (2016) Compassion Fatigue among Healthcare, Emergency and Community Service Workers: A Systematic Review. *International Journal of Environmental Research and Public Health*, 13(6): 618. https://doi.org/10.3390/ijerph13060618.

Cohen, S. (2019) Solidarity and the Future of Global Social Policy: Looking for Direction in Local Social Activism. *Global Social Policy*, 19(1–2) 46–64.

Collins, A.E. (2009) *Disaster and Developments*. New York: Routledge.

Collins, P.H, Maldonado, L., Takagi, D., Thorne, B., Weber, L., and Winant, H. (1995) Symposium: On West and Fenstermaker's 'Doing Difference'. *Gender and Society*, 9: 491–513.

Commins, P. (2004) Poverty and Social Exclusion in Rural Areas: Characteristics, Processes and Research Issues. *Sociologia Ruralis*, 44(1): 60–75.

Comtesse, H., Ertl, V., Hengst, S., Rosner, R. and Smid, G. (2021) Ecological Grief as a Response to Environmental Change: A Mental Health Risk or Functional Response? *Journal of Environmental Research and Public Health*, 18(2): 734. https://doi.org/10.3390/ijerph18020734

Connon, I., and Dominelli, L. (2021) *UNICEF's Children's Climate Risk Index (CCRI): Systematic Review of the Literature: Findings, Outcomes and Policy Recommendations.* Edinburgh: UNICEF and Data for Children Collaborative.

Cook, L. (2017) Making Sense of the Initial Home visit: The Role of Intuition in Child and Family Social Workers' Assessments of Risk. *Journal of Social Work Practice*, 31(4): 431–444. On: https://doi.org/10.1080/02650533.2017.1394826

Corrigan, P., and Leonard, P. (1978) *Social Work Under Capitalism: A Marxist Approach.* London: Macmillan.

Costa, K., and Pospieszna, P. (2015) The Relationship between Human Rights and Disaster Risk Reduction Revisited: Bringing the Legal Perspective into the Discussion. *Journal of International Humanitarian Legal Studies*, 6: 64–86. On https://brill.com/view/journals/ihls/6/1/article-p64_4.xml?language=en

Covey, J., Dominelli, L., Horwell, C., Rachmawati, L., Martin-del Pozzo, A.L., Armienta, M.A., Nugroho, F. and Ogawa, R (2021) Carers' Perceptions of Harm and the Protective Measures Taken to Safeguard Children's Health against Inhalation of Volcanic Ash: A Comparative Study across Indonesia, Japan and Mexico. *International Journal of Disaster Risk Reduction*, 59: 102,194–102,203.

Cuff, M. (2022) Climate Change Could Cause Worst UK Wildfires in Years Warn Fire Chiefs, but Experts Say it's Just the Start. *The Knowledge News.* On https://inews.co.uk/news/climate-change-could-cause-worst-uk-wildfires-in-years-warn-fire-chiefs-but-experts-say-its-just-the-start-1603776

Cunsolo, A., and Ellis, N. (2018) Ecological Grief as a Mental Health Response to Climate Change-Related Loss. *Nature Climate Change*, 8: 275–281. On www.nature.com/natureclimatechange

Curtis, K. (2014) Learning the Requirements for Compassionate Practice: Student Vulnerability and Courage. *Nursing Ethics*, 21(2): 210–223. https://doi.org/10.1177/0969733013478307.

Cutter, S (1996) Vulnerability to Environmental Hazards. *Progress in Human Geography*, 20: 529–539.

Davies, I, P., Haugo, R.D., Robertson, J.C., Levin, P.S. (2018) The Unequal Vulnerability of Communities of Color to Wildfire. *PLoS ONE*: 13(11): e0205825. On https://doi.org/10.1371/journal.

Davis, I., and Alexander, D. (2015) *Recovery from Disaster.* London: Routledge.

Deacon, B., and Cohen, S. (2011) From the Global Politics of Poverty Alleviation to the Global Politics of Welfare State (Re)building. *Global Social Policy*, 11(2): 233–249.

de Silva, S., Pereira, M., and Hansen, G. (eds) (2023) *Sustaining Support for Intangible Cultural Heritage.* Cambridge: Cambridge Scholars Publishing.

Dominelli, L. (2002) *Anti-Oppressive Theory and Practice.* Basingstoke: Palgrave Macmillan.

Dominelli, L. (1988) *Anti-Racist Social Work*. London: Macmillan. 1st Edn. 4ᵗʰ Edn in 2018.

Dominelli, L (2004) Practising Social Work in a Globalising World. In N.-T. Tan and A. Rowlands (eds), *Social Work Around the World III*, pp. 151–173. Berne: International Federation of Social Workers.

Dominelli, L (2006) Women and Community Action. Bristol: BASW/Policy Press.

Dominelli, L. (2009) Social Work Research: Contested Knowledge for Practice. In R. Adams, L. Dominelli and M. Payne (eds), *Practising Social Work in a Complex World*, pp. 240–255. Basingstoke: Palgrave.

Dominelli, L. (2012a) *Green Social Work*. Cambridge: Polity Press.

Dominelli, L. (2012b) Social Work in Times of Disaster: Practising Across Borders. In M. B. Kearnes, F. R. Klauser and S. N. Lane (eds), *Critical Risk Research: Practices, Politics and Ethics*. Oxford: Wiley-Blackwell, chapter 10, pp. 197–218

Dominelli, L (2012c) Empowerment. In P. Stepney and D. Ford (eds), *Social Work Models, Methods and Theories*. Lyme Regis: Russell House Publishing. 2ⁿᵈ Edn.

Dominelli, L. (2013) Mind the Gap: Built Infrastructures, Sustainable Caring Relations, and Resilient Communities in Extreme Weather Events. *Australian Social Work*, 66(2): 204–217.

Dominelli, L (2014) Opportunities and Challenges of Social Work Interventions in Disasters. *International Social Work*, 57(4): 337–44.

Dominelli, L. (2016) *Green Social Work*, Keynote Address, ANZASW (Association of New Zealand and Australian Social Workers) Annual Conference, 27 September to 1 October, James Cook University, Townsville, Australia.

Dominelli, L. (2018a) Green Social Work and the Uptake by the Nepal School of Social Work: Building Resilience in Disaster Stricken Communities. In L. Bracken and H. Ruszczyk (eds), *Evolving Narratives of Hazard and Risk: The Gorkha Earthquake, Nepal, 2015*. London: Palgrave Macmillan.

Dominelli, L. (2018b) Green Social Work in Theory and Practice: A New Environmental Paradigm for the Profession. In L. Dominelli (ed.), *The Routledge Handbook of Green Social Work*, pp. 9–20. London: Routledge.

Dominelli, L. (2019a) Neglected Families: Developing Family-Supportive Policies for 'Natural' and (Hu)man-Made Disasters. In Eydal, G. and Rostgraad, T. (eds) *The Family Handbook*. London: Edward Elgar Publishing, Chapter 27, pp 363–375. On www.e-elgar.com/shop/handbook-of-family-policy

Dominelli, L. (2019b) *Women and Community Action*. Bristol: Policy Press. 3rd Edn. 1st Edn 1990, 2nd Edn 2006.

Dominelli, L. (2020) Rethinking Masculinity in Disaster Situations: Men's Reflections of the 2004 Tsunami in Southern Sri Lanka. *International Journal of Disaster Risk Reduction*, 48, 101594, ISSN 2212-4209, https://doi.org/10.1016/j.ijdrr.2020.101594

Dominelli, L., and Hoogvelt, A. (1996) Globalisation and the Technocratisation of Social Work. *Critical Social Policy*, 16(47): 45–62. https://doi.org/10.1177/026101839601604703

Dominelli, L., and Ku, H.B. (2017) Green Social Work and its Implications for Social Development in China. *China Journal of Social Work*, 10(1): 33–22.

Dominelli, L., and McLeod, E. (1989) *Feminist Social Work*. London: Macmillan.

Dominelli, L. and Vickers, T (2014) Humanitarian Aid in Times of Disasters: Lessons from Responses to the 2004 Tsunami in Sri Lanka. In Hessle, S. (ed.) *Environmental Change and Sustainable Development*, Volume II. Aldershot: Ashgate, pp. 49–52.

Doocy, S., Daniels, A., Dooling, S., and Gorokhovich, Y. (2013) The Human Impact of Volcanoes: a Historical Review of Events 1900–2009 and Systematic Literature Review. *PLOS Currents: Disasters*, 16 April. On https://currents. plos.org/disasters/article/the-human-impact-of-volcanoes-a-historical-review-of-events-1900-2009-and-systematic-literature-review/

Drolet, J., Dominelli, L., Alston, M., Ersing, R., Mathbor, G., and Wu, H. (2015) Women Rebuilding Lives Post-Disaster: Innovative Community Practices for Building Resilience and Promoting Sustainable Development. *Gender and Development*, 23(3): 433–448. On https://doi.org/10.1080/13552074.2015. 1096040

Drolet, J., Lewin, B., and Pinches, A. (2021) Social Work Practitioners and Human Service Professionals in the 2016 Alberta (Canada) Wildfires: Roles and Contributions. *British Journal of Social Work*, 51: 1663–1679. https://doi. org/10.1093/bjsw/bcab141.

Ducy and Stough (2021) Psychological Effects of the 2017 California Wildfires on Children and Youth with Disabilities. *Research in Developmental Studies*, July 103981. On www.sciencedirect.com/science/article/pii/ S089142222100130X?via%3Dihub

Du Cann, C. (2019) Extinction Rebellion Is Creating a New Narrative of the Climate Crisis. *The New York Times*, 28 October. On www.nytimes. com/2019/10/28/opinion/extinction-rebellion-london.html

Easthope, L., and Mort, M. (2014) Techologies of Recovery: Plans, Practices and Entangled Politics in Disaster. *Sociological Review*.

Easthope, L. (2018) *The Recovery Myth: The Plans and Situated Realities of Post-disaster Response*. London: Palgrave Macmillan.

Eashope, L. (2022) *When the Dust Settles*. London: Hodder and Stoughton.

Edwards, R., Franklin, J., and Holland, (2006) *Assessing Social Capital: Concept, Policy and Practice*. Newcastle: Cambridge Scholars Press.

Ehrenreich, B. (2001) *Nickel and Dimed: On (Not) Getting By in America*. London: Picador.

Engelbrecht, L. (2011) The Global Financial Crisis: Response of Social workers to the Financial Capability of Vulnerable Households in South Africa. *Journal of Social Intervention: Theory and Practice*, 20(2): 41–53.

Enarson, E., and Morrow, B. (1998) *The Gendered Terrain of Disaster: Through Women's Eyes*. Westport, CT: Praeger.

Engler, M., and Engler, P. (2016) *This Is an Uprising: How Nonviolent Revolt Is Shaping the Twenty-First Century*. New York: Bold Type Books.

Feng, X., Ma, J., Zhou, Y., England, P., Parsons, B., Rizza, M.A., and Walker, R.T. (2020) Geomorphology and Paleoseismology of the Weinan Fault, Shaanxi, Central China, and the Source of the 1556 Huaxian Earthquake. *Journal of Geophysical Research: Solid Earth*, 125, e2019JB017848. https:// doi.org/10.1029/2019JB017848

Fenton, J., and Kelly, T. (2017) 'Risk is King and Needs to take a Backseat!' Can Social Workers' Experiences of Moral Injury Strengthen Practice? *Journal of*

Social Work Practice, 31(4): 461–475. On https://doi.org/10.1080/02650533.2017.1394827

Ferguson, H. (2018) How Social Workers Reflect in Action and When and Why They Don't: The Possibilities and Limits to Reflective Practice in Social Work. *Social Work Education*, 37(4): 415–427. https://doi.org/10.1080/02615479.2017.1413083.

Finn, D., Chandrasekhar, D., and Xiao, Y. (2019) A Region Recovers: Planning for Resilience after Superstorm Sandy. *Journal of Planning Education and Research*, pp. 1–14. On https://journals.sagepub.com/doi/full/10.1177/0739456X19864145

FireSmart Canada (2019) On www.firesmartcanada.ca/

Folghereiter, F (2003) Relational Social Work: Principles and Practice, *Social Policy and Society*. 6(2): 265–274.

Foote, E.N. (1896) Eunice Newton Foote's Nearly Forgotten Discovery. *Physics Today: People and History*. On https://physicstoday.scitation.org/do/10.1063/pt.6.4.20210823a/full/

Foucault, M. (1980) *Power/Knowledge: Selected Interviews and Other Writings, 1972–1977*. New York: Pantheon Books.

Frank, A.G. (1966) *The Development of Underdevelopment*. New York: Monthly Review Press.

French, M. (1985) *The Power of Women*. Harmondsworth: Penguin.

Friedman, M., and Schwartz, A. (1963) *A Monetary History of the United States, 1867–1960*. Princeton, NJ: Princeton University Press.

Füssel, M. (2007) Vulnerability. *Global Environmental Change*, 17: 155–167.

Gaffney, D. A (2006) The Aftermath of Disaster Children in Crisis. *Journal of Clinical Psychology: In Session*, 62(8): 1001–1016.

Gal, J., Köngeter, S., and Vicary, S. (eds). (2020) *The Settlement House Movement Revisited: A Transnational History*. Bristol: Policy Press.

GHD (Good Humanitarian Donorship) (2003) *Good Humanitarian Donorship Principles*. On https://civil-protection-humanitarian-aid.ec.europa.eu/partnerships/relations/ghd_en

George, S (2003) Globalizing Rights? In M.J. Gibney (ed.), *Globalizing Rights*. Oxford: Oxford University Press.

Giddens, A. (2009) *The Politics of Climate Change*. Cambridge: Polity Press.

Goddard, E., and Sturrock, A. (2017) We Should Be in the Same Neighbourhoods as the Italians – but We're on the Outside. *The Independent*, 13 June. On www.independent.co.uk/news/long_reads/roma-gianturco-camp-settlement-naples-evicted-demolition-homeless-amnesty-european-human-rights-court-a7778571.html

Gordezky, R. (2017) *Fort McMurray Wildfire: A Case Study*. Ottawa: University of Ottawa. On https://ymcawun.files.wordpress.com/2015/04/fort-mcmurray-wildfire-case-study-final-jan-6-2017.pdf

Goulbourne, H. (1998) *Race Relations in Britain since 1945*. London: Macmillan.

Gray, M., Coates, J., and Hetherington, T. (eds) (2013) *Environmental Social Work*. London: Routledge.

Grierson, J. (2019) More than Half of Young People in Jail are of BME Background. *The Guardian*, 29 January. On www.theguardian.com/society/2019/jan/29/more-than-half-young-people-jail-are-of-bme-background

Gubbins, N. (2010) *The Role of Community Energy Schemes in Supporting Community Resilience.* York: JRF.

Gunder Frank, A (1966) The Development of Underdevelopment. *Monthly Review,* September, pp. 27–39.

Gurung, A. and Clark, A. (2018) The Perfect Storm: The Impact of Disaster Severity on Internal Human Trafficking. *International Area Studies Review,* 21(4): 302–322.

Hadborn, H., Hoffmann-Riem, H., Biber-Klemm, S., Grossenbacher-Mansuy, W., Joye, D., Pohl, C., Wiesmann, U., and Zemp, E. (2008) *Handbook of Transdisciplinary Research.* Bern: Springer.

Haigh, I., Ozsoy, O., Wadey, M., Nicholls, R., Gallop, S., Wahl, T., and Brown, J. (2017) An Improved Database of Coastal Flooding in the United Kingdom from 1915 to 2016. *Scientific Data,* 4: 170100. https://doi.org/10.1038/sdata.2017.100. On www.ncbi.nlm.nih.gov/pmc/articles/PMC5827111/pdf/sdata2017100.pdf

Hajat, S., Ebi, K., Kovats, R., Menne, B., Edwards, S., and Haines, A. (2005) The Human Health Consequences of Flooding in Europe: a Review. *Extreme Weather Events and Public Health Responses,* 185–196. On https://link.springer.com/chapter/10.1007/3-540-28862-7_18

Hansard Debates on Grenfell (2019) Grenfell Tower Fire. *Hansard,* Vol 661, 6 June. On https://hansard.parliament.uk/commons/2019-06-06/debates/69CABE5D-68DE-4DBB-A77E-0C33C804762B/GrenfellTowerFire

Haraway, D. (1988) Situated Knowledges: The Science Question in Feminism and the Privilege of Partial Perspective. *Feminist Studies,* 14(3): 575–599.

Haugstvedt, H. (2019) Trusting the Mistrusted: Norwegian Social Workers' Strategies in Preventing Radicalization and Violent Extremism. *Journal for Deradicalization,* 19: 149–184.

Haugstvedt, H. (2022) The Role of Social Support for Social Workers Engaged in Preventing Radicalization and Violent Extremism. *Nordic Social Work Research,* 12(1): 166–179, https://doi.org/10.1080/2156857X.2020.1806102 On www.tandfonline.com/action/showCitFormats?doi=10.1080%2F21568 57X.2020.1806102

Hayes, W. (2022) Tory 'Hostile Environment' Gets More Hostile. *Socialist Appeal,* 13 October. On https://socialist.net/tory-hostile-environment-gets-more-hostile/

Heid, A., Christman, Z., Pruchno, R., Cartwright, F., and Wilson-Genderson, (2016) Vulnerable, But Why? Post-Traumatic Stress Symptoms in Older Adults Exposed to Hurricane Sandy. *Disaster Medicine and Public Health Preparedness,* 10(3): 301–303. On www.cambridge.org/core/journals/disaster-medicine-and-public-health-preparedness/issue/superstorm-sandy/57B8876AD0994C4AD1874CEC99E153FA

Held, D and McGrew, A (eds) (2007) *Globalization Theory: Approaches and Controversies.* Cambridge: Polity Press.

Henry, B., and Henry, L. (2021) *Be Kind, Be Calm, Be Safe.* Toronto: Allen Lane.

Hewitt, K. (1997) *Regions of Revolt: A Geographical Introduction to Disasters.* Edinburgh: Longman.

Hillman, A., Tadd, W., Calnan, S., Bayer, A., (2013) Risk, Governance and the Experience of Care. *Sociology of Health and Illness,* 35(6): 939–955. On https://doi.org/10.1111/1467-9566.12017

Hillman, S., Horwell, C., Densmore, A., Damby., D., Fubini, B., Ishimine, Y., and Tomatis, M. (2012) Sakurajima Volcano: A Physico-chemical Study of the Health Consequences of Long-term Exposure to Volcanic Ash. *Bulletin of Volcanology*, 74: 913–930. https://doi.org/10.1007/s00445-012-0575-3. On www.paho.org/disasters/dmdocuments/SakurajimaVolcPhysico-chemStudy-HealthConsequences.pdf

Hind, D., Allsopp, K., Chitsabesan, P., and French, P. (2021) The Psychosocial Response to a Terrorist Attack at Manchester Arena, 2017: A Process Evaluation. *British Medical Council, Psychology*, On https://bmcpsychology.biomedcentral.com/articles/10.1186/s40359-021-00527-4

HO (Home Office) (2011) *Prevent Strategy*. London: Stationary Office.

HO (Home Office) (2015) *Revised Prevent Duty Guidance: for England and Wales, and Separately for Scotland*. London: HO. On www.gov.uk/government/publications/prevent-duty-guidance

Hollender, J. (2002) Resisting Vulnerability: The Social Reconstruction of Gender in Interaction. *Social Problems*, 49(4): 474–496.

Holtz, D., Zhaoa, M., Benzellb, S., Caoa, C., Rahimiana, A., Yanga, J., Allena, J., Collisb, A., Moehringa, A., Sowrirajan, T., Ghosha, D., Zhanga, Y., Dhillonb, T., Nicolaidesa, C., Ecklesa, D., and Arala, S. (2020) Interdependence and the Cost of Uncoordinated Responses to COVID-19. *PNASS*, 117(33): 19837–19843. On www.pnas.org/doi/pdf/10.1073/pnas.2009522117

Homfeldt, H and Reutlinger, C (2008) Social Development. *Social Work: An International Online Journal*, 6:2 On www.socwork.net/sws/article/view/70/372

Hoogvelt, A. (2007) Globalisation and Imperialism: Wars and Humanitarian Intervention. In Dominelli, L. (ed.) *Revitalising Communities in a Globalising World*, pp. 17–42. Aldershot: Ashgate.

Horwell, C., and Baxter, P. (2006) The Respiratory Health Hazards of Volcanic Ash: A Review for Volcanic Risk Mitigation. *Bulletin of Vulcanology*, 69(1):1–24. https://doi.org/10.1007/s00445-006-0052-y

Horwell, C., Ferdiwijaya, B., Wahyudi, T., and Dominelli, L. (2018) Use of Respiratory Protection in Yogyakarta During the 2014 Eruption of Kelud, Indonesia: Community and Agency Perspectives. *Journal of Volcanology and Geothermal Research*, 382: 92–102.

Hynes, G. (1914) *Defence of the Realm Act (DORA)*. On https://encyclopedia.1914-1918-online.net/home/

IASSW (International Association of Schools of Social Work) (2020) *The In-Country Reports on Covid-19*. On www.iassw-aiets.org

IFRC (International Federation of the Red Cross and Red Crescent Societies) (2018) *The World Disaster Report*, 2018. Geneva: IFRC.

IFRC (International Federation of the Red Cross and Red Crescent Societies) (2020) *The World Disaster Report, 2020*. Geneva: IFRC.

Inter-Agency Standing Committee (IASC)(2007) *IASC Guidelines on Mental Health and Psychosocial Support in Emergency Settings*. Geneva: IASC.

International Labour Organisation (ILO) (2000) *World Labour Report, 2000*. Geneva: ILO.

Ioakimidis, V., Santos, C., Herroro, I. (2014) Reconceptualizing Social Work in Times of Crisis: An Examination of the Cases of Greece, Spain and Portugal. *International Social Work*, 57(4): 285–300. On https://journals.sagepub.com/doi/pdf/10.1177/0020872814524967.

IPCC (Intergovernmental Panel on Climate Change) (2012) *Special Report on Managing the Risks of Extreme Events and Disasters to Advance Climate Change Adaptation. A Special Report of Working Groups I and II of the Intergovernmental Panel on Climate Change* [Field, C.B., V. Barros, T.F. Stocker, D. Qin, D.J. Dokken, K.L. Ebi, M.D. Mastrandrea, K.J. Mach, G.-K. Plattner, S.K. Allen, M. Tignor, and P.M. Midgley (eds)]. Cambridge: Cambridge University Press.

IPCC (Intergovernmental Panel on Climate Change) (2014) Fifth Assessment Report. Available from www.ipcc.ch/report/ar5.

IPCC (Intergovernmental Panel on Climate Change) (2015) *The Paris Agreement.* Paris: UNFCCC COP21 Meeting, 12 December.

IPCC (Intergovernmental Panel on Climate Change) (2018) *Global Warming of 1.5°C.* Report available on: www.ipcc.ch/site/assets/uploads/sites/2/2019/06/SR15_Full_Report_High_Res.pdf

Islam, N., and Winkel, J. (2017) Climate Change and Social Inequality. DESA (Department of Economic and Social Affairs) Working Paper No. 152, ST/ESA/2017/DWP/152. On www.un.org/esa/desa/papers/2017/wp152_2017.pdf

IUCN (International Union for Conservation of Nature) (2021) *Issues Brief: Peatlands and Climate Change,* November, pp. 2. On file:///D:/Peatlands%20iucn_issues_peatlands_and_climate_change_final_nov21.pdf

Jackson, R. (2020) Eunice Foote, John Tyndall, a Question of Priority. *Journal of the Royal Society of the History of Science, Notes and Record,* 74(1): 105–118. On https://royalsocietypublishing.org/doi/epdf/10.1098/rsnr.2018.0066

Jollands, M., Morris, J., and Moffat, A.J. (2011) Wildfires in Wales. *Report to Forestry Commission Wales.* Farnharm: Forest Research. On www.forestry.gov.uk/fr/wildfiresinwales#finalreport

Jones, J. (2012) *Hillsborough: The Report of the Hillsborough Independent Panel.* London: The Stationary Office. On https://assets.publishing.service.gov.uk/government/uploads/system/uploads/attachment_data/file/229038/0581.pdf

Jongman, (2017) Effective Adaptation to Rising Flood Risk. *Nature Communications,* 9: 1986, https://doi.org/10.1038/s41467-018-04396-1.

Kerasidou, A., and Kingori, P. (2019) Austerity Measures and the Transforming Role of A&E Professionals in a Weakening Welfare System. *PLoS ONE,* 14(2): e0212314. On www.ncbi.nlm.nih.gov/pmc/articles/PMC6373963/pdf/pone.0212314.pdf

Keddell, E. (2017) Comparing Risk-Averse and Risk-Friendly Practitioners in Child Welfare Decision-Making: A Mixed Methods Study. *Journal of Social Work Practice,* 31(4): 411–429. On https://doi.org/10.1080/02650533.2017.1394822

Kelly, P.M., and Adger, N. (2000) Theory and Practice in Assessing Vulnerability to Climate Change and Facilitating Adaptation. *Climate Change,* 47(4): 325–352.

Kendall, K. (2010) *Social Work Education: Its Origins in Europe.* Alexandria, VA: CSWE.

Kidson, C. (1953) The Exmoor Storm and the Lynmouth Flood. *Geography,* 38(1): 1–9. On www.jstor.org/stable/pdf/40563346.pdf?refreqid=excelsior%3A14e213942ac8203faf1a275794f9417e

Kirby, (2006) *Vulnerability and Violence. The Impact of Globalization.* London: Pluto Press.

Kirsch, T. D., Wadhwani, C., Sauer, L., Doocy, S., and Catlett, C. (2012) Impact of the 2010 Pakistan Floods on Rural and Urban Populations at Six Months. *PLoS Currents*, 4, e4fdfb212d2432. On https://doi.org/10.1371/4fdfb212d2432

Klein, N. (2007) *The Shock Doctrine: The Rise of Disaster Capitalism*. New York, Metropolitan Books.

Kleinman, A. (1999) Experience and its Moral Modes: Culture, Human Conditions, and Disorder. *Tanner Lectures on Human Values*, 20: 355–420. On https://tannerlectures.utah.edu/_resources/documents/a-to-z/k/Kleinman99.pdf

Knight, S. (2020) Shamima Begum, the ISIS Bride, Is No Longer British: What Does Citizenship Mean? *The New Yorker*, 15 April. On www.newyorker.com/news/letter-from-the-uk/if-shamima-begum-the-isis-bride-is-no-longer-british-what-does-citizenship-mean

Knudsen, RA. (2018) Measuring Radicalisation: Risk Assessment Conceptualisations and Practice in England and Wales. *Behavioral Sciences of Terrorism and Political Aggression*, 1–18. https://doi.org/10.1080/19434472.2018.1509105

Kolbert, E. (2006) *Fieldnotes from a Catastrophe: Man, Nature and Climate Change*. London: Bloomsbury Publishing.

Kokaliari, E. (2016) Quality of Life, Anxiety, Depression, and Stress among Adults in Greece Following the Global Financial Crisis. *International Social Work*, 61(3): 410–424. On https://journals.sagepub.com/doi/abs/10.1177/0020872816651701

Koehler, D., and Fiebig. V. (2019) Knowing What to Do: Academic and Practitioner Understanding of How to Counter Violent Radicalization. *Perspectives on Terrorism*, 13(3): 44–62.

Kruglanski, A., Jasko, K., Webber, D., Chernikova, M., and Molinario, E. (2018) The Making of Violent Extremists. *Review of General Psychology*, 22(1): 107–120. https://doi.org/10.1037/gpr0000144

Ku, H B and Ma, Y N (2015) Rural–Urban Alliance' as a New Model for Post-Disaster Social Work Intervention in Community Reconstruction: The Case in Sichuan, China. *International Social Work*, 58(5): 743–758. https://doi.org/10.1177/0020872815583073

Ku, H B, and Dominelli, L. (2018) Not only Eating Together: Space and Green Social Work. *British Journal of Social Work*, 48(5): 1409–1431.

Kundnani, A. (2009) *Spooked: How Not to Prevent Violent Extremism*. Report. London: Institute.

Landis, M., Edgerton, E., White, E., Wentworth, G., Sullivan, A., and Dillner, A. (2018) The Impact of the 2016 Fort McMurray Horse River Wildfire on Ambient Air Pollution Levels in the Athabasca Oil Sands Region, Alberta, Canada. *Science Total Environment*, March 15, 618: 1665–1676. On www.ncbi.nlm.nih.gov/pmc/articles/PMC6084447/pdf/nihms-983401.pdf

Lane, S., Odoni, N., Landstrom, C., Whatmore, S., Ward, N., and Bradley, S. (2011) Doing Flood Risk Science Differently: An Experiment in Radical Scientific Method. *Transactions of the Institute of British Geographers*, 36(1): 15–36. On www.researchgate.net/publication/227790320_Doing_flood_risk_science_differently_An_experiment_in_radical_scientific_method

Latour, B. (2017) *Facing Gaia: Eight Lectures on the New Climatic Regime*. London: John Wiley Publisher.

Lindell, M., and Perry, R. (2012) The Protective Action Decision Model: Theoretical Modifications and Additional Evidence. *Risk Analysis*, 32(4):616–632, https://doi.org/10.1111/j.1539-6924.2011.01647.x

Liu, Q, J.Q. Wang and Y. N. Qin (2012) Chinese Tibetan Guozhuang Dance from the Perspective of Sports. *Asian Social Science*, 8(7): 240–246.

Loo, YY., Billa, L., and Singh, A. (2015) Effect of Climate Change on Seasonal Monsoon in Asia and its Impact on the Variability of Monsoon Rainfall in Southeast Asia. *Geoscience Frontiers*, 6(6): 817–823.

Lubell, M., Stacey, M., and Humme, M. (2021) Collective Action Problems and Governance Barriers to Sea-Level Rise Adaptation in San Francisco Bay. *Climatic Change*, 167(46): 25–46. On https://link.springer.com/article/10.1007/s10584-021-03162-5

Lundberg, E. (2021) Guardians of Democracy? On the Response of Civil Society Organisations to Right-Wing Extremism. *Scandinavian Political Studies*, 44(2): 170–194. On https://doi.org/10.1111/1467-9477.12193

Makondo, C., and Thomas, D. (2018) Climate Change Adaptation: Linking Indigenous Knowledge with Western Science for Effective Adaptation. *Environmental and Policy*, 88: 83–91. On www.sciencedirect.com/science/article/pii/S1462901118300418

Manyena, S.B. (2006) The Concet of Resilience Revisited. *Disasters*, 30(4): 383–507. On https://onlinelibrary.wiley.com/doi/epdf/10.1111/j.0361-3666.2006.00331.x?saml_referrer

Martin, U. (2015) Health after Disaster: A Perspective of Psychological/Health Reactions to Disaster. *Cogent Psychology*, 2(1): 1–7, 1053741, https://doi.or g/10.1080/23311908.2015.1053741 On https://doi.org/10.1080/23311908.2 015.1053741

Mathbor, G. (2007) Enhancement of Community Preparedness for Natural Disasters: The Role of Social Work in Building Social Capital for Sustainable Disaster Relief and Management. *International Social Work*, 50(3): 357–369. On https://journals.sagepub.com/doi/pdf/10.1177/0020872807076049

Mathias, A.L., and Nähri K. (eds) (2017) *The Ecosocial Transition of Societies*. London: Routledge.

Matlakala FK, Makhubele JC, Nyahunda L. (2022) Social Workers' Intervention during Natural Hazards. *Jamba*. Jun 29,14(1): 1176. https://doi.org/10.4102/jamba.v14i1.1176. PMID: 35812830; PMCID: PMC9257783.

Mattsson, T. (2014) Intersectionality as a Useful Tool: Anti-Oppressive Social Work and Critical Reflection. *Affilia*, 29(1): 8–17. https://doi.org/10.1177/0886109913510659

Maynard, A. (2017) Shrinking the State. *Journal of the Royal Society of Medicine*, 110(2): 49–51. https://doi.org/10.1177/01410 76816 686923

Maynard, N. (2018) Activism across the Lifecourse : Circumstantial, Dormant and Embedded Activisms. *Area*, 50(2): 205–212. On https://dro.dur.ac.uk/21503/1/21503.pdf

McCall, C. (2022) BP Profits 'Utterly Obscene' as Energy Giant Earns £7.1 Billion in Just Three Months. *Daily Record*, 1 Nov. On www.dailyrecord.co.uk/news/politics/bp-profits-utterly-obscene-energy-28377234

McGee, T. (2019) Preparedness and Experiences of Evacuees from the 2016 Fort McMurray Horse River Wildfire. *Fire*, 2, 13. https://doi.org/10.3390/fire2010013 On www.mdpi.com/2571-6255/2/1/13/htm

McKendrick, D., and Finch, J. (2016) Under Heavy Manners? Social Work, Radicalisation, Troubled Families and Non-Linear War. *British Journal of Social Work*, 308–324. https://doi.org/10.1093/bjsw/bcv141.

McKinnon, J., and Alston, M. (eds) (2016) *Ecological Social Work: Towards Sustainability*. London: Palgrave Macmillan.

McLeod, G. (2018) The Grenfell Tower Atrocity: Exposing Urban Worlds of Inequality, Injustice, and an Impaired Democracy. *City, Analysis of Urban Trends, Culture, Theory, Policy, Action*, 22(4): 460–489. https://doi.org/10.10 80/13604813.2018.1507099. On www.tandfonline.com/loi/ccit20

McTeer Toney, H. (2019) *Moving Past Stereotypes: Climate Action IS the Social Justice Issue of Our Time*, Paper Delivered at the Bioneers 2019 30th Conference, Seeding the Field, Growing Transformative Solutions. Transcript on https://bioneers.org/moving-past-stereotypes-climate-action-social-justice-heather-mcteer-toney-zstf1911/

Meacher, M. (1975) [to be completed]

Meadows, D. (2008) *Thinking in Systems*. White River Junction, VT: Chelsea Breen Publishing.

Meadows, D., Meadows, D., Randers, J., and Behrens, W. (1972) *The Limits to Growth*. Washington, DC: Potamac Associate Books. On www.donellameadows.org/wp-content/userfiles/Limits-to-Growth-digital-scan-version.pdf

Mitchell, T., and Harris, K. (2012) *Resilience: A Risk Management Approach*. London: ODI. On www.odi.org/sites/odi.org.uk/files/odi-assets/publications-opinion-files/7552.pdf

Monbiot, G. (2019) Today, I Aim to Get Arrested. It Is the Only Real Power Climate Protesters Have. *The Guardian*, 16 October. On www.theguardian.com/commentisfree/2019/oct/16/i-aim-to-get-arrested-climate-protesters

Moore-Bick (2019) *Grenfell Tower Inquiry: Phase 1 Report*. On https://assets.grenfelltowerinquiry.org.uk/GTI%20-%20Phase%201%20full%20report%20-%20volume%201.pdf

Moore-Bick, (2021) *The Grenfell Tower Fire Inquiry*. Phase 1, Volumes 1–4. On www.grenfelltowerinquiry.org.uk/phase-1-report

Mor, F. (2018) *Bank rescues of 2007–09: Outcomes and Cost*. London: House of Commons Library, Briefing Paper, 5748. 8 October. On https://researchbriefings.files.parliament.uk/documents/SN05748/SN05748.pdf

Musso, M., and Crouzet, G. (2020) Energy Imperialism? *Journal of Energy History*, 3, pp 1–5. On https://energyhistory.eu/sites/default/files/pdf/04_Energy%20Imperialism.pdf

Mutascu, M. I., Albulescu, C. T., Apergis, N., and Magazzino, C. (2022). Do Gasoline and Diesel Prices Co-move? Evidence from the Time–Frequency Domain. *Environmental Science and Pollution Research*, 29(45): 68776–68795. On https://doi.org/10.1007/s11356-022-20517-2

Narayanan, A., Finucane, M., Acosta, J., and Wicker, A. (2020). From Awareness to Action: Accounting for Infrastructure Interdependencies in Disaster Response and Recovery Planning. *GeoHealth*, 2, e2020GH000251. https://doi.org/ 10.1029/2020GH000251, On www.ncbi.nlm.nih.gov/pmc/articles/PMC7415906/pdf/GH2-4-e2020GH000251.pdf

Neumayer, E., and Plümper, T. (2007) The Gendered Nature of Natural Disasters: The Impact of Catastrophic Events on the Gender Gap in Life Expectancy, 1981–2002. *Annals of the Association of American Geographers*, 97:3, 551–566, https://doi.org/10.1111/j.1467-8306.2007.00563.x On https://doi.org/10.1111/j.1467-8306.2007.00563.x

Newsinger, J. (1999) *Orwell's Politics*. London: Macmillan.

Nikku, B. (2016) *Prostitution in Post-Earthquake Nepal*. Durham: Durham University, SASS Seminar Lecture, March.

Nishimura, L. (2015) Climate Change Migrants': Impediments to a Protection Framework and the Need to Incorporate Migration into Climate Change Adaptation Strategies. *International Journal of Refugee Law*, 27(1): 107–134. On https://doi.org/10.1093/ijrl/eev002

Nordhaus, W. (2018) Projections and Uncertainties about Climate Change in an Era of Minimal Climate Policies. *American Economic Journal: Economic Policy Review*, 10(3): 333–360. On https://doi.org/10.1257/pol.20170046

Nordtveit, B. (2010) Towards Post-Globalisation? On the Hegemony of Western Education and Development Discourses. *Globalisation, Societies and Education*, 8(3): 321–337, https://doi.org/10.1080/14767724.2010.505094.

Nyong, A., Adesina, E., and Osman Elasha, B. (2007) The Value of Indigenous Knowledge in Climate Change Mitigation and Adaptation Strategies in the African Sahel. *Mitigation and Adaptation Strategies for Global Change*, 12: 787–797. On www.researchgate.net/publication/46537001_The_Value_of_Indigenous_Knowledge_in_Climate_Change_Mitigation_and_Adaptation_Strategies_in_the_African_Sahel

O'Toole, Meer, N., Nilsson De Hanas, D., Jones, S., and Modood, T. (2016) Governing through Prevent? Regulation and Contested Practice in State–Muslim Engagement. *Sociology*, 50(1): 160–177.

Oxfam (2016) *An Economy for the 1%*. Oxford: Oxfam. On www.oxfam.org/en/research/economy-1#:~:text=The%20global%20inequality%20crisis%20is, the%20richest%20and%20the%20rest

Parker, D. (2017) Grenfell | Burning Questions Unanswered. *New Civil Engineer*, 18 August. On www.newcivilengineer.com/archive/grenfell-burning-questions-unanswered-16-08-2017/

Parker, D. (2020) Disaster Resilience – a Challenged Science. *Environmental Hazards*, 19(1): 1–9. On https://doi.org/10.1080/17477891.2019.1694857

Parkinson, D., and Zara, C. (2013) The Hidden Disaster: Domestic Violence in the Aftermath of Natural Disaster. *The Australian Journal of Emergency Management*, 28(2): 28–35.

Parsons, T., and Smelser, J. (1957) *Economy and Society*, Glencoe, IL: The Free Press.

Pelling, M. (2003) *Natural Disasters and Development in a Globalizing World*. London: Routledge.

Pelling, M., and Manuel-Navarette, M. (2011) From Resilience to Transformation: The Adaptive Cycle in two Mexican Urban Centers. *Ecology and Society*, 6: 11. On www.ecologyandsociety.org/vol16/iss2/art11/

Pistone, I., Eriksson, E., Beckman, U., Mattson, C., and Sager, M. (2019) A Scoping Review of Interventions for Preventing and Countering Violent Extremism: Current Status and Implications for Future Research. *Journal for Deradicalization*, 19: 1–84.

Pittaway, E., Bartolomei, L., and Rees, S. (2007) Gendered Dimensions of the 2004 Tsunami and a Potential Social Work Response in Post-Disaster Situations. *International Social Work*, 50(3): 307–319. On https://journals.sagepub.com/doi/pdf/10.1177/0020872807076042

Polka, E. (2018) Global Flood Risk under Climate Change. *Public Health Post*, 17 April. On www.publichealthpost.org/databyte/global-flood-risk-under-climate-change/ Accessed 16/06/22.

Pomerantsev, P. (2014) *Non-Linear War*. 28 March. On www.lrb.co.uk/blog/2014/march/non-linear-war

Ponsot, AS., Autixier, C., and Madriaza, P. (2017) Factors Facilitating the Successful Implementation of a Prevention of Violent Radicalization Intervention as Identified by Front-Line Practitioners. *Journal for Deradicalization*, 18(16): 1–33.

Post, R. (2009) Debating Disciplinarity. *Critical Inquiry*, 35: 749–772. On https://digitalcommons.law.yale.edu/cgi/viewcontent.cgi?referer=www.google.com/&httpsredir=1&article=1163&context=fss_papers

Pottick, E.K., and Pottick, J. (2014) *Superstorm Sandy and Social Work Responses*. On https://blog.oup.com/2014/03/superstorm-sandy-social-work-resources/

Poynting, S. (2012) *Counter-Terrorism and State Political Violence*. London: Routledge.

Prainsack, B. and Buyx, A. (2011). *Solidarity: Reflections on an Emerging Concept in Bioethics*. London: Nuffield Council on Bioethics.

Putnam, R. (2000) *Bowling Alone: The Collapse and Revival of American Community*. New York: Simon and Schuster.

Pyles, L. (2006) Toward a Post-Katrina Framework: Social Work as Human Rights and Capabilities. *Journal of Comparative Social Welfare*, 22(1), pp. 79–87.

Pyles, L. (2007) Community Organizing for Post-Disaster Social Development. *International Social Work*, 50(3), pp. 321–33.

Pyles, L. (2011) Neoliberalism, INGO Practices and Sustainable Disaster Recovery: A Post-Katrina Case Study. *Community Development Journal*, 46(2), pp. 168–80.

Pyles, L. (2015) Participation and Other Ethical Considerations in Participatory Action Research in Post-Earthquake Rural Haiti. *International Social Work*, 58(5), pp. 628–45.

Pyles, L. (2016) Decolonising Disaster Social Work: Environmental Justice and Community Participation. *British Journal of Social Work*, 1–18. On www.researchgate.net/profile/Loretta_Pyles/publication/301830989_Decolonising_Disaster_Social_Work_Environmental_Justice_and_Community_Participation/links/5a7324940f7e9b20d48eec9d/Decolonising-Disaster-Social-Work-Environmental-Justice-and-Community-Participation.pdf

Pyles, L., Kulkarni, S. and Lein, L. (2008) Economic Survival Strategies and Food Insecurity: The Case of Hurricane Katrina in New Orleans. *Journal of Social Service Research*, 34(3), pp. 43–53.

Pyles, L., Svistova, J. and Andre, J. (2015) *Disaster Recovery in Post-Earthquake Rural Haiti: Research Findings and Recommendations for Participatory, Sustainable Recovery*, Albany, NY, University at Albany.

Qurashi, F. (2018) The *Prevent* Strategy and the UK 'War on Terror': Embedding Infrastructures of Surveillance in Muslim Communities. *Palgrave Communications*, 4(17). On https://doi.org/10.1057/s41599-017-0061-9

Rinkel, M., and Powers, M. (eds) (2016) *Social Work Promoting Social and Environmental Sustainability*. Berne: IFSW.

Robinson, F. (2011) *The Ethics of Care. A Feminist Approach to Human Security*. Philadelphia, PA: Temple University Press.

Rosenfeld, L.B. J. S. Caye, O. Avalon, and M. Lahad (2005) *When their World Falls Apart: Helping Families and Children Manage the Effects of Disasters*. Washington, DC: NASW Press.

Ross, S. (2022) *Major Regulations Following the 2008 Financial Crisis*. On www.investopedia.com/ask/answers/063015/what-are-major-laws-acts-regulating-financial-institutions-were-created-response-2008-financial.asp

Rowlatt, J. (2022) Peat Soil Fires: Campaigners Say England's 'Rainforests' Illegally Burned. *BBC News*, 30 May. On www.bbc.co.uk/news/science-environment-61607510

Ruskin, J., Rasula, R., Schneider, S., Bevilacqua, K., Taiolic, E., Schwartz, R. (2018) Lack of Access to Medical Care during Hurricane Sandy and Mental Health Symptoms. *Preventative Medicine Reports*, 10: 363–269. On www.sciencedirect.com/science/article/pii/S221133551830069X?via%3Dihub

Sadri, N., Hasan, S., Ukkusuri, S., and Cebrian, M. (2018) Crisis Communication Patterns in Social Media during Hurricane Sandy. *Transportation Research Record*, 2672(1): 125–137. On https://journals.sagepub.com/doi/pdf/10.1177/0361198118773896

Said, E (1978) *Orientalism*. New York: Random House.

Sammonds, P. (2018) Transdisciplinary Collaboration between Physical and Social Scientists – Drawing on the Experiences of an Advisor to Earthquakes without Frontiers (EwF). In L. Dominelli, (ed.), *The Routledge Handbook of Green Social Work*, pp. 21–34. Abingdon: Routledge.

Santos, J., Castro Herrera, L., Danielle, K., Yu, S., Pagsuyoin, A., and Tan, R. (2014) State of the Art in Risk Analysis of Workforce Criticality Influencing Disaster Preparedness for Interdependent Systems. *Risk Analysis*, 34(6): 1–13. On https://onlinelibrary.wiley.com/doi/epdf/10.1111/risa.12183?saml_referrer

Satterthwaite, D. (2009) The Implications of Population Growth and Urbanization for Climate Change. *Environment and Urbanization*, 21(2): 545–567. On www.environmentportal.in/files/population%20growth%20and%20climate%20change.pdf

Saunders, J. (2022) *The Manchester Arena Inquiry*, Vols 1 and 2. On https://manchesterarenainquiry.org.uk/report-volume-one and https://manchesterarenainquiry.org.uk/report-volume-two

Schmeltz, M., González, S., Fuentes, L., Kwan, A., Ortega-Williams, A., and Pilar Cowan, L. (2013) Lessons from Hurricane Sandy: A Community Response in Brooklyn, New York. *Journal of Urban Health*, 90(5). On https://doi.org/10.1007/s11524-013-9832-9.

Scottish Fire and Rescue Service (n.d.) *Wildfires*. On www.firescotland.gov.uk/your-safety/outdoors/wildfires/

Scottish Fire and Rescue Service (n.d.) Advice on Dialing 999. On https://www.firescotland.gov.uk/

SDGs (Sustainable Development Goals) (2015) *The 17 Sustainable Development Goals*. On www.fivetalents.org.uk/un-sustainable-development-goals/?gclid=EAIaIQobChMIpZKQpYjV2AIVQ40bCh0khga8EAAYAiAAEgJ9DPD_BwE Accessed 12/12/2017 and https://sustainabledevelopment.un.org/?menu=1300

Seton, A. (2022) Scottish Fire and Rescue Service (SFRS) – *Wildfire: Incident Reporting System – Data Analyses*. On www.gov.scot/publications/provision-analyses-scottish-fire-rescue-service-sfrs-incident-reporting-system-irs-data-relation-wildfire-incidents/pages/8/

Shildrick, T. (2018) Lessons from Grenfell: Poverty Propaganda, Stigma and Class Power. *The Sociological Review*, 66(4): 783–798. On https://doi.org/10.1177/0038026118777424

Sim T (2015) Psychosocial Work. In D.W. James (ed.), *International Encyclopedia of the Social and Behavioral Sciences*, 19: 477–483. 2nd edn. Oxford: Elsevier.

Sim, T and Dominelli, L (2017) When the Mountains Move: A Chinese Post-Disaster Psychosocial Social Work Model. *Qualitative Social Work*, 16(5): 594–611 On http://journals.sagepub.com/doi/pdf/10.1177/1473325016637912

Sim, T., Lau, J., and Su, G. (n.d.) *Transdisciplinarity in the Earthquake Without Frontiers Project*. Personal communication to author.

Sliwinski, S. (2009) The Aesthetics of Human Rights. *Culture, Theory and Critique*, 50(1): 23–39. On www.tandfonline.com/doi/full/10.1080/14735780802696336?needAccess=true

Smit, B., and Wandel, J. (2006) Adaptation, Adaptive Capacity and Vulnerability. *Global Environmental Change*, 16(3): 282–292.

Smith, C., and Sorrell, K. (2014). On Social Solidarity. In V. Jeffries (eds), *The Palgrave Handbook of Altruism, Morality, and Social Solidarity*. London: Palgrave Macmillan, pp. 219–247. https://doi.org/10.1057/9781137391865_10

Smith, G.P., and Wenger D. (2007) Sustainable Disaster Recovery: Operationalizing an Existing Agenda. In H. Rodriguez, E. Quarantelli and R. Dynes (eds), *Handbook of Disaster Research*. New York: Springer. On https://doi.org/10.1007/978-0-387-32353-4_14

SPF (2015) *Social Protection Floor*. On http://www.ilo.org/secsoc/areas-of-work/policy-development-and-applied-research/social-protection-floor/lang--en/index.htm accessed 30 Jan 2015.

Sovacool, B.K., Martiskainen, M., Hook, A. and Baker, L. (2019) Decarbonization and its Discontents: A Critical Energy Justice Perspective on Four Low-Carbon Transitions. *Climatic Change*, 155: 581–619. On https://doi.org/10.1007/s10584-019-02521-7

Stec, A., Dickens, A., Salden, K., Hewitt, M., Watts, F., Houldsworth, P., and Martin, F. (2018). *Occupational Exposure to Polycyclic Aromatic Hydrocarbons and Elevated Cancer Incidence in Firefighters*. On http://clok.uclan.ac.uk/21626/

Stern, N. (2007) *The Economics of Climate Change: The Stern Review*. Cambridge: Cambridge University Press.

Stromquist, N. (1990) Women and Illiteracy. *Comparative Education Review*, pp. 190–111.

Summers, J. K., Harwell, L. C., Smith, L. M., and Buck, K. D. (2018). Measuring community resilience to natural hazards: The Natural Hazard Resilience

Screening Index (NaHRSI)— Development and application to the United States. *GeoHealth*, 2, 372–394. https://doi.org/10.1029/2018GH000160

Sun, C. Q (2005) Entertaining and Body-Building Values of Tibetan Folk Dance. *Journal of Xian Institute of Physical Education*, 22(22): 89–91.

Svistova, J., and Pyles, L. (2018) *Production of Disaster and Recovery in Post-Earthquake Haiti*. London: Routledge.

Swift, K. (1997) *Manufacturing 'Bad' Mothers*. Toronto: University of Toronto Press.

Tarnoff, C. (2018) *The Marshall Plan: Design, Accomplishments, and Significance*. Report for Members and Committees of Congress. On https://sgp.fas.org/crs/row/R45079.pdf

Taylor, D. (2018). Grenfell Inquiry Cuts Ties with KPMG Following Complaints. *The Guardian*, 7 Jan. On www.theguardian.com/uk-news/2018/jan/07/grenfell-inquiry-cuts-ties-kpmg-following-complaints

Ten Have, H. (2018) *Disasters, Vulnerability and Human Rights*. London: Springer. On https://link.springer.com/chapter/10.1007/978-3-319-92722-0_11

Thomas P. (2012) *Responding to the Threat of Violent Extremism: Failing to Prevent*. London: Bloomsbury.

Thomas, A., Baptiste, A., Martyr-Koller, R., Pringle, P., and Rhiney, K. (2020) Climate Change and Small Island Developing States. *Annual Review of Environmental Resources*, 45: 1–27. On www.annualreviews.org/doi/pdf/10.1146/annurev-environ-012320-083355

Thomson, M., Kentikelenis, A. and Stubbs, T. (2017) Structural Adjustment Programmes Adversely Affect Vulnerable Populations: A Systematic-Narrative Review of Their Effect on Child and Maternal Health. *Health Reviews*, 38(13) 1–18. On https://publichealthreviews.biomedcentral.com/articles/10.1186/s40985-017-0059-2

Throsby, D., and Petetskaya, E. (2016) Sustainability Concepts in Indigensous and Non-Indigenous Cultures. *International Journal of Cultural Property*, 23: 119–140. On www.cambridge.org/core/journals/international-journal-of-cultural-property/article/sustainability-concepts-in-indigenous-and-nonindigenous-cultures/00C9321FC8ED4EA427B66A787CBAEE61

Thurston, AM., Stöckl, H., Ranganathan, M. (2021) Natural Hazards, Disasters and Violence against Women and Girls: A Global Mixed-Methods Systematic Review. *British Medical Journal, Global Health*, 6:e004377. https://doi.org/10.1136/bmjgh-2020-004377 On https://gh.bmj.com/content/bmjgh/6/4/e004377.full.pdf

To, P., Eboreime, E. and Agyapong, V.I.O. (2021) The Impact of Wildfires on Mental Health: A Scoping Review. *Behavioural Sciences*, 11: 126–144. https://doi.org/10.3390/ bs11090126.

UIA (2021) Illiteracy Among Women in *Encyclopedia of World Problems and Human Potential*. On http://encyclopedia.uia.org/en/problem/154236#:~:text=Further%2C%20female%20illiteracy%20confirms%20society's, and%20those%20of%20their%20children.

UN (United Nations) (2016) *Leaving No One Behind: The Imperative of Inclusive Development. The World Social Situation, 2016*. New York: UN DESA. On https://desapublications.un.org/?keywords=leaving%20no%20one%20behind

Ungar, M. (2002) A Deeper, More Social Ecological Social Work Practice. *Social Service Review*, 76(3): 480–97. On *JSTOR*, https://doi.org/10.1086/341185

UN-REDD (2016) *UN-REDD Programme Strategic Framework 2016–2020, Draft for Consultation.* Geneva: UN-REDD. On www.un-redd.org/sites/default/files/2021-10/UNRP%20strategic%20framework%202016-2020%20draft%20for%20consultation%20%282%29.pdf

UNICEF (UN Children's Fund) (2018) *Children Recruited by Armed Forces or Armed Groups.* On www.unicef.org/protection/children-recruited-by-armedforces

UNISDR (UN International Strategy for Disaster Reduction, now UNDRR (Disaster Risk Reduction). (2009) *Terminology on Disaster Risk Reduction.* Geneva: United Nations.

UNISDR (2015) *Global Assessment Report on Disaster Risk Reduction, Making Development Sustainable: The Future of Disaster Risk Management.* Geneva: United Nations.

Van Berkel, R., De Graff, W., and Sirovátka, T. (2011) *The Governance of Active Welfare States in Europe.* London: Palgrave Macmillan.

Van Eck, R., Gullett, H., Lamb, S., Krouse, H., Mazzurco, L., Lage, O., Lewis, J., and Lomis, K. (2021) The Power of Interdependence: Linking Health Systems, Communities, and Health Professions: Educational Programs to Better Meet the Needs of Patients and Populations. *Medical Teacher*, 43(2): S32–S38. On https://doi.org/10.1080/0142159X.2021.1935834

Västfjäll, D., Slovic, P., Mayorga, M., and Peters, E. (2014) Compassion Fade: Affect and Charity Are Greatest for a Single Child in Need. *PLOS One*, 9(6): e100115, 1–10. On https://journals.plos.org/plosone/article?id=10.1371/journal.pone.0100115

Veleva, V. (2020) The Role of Entrepreneurs in Advancing Sustainable Lifestyles: Challenges, Impacts, and Future Opportunities. *Journal of Cleaner Production*, 283: 0959-6526. Online version published later on www.sciencedirect.com/science/article/pii/S0959652620347028?via%3Dihub

Vertovec, S. (2007) Super-diversity and its Implications. *Ethnic and Racial Studies*, 30(6): 1024–1054. On: https://doi.org/10.1080/01419870701599465.

Vincent, K., Naess, L.O. and Goulden, M. (2013) National Level Policies versus Local Level Realities – Can the Two Be Reconciled to Promote Sustainable Adaptation? In Sygna, L., O'Brien, K., and Wolf, J. (eds), *A Changing Environment for Human Security. Transformative Approaches to Research, Policy and Action.* London: Routledge.

Virtanen, P., Siragusa, L., and Guttorm, H. (2020) Introduction: Toward More Inclusive Definitions of Sustainability. *Science Direct*, On www.sciencedirect.com/science/article/pii/S1877343520300300

Wallerstein, I. (1974) The Rise and Future Demise of the World Capitalist System: Concepts for Comparative Analysis. *Comparative Studies in Society and History*, 16(4)L: 387–415.

Wang, Y.L. (2015) *Lives Displaced By Central Park Take Center Stage In New Play.* 4 September. On www.npr.org/2015/09/04/436938527/lives-displaced-by-central-park-take-center-stage-in-new-play

Warner, K., Hamza, M., Oliver-Smith, A., Renaud, F., and Julca, A. (2010) Climate Change, Environmental Degradation and Migration. *Natural Hazards*, 55: 689–715. On www.researchgate.net/profile/Alex-Julca-2/

publication/225452578_Climate_change_environmental_degradation_migra-tion/links/54e3640f0cf2748d3a9d6387/Climate-change-environmental-degra-dation-migration.pdf

Watts, M. (1993) Hunger, Famine and the Space of Vulnerability. *Geojournal*, 30(2): 117–125.

WCCD (World Commission on Cultural Diversity) (1995) *Our Creative Diversity: Report of the World Commission on Culture and Development*. Paris: UNESCO. On https://unesdoc.unesco.org/ark:/48223/pf0000101651

Weaver, M. (2019) UK Government Loses Supreme Court Fight over Bedroom Tax. *The Guardian*, 13 November. On www.theguardian.com/society/2019/nov/13/uk-government-loses-supreme-court-fight-over-bedroom-tax

West-Oram, P., and Buyx, A. (2017) Global Health Solidarity. *Public Health Ethic*, 10(2): 212–224.

Whittaker, A., and Taylor, B. (2017) Understanding Risk in Social Work. *Journal of Social Work Practice*, 31:4, 375–378. https://doi.org/10.1080/02650533.2 017.1397612

WHO (World Health Organization) (2018) *Heat and Health*. On www.who.int/news-room/fact-sheets/detail/climate-change-heat-and-health

WHO (World Health Organization) (2022) *The World Health Statistics, 2022*. Geneva: WHO.

Wiltshire, J. (2019) *Carbon Loss and Economic Impacts of a Peatland Wildfire in North-east Sutherland, Scotland*, 12–17 May 2019. On www.wwf.org.uk/sites/default/files/2019-11/Carbon%20loss%20and%20economic%20impacts%20of%20a%20peatland%20wildfire%20in%20north-east%20Sutherland.pdf

Winston, A. (2019) *Is the Green New Deal Realistic?* On https://andrewwinston.com/is-the-green-new-deal-realistic/

Wisner, B., Blaikie, P., Cannon, T., and Davis, I. (2004) *At Risk: Natural Hazards, People's Vulnerability, and Disasters*, 2nd Edn. London: Routledge.

Woolcock, M.(1998) Social Capital and Economic Development: Toward a Theoretical Synthesis and Policy Framework. *Theory and Society*, 27(1):151–208.

Woolcock, M. (2001) Microenterprise and Social Capital: A Framework for Theory, Research, and Policy. *The Journal of Socio-Economics*, 30: 193–198.

World Economic Forum. (2020) *Global Gender Gap Report 2020*. Davos: WEF. On www3.weforum.org/docs/WEF_GGGR_2020.pdf

World Vision (2012) *Hurricane Sandy: Facts, FAQs and How to Help*. On www.worldvision.org/disaster-relief-news-stories/2012-hurricane-sandy-facts

World Vision (2013) *Typhoon Haiyan: Facts, FAQs, and How to Help*. www.worldvision.org/disaster-relief-news-stories/2013-typhoon-haiyan-facts

Worldometer (2022) *Covid-19: Coronavirus Pandemic*. On www.worldometers.info/coronavirus/

WWF (World Wildlife Fund) (2020) *Covid-19: Urgent Call to Protect People and Nature*. On https://www.worldwildlife.org/publications/covid19-urgent-call-to-protect-people-and-nature

Yamada, S., and Galat, A. (2014) Typhoon Yolanda/Haiyan and Climate Justice. *Concepts in Disaster Medicine*, 8(5): 432–436. https://doi.org/10.1017/dmp.2014.97. On www.cambridge.org/core/journals/disaster-medicine-and-public-health-preparedness/article/typhoon-yolandahaiyan-and-climate-justice/0F30290EB22C367D10652E3F44382B06

Younghusband, E. (1978) *Social Work in Britain, 1950–1975*. London, Allen and Unwin.

Zastrow, C. (2010) *Introduction to Social Work and Social Welfare: Empowering People*. Boston, MA: Brooks/Cole.

Zhang, L.L., X. Liu, Y. P. Li, Y. Liu, Z. P. Liu, J. C. Lin, J. Shen, X. F. Tang, Y. Zhang and W. N. Liang (2012) Emergency Medical Rescue Efforts after a Major Earthquake: Lessons from the 2008 Wenchuan Earthquake. *Lancet*, 379: 853–861.

Author Index

Subject Index

Printed in the United States
by Baker & Taylor Publisher Services